RAILWAY CRANES

Volume 2: The story of breakdown cranes on the railways of Britain

Peter Tatlow CEng MICE

crecy.co.uk

Dedicated to members of breakdown gangs
and the crane-men of all railways

First published in 2013

This edition published 2022

A CIP record for this book is available from the British Library

Printed in Turkey by Pelikan

ISBN 9781910809921

Crécy Publishing Limited
1a Ringway Trading Estate, Shadowmoss Road,
Manchester M22 5LH
www.crecy.co.uk

Front Cover Brand-new 75-ton steam breakdown crane No RS 1092/75 from Willesden is seen lifting into position a new pre-cast concrete footbridge span on 1 April 1962 at Bridge No 81, Apsley. This work will have been part of the Modernisation Plan and required in connection with the provision of overhead clearance for the electrification of the West Coast mainline to Euston. These 75-ton cranes, together with the concurrently supplied 30-ton cranes, were British Railways' first acquisition of breakdown cranes following nationalisation 15 years earlier. *M.S. Welch*

Back Cover No ADRC96713 at work at Chinley N. Jct on 11 October 1983. *M.S. Welch*

Wherever possible drawings have been reproduced to the standard modellers specification of 4mm to the foot. However care should be taken on scaling these from the printed pages and a cross check made with the written dimensions whenever possible.

Contents

On a wintery day ex-LNER 45-ton Cowans Sheldon steam crane No. DE331156/ADRC95217 darkens the sky of Stockton as it prepares to undertake a lift within station limits. *ColourRail*

Preface

The manner in which this book came about was set out in the Preface to Volume 1 and little can be added other than to express my pleasure at the way in which Volume 1 has been received and to hope that this volume will equally satisfy readers' interests.

This volume introduces the concept of relieving bogies, touched upon in Volume 1, but fully explored here. This necessarily introduces a degree of complexity which I have done my best to describe and explain in straightforward terms. I hope, however, that less scientific and less engineering-minded readers will not be put off. For the historical record I feel these details should be set out in print.

Peter Tatlow, 2012

Note on the Author

Peter Tatlow is well known for his contribution to railway research over 60 years. An interest in railways and railway modelling has been his main pastime for as long as he can remember. Born during the age of the 'Big Four', some of his earliest memories are of journeys undertaken during the Second World War. Following military service in the Royal Engineers, he joined the Chief Civil Engineer's Department of the Southern Region of British Railways. He left BR over ten years later, having qualified as a chartered civil engineer, then worked on the design and construction of bridges, both in the United Kingdom and overseas. He is now retired from full-time employment.

His interest in railways and modelling has led to him writing numerous articles in the prototype and model railway press and in specialist journals on a wide range of subjects including locomotives, coaches, wagons, travelling cranes, bridges, train ferries and civil engineering activities.

His books include:

A pictorial record of LNER wagons (OPC, 1976, reprinted twice)
A history of Highland Locomotives (OPC 1979, reprinted 1989)
Highland Railway Miscellany (OPC 1985)
Historic Carriage Drawings, Volume 3 – Non-Passenger Coaching Stock (Pendragon 2000)
Harrow & Wealdstone Accident, 50 years on, clearing up the aftermath (The Oakwood Press, 2002, reprinted 2008)
St John's Lewisham, 50 years on, restoring traffic (The Oakwood Press, 2007)
Return from Dunkirk, Railways to the rescue, Operation Dynamo (1940) (Oakwood 2010)
Railway Breakdown Cranes, Volume 1 (Noodle Books, 2012, reprinted 2014)
Railway Cranes, Volume 3 (Crécy Publishing, 2018)
Highland Railway Carriages & Wagons (Noodle Books, 2014)
Dingwall & Skye Railway, A pictorial record of the line to Kyle of Lochalsh (Crécy Publishing, 2016)

He has recently revisited the subject of his first work with *An Illustrated History of LNER Wagons* in five volumes, published by Wild Swan in 2005, 2007, 2009, 2012 and 2015.

Introduction

In Volume 1, the development of steam-powered cranes primarily intended for breakdown work was explored, beginning with Appleby's 5-ton-capacity machine mounted on just two axles. Over the years, as this type of crane gradually became accepted as a necessary adjunct to the contemporary railway, the required capacity steadily increased from an initial 10 and 15 tons to 20, 25, 30 tons and on to 35/36 tons. The inevitable consequence of this was that their size also grew, with the need for increasing numbers of axles to contain the maximum axle loads within acceptable bounds and thereby avoid overloading the rail section or under-line bridges over which the crane might be expected to pass. In the end, the length of the carriage itself became a hindrance to the crane's ability to approach sufficiently close to the load to be able to effectively handle it at its maximum lifting capacity.

A bold attempt had been made in 1908 to address this problem when the Great Western Railway commissioned a pair of 36-ton long-jib cranes on five-axle carriages. However, on the down-side, these suffered from the disadvantage that their crew had to expend time while attaching the counterweight and installing the propping girders just to ensure that the maximum axle loads when in train formation were low enough to satisfy the line's Engineer. Although some other companies quickly followed suit, when the LNER needed even greater capacity to handle Gresley's and Raven's Pacifics and other heavy locomotives, an extremely high axle load was tolerated when two 45-ton cranes mounted on a pair of two-axle bogies were ordered in 1926. Nonetheless, this resulted in restricted route availability and no other British company followed suit, although similar cranes did appear in Australia.

This volume will now go on to consider the solution to this difficulty in the form of the relieving bogie patented by Wilfrid Stokes in 1904. Details will be considered later, but briefly this consists of, usually, a pair of detachable bogies, one at each end of a not-too-long carriage; one, or both, of which can be removed at the site of operations, but which help to distribute the load of the crane over a greater length while in train formation. Only one example was acquired by a British company prior to 1931.

Thereafter, however, most cranes supplied for breakdown work adopted the relieving bogie system, apart from some modern long-jib 30-ton cranes obtained to replace old life-expired small cranes. Capacity was generally 36 to 45 tons until 1961, when a dozen 75-ton cranes were acquired as part of the British Railways Modernisation Plan. By then, however, the railways were changing. Firstly, the substitution of diesel for steam traction meant that the facility for lifting a heavy locomotive anywhere along the main frames was no longer feasible. Due to the design of their frames, diesel and electric locomotives could only be lifted some way back from the buffer beam, usually over the bogie centre, for which special lifting attachments were inevitably required. This soon rendered all but the largest cranes unsuitable.

Secondly, at the opposite end of the scale, whereas the public perception of a breakdown crane at work might have been as a result of seeing newspaper photographs of them clearing up the aftermath of some major accident involving a passenger train, the everyday bread and butter of a breakdown gang was actually more often re-railing a couple of loose-coupled goods wagons hidden away out of view in some goods yard. By the 1970s, after more than a century of often single-wagon loads transported in unfitted vehicles, the freight traffic that the railway retained was generally bulk goods conveyed in fully brake-fitted block trains. In these circumstances there was little call for a crane limited to 30 tons capacity or less and all were soon withdrawn.

Finally, following developments in the field of road-mobile cranes, telescopic jibs were adopted for the final batch of six 75-tonne diesel-powered breakdown cranes supplied to British Railways in 1977. Before the last of the steam cranes were withdrawn, however, the opportunity was taken to convert the 75-ton steam cranes to diesel power, followed also by a small number of 45-ton cranes, the latter having their capacity enhanced to 50-tonnes.

Following the Second World War, there had been advances in the alternative means of re-railing errant

Two 45-ton steam breakdown cranes confront each other, one the last of the old generation, the other the shape of things to come and to be described in this volume. The Cowans Sheldon 45-ton crane on just four axles on the left should be compared with the Ransomes & Rapier crane of the same capacity on the right. The significance of the latter crane lies in the method of distributing the crane's weight onto the track with regard to the total load, the maximum axle load applied and the crane's ability to traverse reasonable curves within the loading gauge. Detachable bogies were provided at each end to which some of the crane's weight could be transferred while in train formation. The work underway is an under-bridge deck renewal at Chesterfield on 22 August 1976.
53A Models of Hull collection

vehicles, providing a means for coping without the use of a crane, particularly relevant with the increasing lengths of overhead-electrified line. All of this meant that there was a declining need for the conventional railway breakdown crane, hastened yet further by the vast increase in the use of mobile cranes, which could be hired in from outside as the occasion demanded, subject only to the site being accessible to such beasts.

At the time of writing, just four breakdown cranes remain in service with Network Rail. On the other hand, over thirty have found homes on heritage railways, of which perhaps half are serviceable.

1
Entry of Relieving Bogies

Stokes Patent Relieving Bogie

The design of a rail-mounted crane that is capable of lifting any substantial load and yet can remain stable while standing 'free on rail' while also staying within a limited maximum axle load invariably leads to some compromises. As elaborated upon in Volume 1, pp.20–24, the narrowness of the distance between the rail heads limits the stability when 'free on rail'. For a given load and radius this can be counteracted by increasing the counterbalance at the tail end of the crane superstructure, but that increase is in turn restricted by the risk of overturning backwards with no load. This risk can be offset by increasing the total dead load acting about the centre of gravity of the crane and weight is usually put in the carriage. For a given number of axles, however, the maximum permissible axle load will constrain the extent to which the overall weight can be raised. This might be overcome by adding to the number of axles, but the minimum axle spacing means that the length of the carriage has to be increased, which in turn has an adverse effect on the reach to the point of lift for maximum load in front of the crane.

As we have already seen in Volume 1, p.125, the Great Western Railway initiated a design of crane that relied on detachable counterweights and placing the propping girders in the accompanying match or weight wagon. As an alternative, Sir Wilfrid Stokes of Ransomes & Rapier invented his patent system of relieving bogies in 1904. This concept consisted of a pair of bogies structurally attached, in the vertical sense, but free to move laterally, one at each end of a four-axle crane carriage. Yet both bogies were capable of being removed, one or both as required, and shunted or placed to one side prior to the commencement of lifting operations. Before moving off again in train formation, it was of course necessary to refit the bogies and to transfer a significant proportion of the dead weight of the crane onto the bogies using a system of levers and jacks. Thus the spread of load over a greater length enabled the crane to be heavier (i.e. equipped with more ballast) without exceeding the maximum permitted axle loads or reducing route availability, while still allowing it to traverse reasonable curves.

A British patent was applied for on 8 June 1904, fully specified on 4 March 1905 and granted as Patent No. 12,927 on 6 April 1905. The principle of the relieving bogie for railway breakdown cranes and other similar roles is depicted firstly in the drawings on pp.11-19 (Figures 1 to 7), as shown in the patent and as applied to the Midland (drawings on pp.22 and 23 (Figures 8 and 9)) and subsequent cranes.

The diagram attached to the Patent showed an eight-wheel crane carriage, at each end of which were short four-wheel bogies. Unlike the system actually adopted however, between the crane and each bogie, a longitudinal structural beam passed from within the carriage frame to a bogie, where it was supported. At its centre, this beam passed through an opening in the headstock, where it was vertically constrained by and pivoted on a pin within a socket, which was mounted on strengthening to the end plates of the carriage in the vicinity of the outer propping girder boxes.

At its ends the beam bore on a pair of stout crossmembers, one within the carriage of the crane, near the bedplate, which slid transversely. The other end passed through the headstock of the adjacent relieving bogie, and

SIR WILFRID STOKES

Frederick Wilfrid Scott Stokes was born on 9 April 1860 in Worcester. Following his education at Kensington Catholic Public School and the Catholic University College, Kennington, he trained under the New Works Engineer to the Great Western Railway and subsequently worked for the Hull & Barnsley Railway on bridges. In 1896, he was appointed a director of Ransomes & Rapier, where his railway experience would have been invaluable, and was made Managing Director a year later. He soon perceived how the larger railway crane was limited by the combination of the maximum allowable axle load, the practical limit of the carriage and flexibility requirements, and devised his patent relieving bogies. He was the innovator behind many inventions, including devising the Stokes trench mortar in 1915, for which he was made a Knight of the British Empire in 1917. He died on 7 February 1927.

was encompassed by the bogie, or extension truck, about which it was able to rotate in plan at the vertical spindle at the centre of the bogie. This end of the beam was attached to a nut, through which the threaded spindle passed. Traction forces were transmitted between the carriage and bogie through the pin and spindle connected by the beam, assisted in compression by the rounded abutment plates mounted on the inner ends of the bogies.

Load was taken up by operating ratchet levers mounted on a transverse shaft supported by brackets, moving a worm at the centre to rotate a worm wheel on the vertical spindle. As this was threaded and encompassed by a nut, the beam was raised or lowered. The bottom end of the spindle thrust against a stepped block mounted on a transverse bearer, while at the top the shaft was located by an abutment collar bearing held in place by a collar mounted on an upper transverse bearer.

By this means, part of the weight of the crane could be taken by the bogie, thereby increasing the effective wheel base and spreading the load while in train formation, yet the crane and bogies were capable of flexing sufficiently to negotiate curves in the track. Once on site, the pin(s) could be withdrawn and the bogie(s) separated from the carriage.

Whilst this arrangement distributed the load effectively, it was clearly cumbersome, with the beams passing through much of the carriage, and one suspects considerable friction would have been set up between the top of beam and the underside of the bedplate. It is not known whether any cranes were made incorporating such beams, but certainly none were built in Britain. The wording of the Patent, nonetheless, also covered the possibility of pinning a cantilever framework to the headstock of the crane, thereby avoiding the beam projecting further into the carriage. In the event, this was found to be more practical, probably because it suffered from less friction when changing curvature and was less unwieldy than the beam projecting from the bogie when disconnected. This method was preferred for all future cranes provided with relieving bogies and was eventually developed to make use of paired hinged outriggers at each end of the carriage.

The first crane supplied by Ransomes & Rapier to utilise the relieving bogie principle was a 20-ton crane for the Great Indian Peninsular Railway, the order for which was placed on 26 February 1906, Order No B6655. The second was a 36-ton crane for the Midland Railway, which is considered later in this chapter. Thereafter, customers worldwide seem to have been slow to adopt the system, with only one 40-ton ordered by the East Indian Railway on 1 January 1923 and one 35-ton ordered on 8 February 1926 by the Crown Agents Commission for Uganda Railways, being built before the patent is likely to have expired.

On 4 October 1928, Antony Scott Stokes applied for a British patent relating to travelling cranes, granted as Patent No 323,723 on 6 January 1930. This was a development of the scheme devised by his uncle, Sir Wilfrid, in which the connection between the cantilever girder and the bogie was revised to permit rolling and pitching movements of the bogie, as well as pivotal movement about a vertical axis.

The first example of a crane equipped with relieving bogies was a 20-ton machine supplied to the Great Indian Peninsular Railway of 5ft 6in gauge in 1906. Designed to be capable of lifting 20 tons to a radius of 19ft when propped, or 11 tons when 'free on rail' and 15 tons at 14ft, presumably its minimum radius. It is seen here at Rapier's Waterside Works following a test to 24 tons at 19ft radius and 30 tons at 15ft. The Specification required that about 10½ tons of the crane's weight was to be transferred to the bogies. Ratchet levers are in place on the ends of the transverse shaft on the bogies. *Ransomes & Rapier, author's collection*

The first breakdown crane equipped with Sir Wilfrid Stokes's patent relieving bogie system to be supplied to a British railway company was the 36-ton machine ordered by the Midland Railway on 18 April 1914. Delivery of the crane was quoted as 10 months or earlier, but due to the outbreak of the First World War, delivery is believed to have been delayed until as late as early 1916. Instead of depending on the time-consuming method of removing counterweights and propping girders accepted by the Great Western Railway and others, detachable four-wheel bogies were provided at each end which relieve some of the crane's weight while in train formation. *London Midland Region, author's collection*

As before, the diagram attached to the Patent showed four-wheel relieving bogies B and B1 attached at each end of the eight-wheel crane carriage A, but instead of the longitudinal structural beam of the original Patent running from within the end of the carriage frame to each bogie, a cantilever D was used to connect to the bogie B, and was supported on it, as originally envisaged as an alternative. This cantilever was vertically constrained by and pivoted to the headstock of the crane by a pin P passing through upper and lower lugs N and N1 on the carriage and M and M1 on the cantilever. The headstock of the bogie was bifurcated and a slot in the web of the cantilever girder allowed the lower member of the headstock to pass freely through.

In the new Patent, however, at the bogie end the cantilever girder was provided with a pair of vertical, inward-facing, cup-shaped bearings E and E1, which encompassed a ball, F, and were free to move, within limits, around it, the ball itself supported by a collar G2 on the vertical spindle G. The cantilever was therefore free to pivot on the balljoint both laterally and longitudinally to a limited extent, but sufficiently to accommodate curvature and changes in crossfall in the track traversed by the crane and its bogies. Because the worm wheel was restrained from moving vertically downwards by the upper crossmember, as it is rotated it raised the vertical shaft, or conversely allowed the shaft to be gradually lowered. Using hand-gear J2, the spindle G could therefore be raised, thereby taking load off

the crane, and lowered, thus releasing load off the bogie, in bearings within transverse members H and H1.

Load was taken up by the operation of a capstan fitted over the squared ends at either or both ends of the cross-shaft K, supported by brackets L and L1 attached to the upper crossmember H. Rotation of the shaft K caused the worm J2 at the centre of K to rotate worm wheel J1 on the vertical threaded spindle G. In practice, the worm wheel was resting on a ball-bearing race seated on a thrust block bolted to member H. The worm wheel carried an internally threaded bush which engaged with, and ran freely on, the threaded upper portion of the vertical spindle. This was thereby raised or lowered, and in turn so was the cantilever D. The lower end of the spindle G was located in the lower crossmember H1, within which it was free to move vertically, but was prevented from rotating by a sliding key.

When disconnected from the carriage, the crane end of the cantilever beam D in the bogie settled to some extent. This was constrained by a spring R. A nut and lock-nut at the top of a long vertical rod S through the spring afforded a means of adjusting the height of the free end of the cantilever, thereby easing reconnection to the bogie. The crane end of the cantilever was provided at the top and bottom with upper and lower lugs M and M1. The projections of these lugs were shaped in plan to create curved ends, so that during reconnection they were guided between matching lugs N and N1 on the crane carriage. The lugs M on the bogie and N on the

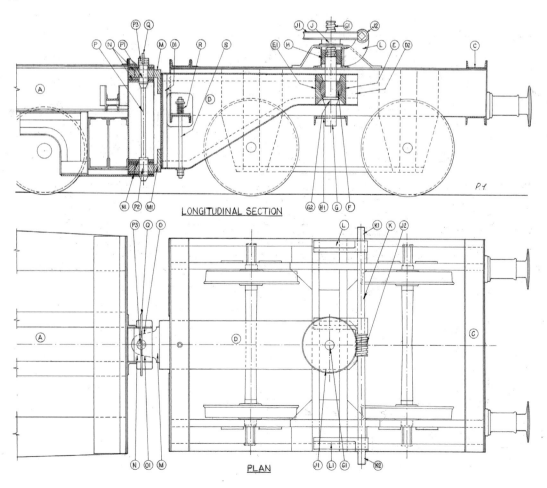

Figure 1 A drawing showing Stokes modified patent relieving bogie, as applied to Ransomes & Rapier 35/36-ton cranes supplied to the LMS and the LNER in 1931 and 1932. *Author*

crane were connected by means of a long removable vertical pin P, thereby allowing horizontal, but not vertical rotation. This pin was of reduced diameter between the lugs, and once in position was secured by a locking bar Q engaging with recesses in the pin and in the lugs.

On reconnecting the crane to the bogie, as the vertical spindle was raised upwards, once slack was taken up, it lifted the cantilever beam and hence relieved some of the load of the crane, transferring this to the bogie, loading its wheel springs. However, these four-handle capstans used to rotate the worm shaft were hard work to turn, especially with the operator standing on the formation beside the crane. The crane relieving and traction forces were passed into the bogie via the beam and the balljoint. Typically, the two bogies together relieved up to 35% of the crane's weight, reducing the axle-load from, say, 20 tons to less than 13 tons.

In an alternative scheme, the bogie end of the cantilever D carried a longitudinal pin journaled in a yoke provided with transverse pins, themselves journaled in a vertically adjustable yoke, in effect a universal joint. As far as known, however, this scheme was not implemented in a British crane.

In either case, the bogies were free to pitch and roll relative to the crane as they traversed uneven sections of track.

All well and good, that was the theory and no doubt by careful and time-consuming adjustment of the spring hangers, these optimum axle loads could be achieved for

The connection between the crane and relieving bogie of a Ransomes & Rapier 36/40-ton crane supplied to the LMS in 1931. Vertical pins through sockets at the top and bottom of the triangular-shaped cantilever projecting from the bogie on the left engage with sockets within the pair of large vertical angles on the end of the carriage. *Author*

COMPONENTS OF THE IMPROVED STOKES PATENT RELIEVING BOGIE		
Component	**Within**	**Description**
A	Crane	Carriage or main truck of crane
B & B1	Bogie	Relieving bogies, subsidiary trucks
C	Bogie	Headstock
D	Crane & bogie	Tapered cantilever relieving girder
D2	Crane & bogie	Bogie end of cantilever relieving girder D
E & E1	Cantilever	Pair of opposing cup-shaped members
F	Cantilever	Ball-shaped member within E & E1
G	Bogie	Vertical spindle passing through F
G2	Bogie	Shoulder upon which ball F rests
H	Bogie	Bearing on top of bogie frame
H1	Bogie	Guide bearing at bottom of bogie frame
J	Bogie	Nut on spindle G
J1	Bogie	Worm wheel on nut J
J2	Bogie	Worm on shaft K
K	Bogie	Transverse shaft with squared ends
L & L1	Bogie	Brackets secured to H to support K
M & M1	Cantilever	Upper & lower lugs to connect to A
N & N1	Crane	Upper & lower lugs to connect to B
O & O1	Cantilever	Nose shape to N & N1
P	Crane	Vertical pin connecting M & M1 and N & N1
P1 &P2	Crane	Enlarged portions of P
P3	Crane	Transverse holes in N & P to receive Q
Q	Crane	Locking lever to secure P
R	Bogie	Compression spring to support D
S	Bogie	Vertical rod through R

The small brass load-indicator plate affixed to the horn guide, and the pointer attached to the axle box of a relieving bogie on an ex-LMS 40-ton Ransomes & Rapier crane. As the springs deflected, the pointer indicated that the bogie had taken on sufficient load from the crane, for the jib end above the horizontal line, or at the tail end below the line. *S. Bell*

The more-sophisticated load indicator on the side of a relieving bogie of an ex-LMS 40-ton Ransomes & Rapier crane. Note the brass plates inscribed 'Coupling position', 'Tail bogie' and 'Jib bogie'. *S. Bell*

the Works acceptance trials and perhaps after overhaul, but how were the men out on the track supposed to obtain the same loads? Measuring the deflection of multiple-leaf springs is a notoriously inaccurate method of measuring load, yet in one way or another it appears this was all there was to rely upon.

The early Rapier cranes were fitted with a small brass plate on each of the four horn guides. The plates were graduated with two closely-spaced horizontal lines marked: 'Running position jib end' and 'Running position tail end'. The intention was that the load should continue to be applied to the bogie until the springs had deflected sufficiently for a pointer on the axle box to line up with the appropriate inscription.

A more sophisticated supplementary system was subsequently devised and fitted to at least one crane which, by a means of rods and fulcrums, detected the rise and fall of all four axle boxes within their horn guides, compensating for the differences in the various readings. A pointer mounted on one side of the bogie activated by this linkage responded to this movement and hence the degree of load transferred to the bogie. A sector plate behind the pointer was graduated as: 'Coupling position'; 'Tail bogie'; and 'Jib bogie'. This, however, was rather complex and does not appear to have been any more accurate as an indicator of the actual load transferred.

A feature sadly lacking on the bogies of the first two cranes was any form of handbrake and once separated from the crane, the bogies needed wheel-chocking to prevent them running away. From Order No. D4648 of 1932, however, bogies were fitted with a screw handbrake.

On subsequent Stokes bogie cranes built by Ransomes & Rapier from 1938 onwards, the load was transferred onto and off each bogie by means of handwheels fitted at a lower height on both sides, rather than the high four-spoke capstan of the earlier cranes. These drove a chain-reduction gearing system to rotate the primary cross-shaft carrying the worm, as before.

On this design, a longitudinal wedge passed through a slot in the lower end of the vertical shaft and acted as a moveable hard stop to the loading mechanism. Its position could be adjusted via a linkage and cross-shaft, at the outer end of which was a pointer in front of a sector plate on one side of the bogie frame. The position of this pointer could be selected by hand and clamped in line with one of two arrow heads on the quadrant plate, above which were inscriptions reading 'Front' and 'Rear', referring of course to the placing of the bogie relative to the crane. Once correctly set up, overloading was avoided, since the wedge prevented the vertical shaft from being raised any further, see drawing on p.14 (Figure 2).

A substantial redesign of the bogie, though still using the earlier principles, was undertaken for Orders E8136/8 (GW and SR 45-ton) onwards, whereby the frame was lowered, with the whole of the inner headstock passing through the cantilever framework, rather than being bifurcated as before.

The two bogies were identical in construction and hence, in theory at least, interchangeable. However, because unequal loads were generally transferred to each bogie, once correctly set-up without readjustment – which required weighing equipment only available at Works – they ceased to be interchangeable. For this reason, the two ends of most cranes and their matching relieving bogies were clearly marked 'A' and 'B'.

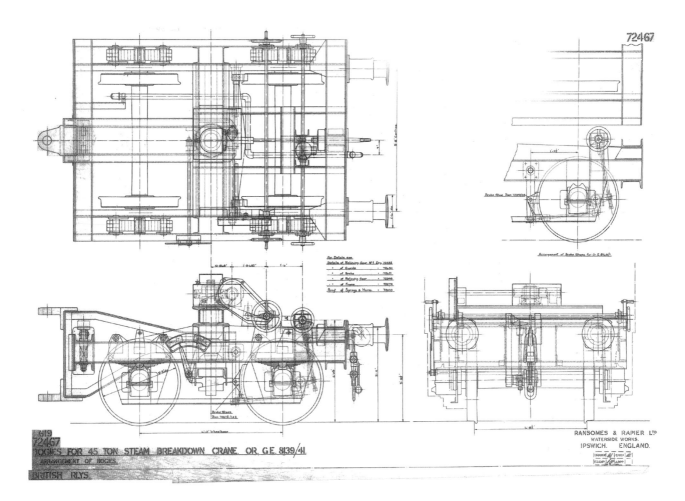

72467

RANSOMES & RAPIER LTD
WATERSIDE WORKS.
IPSWICH.   ENGLAND.

BOGIES FOR 45 TON STEAM BREAKDOWN CRANE. OR. G.E. 8139/4II.
ARRANGEMENT OF BOGIES.
BRITISH RLYS.

Figure 2 The modified design of Ransomes & Rapier relieving bogie fitted to the 45-ton cranes from 1940. Written in pencil in the tablets on each corner of the sector plate are 'Front' and 'Rear', while not shown is the small clamp on the pointer to lock this opposite the appropriate description. *Ransomes & Rapier, author's collection*

Notable from Order No GF5937/49 (MoS) was the introduction of a hand-pumped hydraulic system for load transference from crane carriage to bogie. In this design, a heavy cradle beneath the central crossmember of the bogie supported a hydraulic jack bearing directly on the underside of the load-supporting shaft. At the top of the shaft there was a transverse slot, through which a removable cotter could slide, operated by hand levers on either side of the carriage. At the top of the vertical shaft, a substantial screw with locknut permitted adjustment against the upper surface of the cotter.

By pumping the jack to lift the central shaft until such time as the shaft had been raised sufficiently to allow the cotter to pass under the adjusting screw and enter the slot, the bogie was loaded. The cotter was then held in position by a catch, and the jack released until the central shaft rested on the cotter; thereby taking that portion of the weight of the crane carried by the bogie. To release the bogie, the jack was raised until the load was taken off the cotter, which was then withdrawn, and the jack released to lower the central shaft. The instructions on the operation of the bogies are reproduced in the accompanying box.

Unless it was necessary for the crane to approach particularly close to the load or some other obstruction, it would be normal practice to leave the relieving bogies coupled, however, they had to be in the unloaded condition.

Right, Figure 3 The final design of Ransomes & Rapier relieving bogie utilising a hydraulic jack and applied to the 45-ton cranes built from 1943, as pertaining to the Southern Railway crane of 1946. *Ransomes & Rapier, author's collection*

SEQUENCE OF OPERATION FOR RANSOMES & RAPIER CRANE FITTED WITH HYDRAULIC JACK

1. Operation for attaching bogie to crane

(a) Cotter must be in 'Withdrawn' position.

(b) Run bogie up to crane, allowing the tongues on relieving bogie girder to enter into sockets on the crane headstock.

(c) Insert bottom connecting or pivot pin.

(d) Raise end of relieving girder in bogie, by means of hydraulic jack until top connecting or pivot pin can be dropped into position.

(e) Continue to operate hydraulic jack until removable cotter can be inserted.

(f) Release pressure in hydraulic jack and allow load to be carried by cotter

2. Operation to release bogie (bogie brake applied)

(a) Operate hydraulic jack to release and withdraw cotter, keeping the bogie load on the jack

(b) Remove top connecting pin

(c) Release fluid pressure in jack

(d) Remove bottom connecting pin and withdraw bogie away from crane

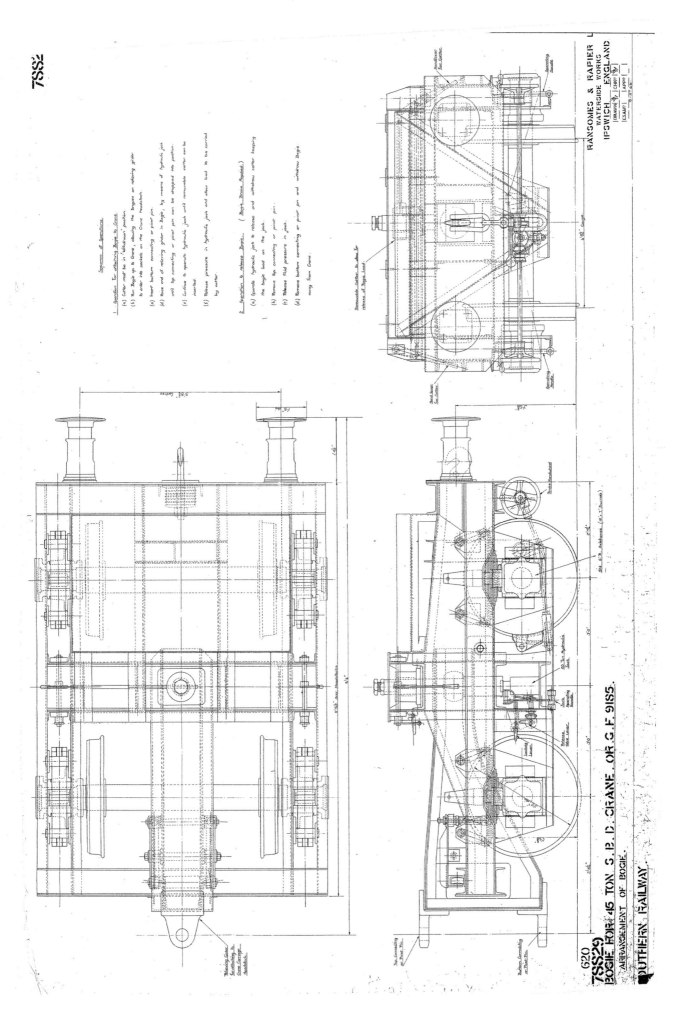

Other Forms of Relieving Bogie

From between the First and Second World wars, in due course, the usual compromise for all larger cranes in the UK was to adopt four-axle carriages with two-axle relieving bogies at each end. Even then, to make the most of the permitted axle loads, it was desirable to utilise the maximum load on each axle. In train formation, however, with the weight of the jib largely resting on the match wagon, the counterweight in the tail of the crane would place the longitudinal centre of gravity well to the rear of the middle of the carriage, and hence there would be an unequal distribution of axle loads were the king pin to remain at the centre of the carriage. This and the desire to improve the portée at the front end of the crane, albeit with a corresponding disadvantage at the other end, frequently led to the pin being placed just forward of the second axle. During this period, both Cowans Sheldon and Craven Bros were to develop their own design of relieving bogie, as described in the following sections.

Cowans Sheldon design of relieving bogie

In the Cowans design, the cantilever beam was replaced by a triangular system of tie and strut. At the crane end, the nearly horizontal strut rested in a knuckle socket at the top of the headstock of the crane, while the tie was pinned horizontally to a bracket on the lower edge, presumably with some lateral flexibility. At the bogie end, the tie was connected to the strut by another pin close to a steel casting supported by a lever and fulcrum at the centre of the bogie on the 'steelyard' principle. The other end of the lever could, through a hole in the bogie floor, be raised by the crane hook so as to transfer load to the bogie by the specified amount, and a locking pin could then be inserted through a hole in the lever once two marks lined up. Release was again by raising the lever with the hook and withdrawing the pin. This method eliminated the need for crane carriage weight to be transferred on and off the bogie by manual effort. Alternatively, however, the lever could be raised by a manually operated screw jack or, from 1940 by hydraulic jack to transfer the load; the hook-

raising arm being retained for emergency use. A set of hard marks on the axle boxes and horn-block guides were supposed to coincide when the crane was in running order on level track.

Trouble was sometimes experienced in disengaging and re-engaging the relieving bogies of Cowans cranes, a problem which was traced to wear in the ball-and-socket joint of the top cantilever arm, there being no method of lubricating this other than by applying grease by hand with the bogie separated from the carriage. With many cranes stabled outside, and frequently out on a job subject to all weathers, this grease rapidly disappeared from the working surfaces, causing them to wear. The result was that the vertical position of the cantilever altered, and as a result incorrect loads were applied to the relieving bogie. At Darlington, local arrangements were made for holes to be drilled through the socket so that a drip-feed lubricator could be fitted, after which wear was much reduced. Due to a lack of lateral flexibility of the cantilever, further difficulties were encountered in coupling up and uncoupling on curved and super-elevated track.

INSTRUCTIONS ON THE RESETTING OF COWAN SHELDON CRANE
1 Raise carriage by means of portable jacks, one at each corner to the correct height i.e. specified height from rail level to top flange of side girder angle, less any tyre wear
2 Screw down spring jacking screws until reasonably tight
3 Remove portable jacks
4 Connect up the relieving bogies and take part weight of crane
5 Adjust spring links until the carriage springs take the load sufficiently to just slacken jacking screws
6 Axle loadings should now be approximately correct, but relieving screws over springs should be slackened right off and axle loads weighed and, if necessary, spring adjusting screws should be further adjusted
Note: It is not possible to raise crane carriage, if this has dropped from any cause either by means of the spring adjusting screws or by means of the relieving bogies.

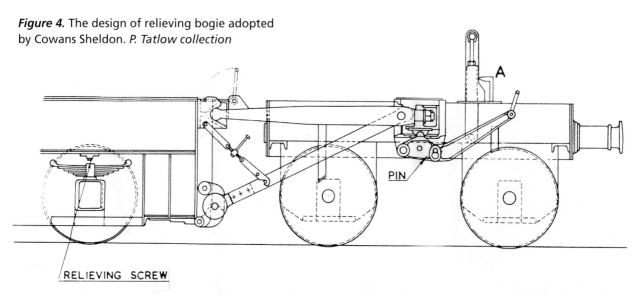

Figure 4. The design of relieving bogie adopted by Cowans Sheldon. *P. Tatlow collection*

RELIEVING SCREW

PIN

A

COWANS SHELDON & Co. LTD.

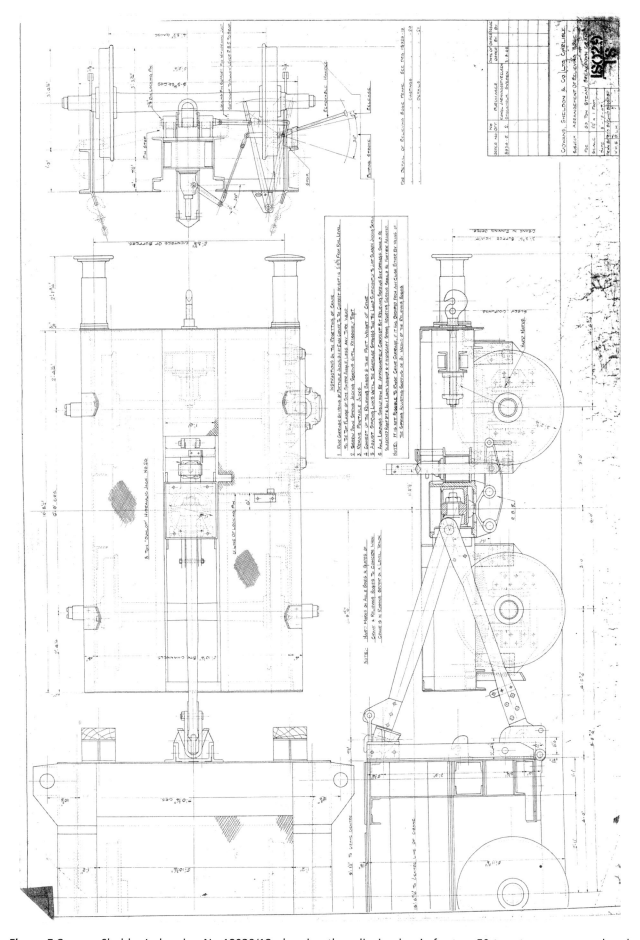

Figure 5 Cowans Sheldon's drawing No 18029/18, showing the relieving bogie for two 50-ton steam cranes ordered by Kungl Jarnvagsstyrelsen (Swedish State Railways), Stockholm, Sweden, on 3 August 1946. This shows the detail of a bogie fitted with an 8-ton 'Dunlop' hydraulic jack No 26. These cranes, however, were fitted with hinged outriggers instead of telescopic propping girders, which accounts for the steep incline of the strut. The instructions on the resetting of the crane are reproduced in the box. *Cowans Sheldon, author's collection*

The relieving bogie and match wagon of a Cowans 45-ton crane standing separately and showing the upper ball of the strut and lower pin of the diagonal tie which engage with the crane. *J. Templeton*

The horizontal strut with cupped socket at the left-hand end and inclined tie connection devised by Cowans Sheldon to couple the relieving bogie to the crane. *Author*

Craven Bros design of relieving bogie

With the Craven method, the cantilever beam was a large steel casting, which at the crane end fitted into a cast-steel socket at the top of the headstock, and at the bottom was pinned to a short vertical shaft between the underside of the socket and a projection beneath the headstock. Within the bogie, the means of support for the cantilever from the crane employed a table mounted on a pair of scissor arms capable of being raised and lowered by a double-acting horizontal screw jack between the scissors. Loading was applied by rotating a six-handle capstan, which was similar in form to a ship's wheel, on one side of the bogie, placed between the axle boxes and therefore easier to turn than the high-level versions on the early Rapier cranes. During the taking up of load, the capstan was prevented from slipping back by a ratchet and pawl. Once the correct load had been achieved, a pin was inserted into an arm projecting from the upper part of the scissors, which passed through a slot in one side of the bogie frame. The only Craven cranes with weight-relieving bogies provided to a British railway were the two 36-ton breakdown cranes for the LMS in 1931, however their design of bogie was later taken up by some continental crane builders.

The alternative versions of relieving bogie are illustrated in the drawings on p.19 (Figures 6 to 7). All types had their merits and disadvantages in use, the Craven being the best liked and Cowans least favoured, particularly due to the lack of a facility to lubricate the knuckle and difficulties when engaging or disengaging the bogie on curved track.

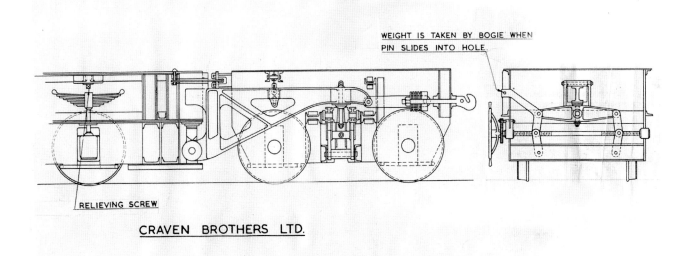

Figure 6 The form of relieving bogie developed by Craven Bros. *P. Tatlow collection*

Figure 7 A general arrangement drawing for the Craven Bros version of relieving bogie applied to the two 36-ton cranes supplied to the LMS in 1931. *Craven Bros, courtesy Herbert Morris*

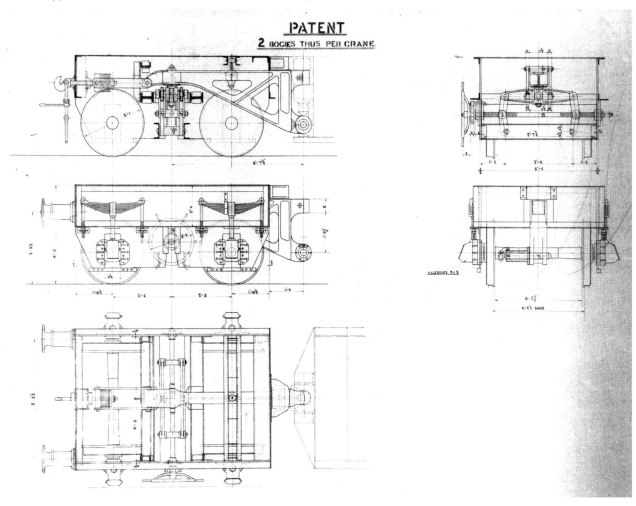

Craven Bros' form of large steel casting for the cantilever connection between the bogie on the left and crane on the right. *Author*

MIDLAND RAILWAY RANSOMES & RAPIER 36/40-TON								
Date ordered: delivered	Order No	Cost	Running No			Match wagon No	Allocation	Disposal
			MR	1st LMS	2ndLMS/BR			
18/4/14: 1916	B7608	£3,703	249	MP1	RS1038/40	1600	Derby 1916–5/58, Kentish Town 1962, Cricklewood 3/64, Banbury 12/7/66, Toton (store) 10/66	Withdrawn 4/67, sold for scrap 12/8/67

36-ton Crane for the Midland Railway (MR)

The first crane incorporating relieving bogies supplied by Ransomes & Rapier to a British railway company was the 36-tonner ordered on 18 April 1914, by the Midland Railway. A delivery period of 10 months, or earlier if possible, was agreed, but the outbreak of the First World War meant that it was not delivered until early 1916. The crane's superstructure was similar to the previous GW and LNWR cranes, which had detachable counterweights, with the same cast-steel bedplate inside the crab sides and bearing springs as the LNWR crane. The crane alone weighed about 82½ tons. When complete with its bogies, this increased to 96¾ tons, but redistribution of the crane's load enabled the ensemble to achieve a maximum axle load of 12¼ tons. As this crane clearly predates the Patent of 1930, it is presumed not to have included the balljoint within the bogie, and hence lacked the improved ability to accommodate pitch and roll of the bogie relative to the crane.

An option to fit either a 4ft 6in-diameter by 7ft 2in-high ER & F Turner boiler, or a 4ft 6in-diameter by 6ft 3in-high Spencer Hopwood unit, both at a working pressure of 80psi, and lagged with wood, was left to the makers, and depended on whether the first type could be accommodated within the restricted loading gauge of the Midland Railway. In the event, the boiler fitted was a Spencer Hopwood and the working pressure later increased to 120psi with subsequent replacement boilers. The buffers, draw gear, boiler pressure gauge and cab windows in the rear of the shelter were supplied free of charge by the MR. To allow a four-axle carriage to pass slowly round a four-chain curve, the journals of the axles were provided with side play and the flanges of the inner wheels of the carriage were thinner than normal.

One of the advantages of adopting the relieving bogie arrangements was that the propping girders could be permanently carried in the carriage of the crane, rather than having to be taken from the match wagon and inserted prior to commencing work. In this case however, the propping girders were not initially fitted with jacks, but merely vertical stiffeners at the ends, a feature which would have saved some weight to be carried by the crane. Instead, the makers were required to provide short auxiliary girders and two screw jacks per propping girder, which were carried on the match wagon. An auxiliary girder was placed across the end of each propping girder and supported on a pair of screw jacks standing on the usual timber packing. At some point later, probably coinciding with an update, conventional screw jacks were fitted to the outer ends of each propping girder.

The four-wheeled match wagon was built at Derby to Lot 890 and drawing No 4223, ordered on 8 October 1914. Its design appears to owe a lot to that company's 20-ton flat wagon to diagram D585, with four shackles attached to the solebars on each side. The roller-jib carrier and swivel plate were supplied by Rapier at an additional cost of £25. The jib rest on the crane's match wagon was changed by early BR days to one which more readily permitted transverse movement as the crane negotiated a curve, and was similar to those on the match wagons used with the LMS 30-ton cranes described in Chapter 6.

The superstructure revolved on a live roller ring running on a machined roller path which incorporated the external-tooth slew rack. A slipping clutch in the drive protected the slew gear from excessive load or shocks. The crane was fitted with two horizontal engines, each with a 9in x 14in single cylinder and link reversing gear, one on either side of the machinery frame.

The crane was capable of lifting 36 tons at a radius of 20ft with a 38ft lift above rail level, 24 tons at 30ft radius, or 16 tons at 40ft radius in propped condition, or 14 tons at 20ft when 'free on rail'. The load was lifted on a 4¼in-circumference steel wire rope, reeved in four falls, one winding on the barrel; the ram's-horn hook was fitted with a ball-bearing race. The derricking tackle was a 4in-circumference steel wire rope, reeved in ten falls, two winding on the barrel.

This crane remained the only example with relieving bogies in Britain until 1931, when the MR's successor, the LMS, acquired more, after which other railway companies followed suit. As the largest on the system, the Midland's 36-ton crane was located at Derby for much of its life, from where it could be sent to most parts of its system to assist the numerous locally based 15-ton cranes. Numbered 249 by the MR, it was soon designated MP1 by the LMS, only to be renumbered RS1038/40 in May 1941, a number it kept until the end of its days.

As part of the LMS's review and upgrading of cranes in 1937/8, discussed in Chapter 2, it was uprated from 36 tons to 40 tons at its minimum radius of 18ft – a token gesture. By the early 1940s, a small platform had been fitted for the supervisor on the front right-hand corner of the superstructure, and a water tank added under the driver's position. Once displaced at Derby by the arrival of a new 75-ton crane in 1962, RS1038/40 commenced a more peripatetic life and after short sojourns at Cricklewood, Banbury and in store at Toton, further possibilities being somewhat limited by its extreme height of 13ft 4¼in, it was withdrawn in April 1967 and sold for scrap on 12 August.

Overleaf, Figure 8 Elevation of the first crane equipped with relieving bogies for a British railway company, a Ransomes & Rapier 36-ton steam crane which was supplied to the Midland Railway in 1915/6 and later uprated to 40-ton capacity. *Author*

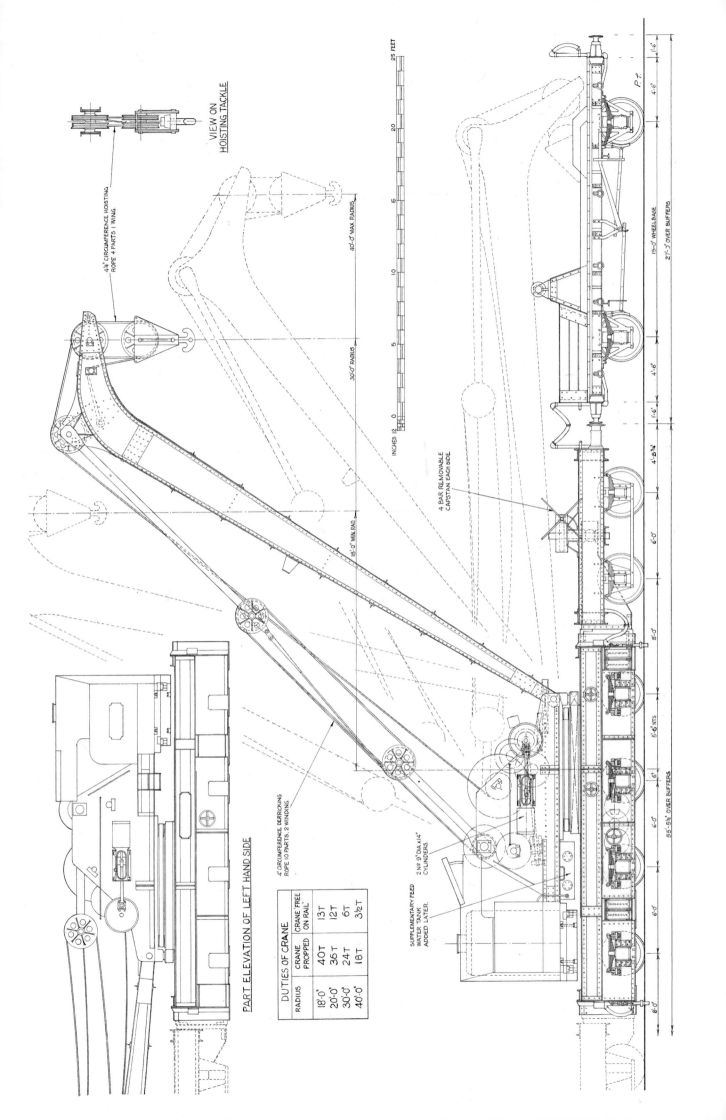

VIEW ON
HOISTING TACKLE

4¼" CIRCUMFERENCE HOISTING
ROPE 4 PARTS 1 WING.

40'-0" MAX RADIUS.

30'-0" RADIUS

16'-0" MIN. RAD.

25 FEET

20

15

10

5

0

INCHES 12

PART ELEVATION OF LEFT HAND SIDE

4 BAR REMOVABLE
CAPSTAN EACH SIDE.

4" CIRCUMFERENCE DERRICKING
ROPE 10 PARTS, 2 WINDING.

2 No 9" DIA x 14"
CYLINDERS.

SUPPLEMENTARY FEED
WATER TANK
ADDED LATER.

DUTIES OF CRANE		
RADIUS	CRANE PROPPED	CRANE FREE ON RAIL
18'-0"	40T	13T
20'-0"	36T	12T
30'-0"	24T	6T
40'-0"	18T	3½T

P.T.

1'-6"

4'-6"

15'-0" WHEELBASE

27'-3" OVER BUFFERS

4'-6"

1'-6"

4'-8¾"

6'-0"

8'-0"

5'-6 KTS

6'

6'-0"

6'-0"

8'-0"

55'-5⅝" OVER BUFFERS

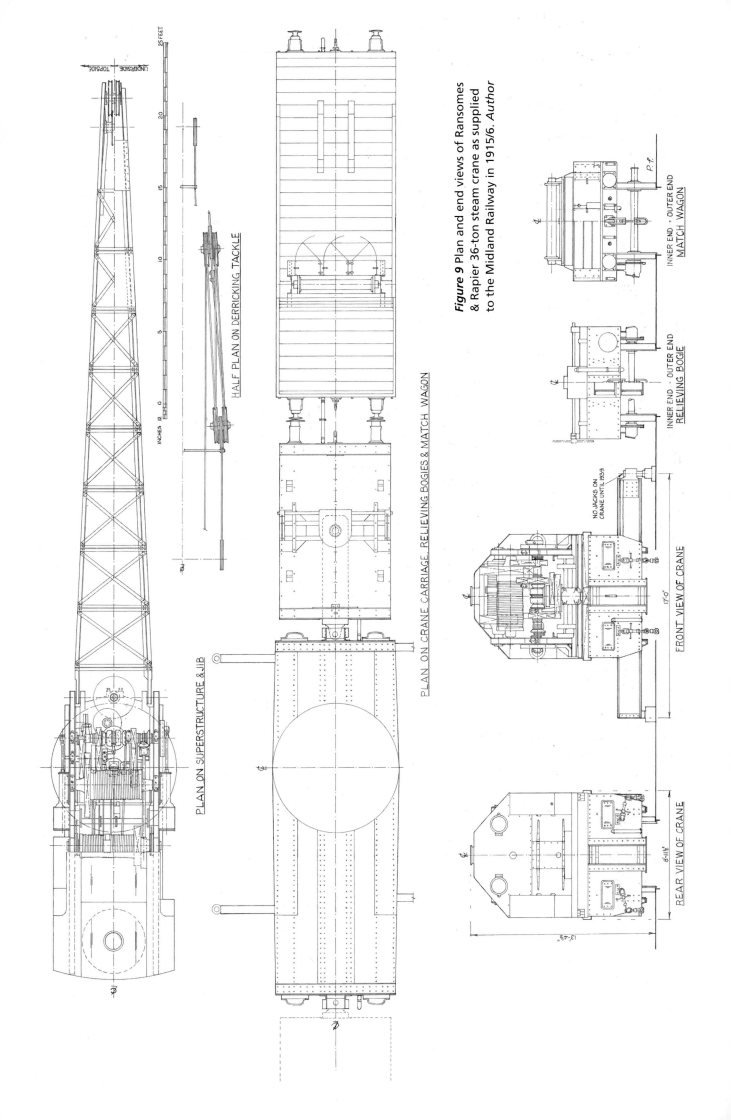

HALF PLAN ON DERRICKING TACKLE

PLAN ON SUPERSTRUCTURE & JIB

PLAN ON CRANE CARRIAGE, RELIEVING BOGIES & MATCH WAGON

TOPSIDE.
UNDERSIDE.

UNDERSIDE. TOPSIDE.

25 FEET

20

15

10

5

0

INCHES 12 0

INNER END - OUTER END
MATCH WAGON

INNER END - OUTER END
RELIEVING BOGIE

NO JACKS ON
CRANE UNTIL 1939

FRONT VIEW OF CRANE

REAR VIEW OF CRANE

Figure 9 Plan and end views of Ransomes
& Rapier 36-ton steam crane as supplied
to the Midland Railway in 1915/6. *Author*

Ransomes & Rapier were responsible again for introducing the next development of railway cranes in the form of detachable relieving bogies at each end of the crane's carriage, invented by Wilfrid Stokes to limit the maximum axle load imposed by the crane in train formation. The Midland Railway took advantage of the system by acquiring a 36-ton crane in 1915/6. It was allocated to Derby for many years from where it could be dispatched to anywhere on the system to assist the company's 15-ton cranes with heavy lifts. It is seen here with the rest of the breakdown train at Derby North Side Goods Yard in early LMS days behind ex-MR 0-6-0 3F No 3637. *London Midland Region, author's collection*

One of the more unpleasant training exercises necessitated
by war was that of operating the crane under gas attack.
Here the crew of No RS1038/40 practice their skills dressed in
oilskins. Note the supervisor standing at the front right-hand
corner of the superstructure from where he had a good view.
The four-arm capstan on the relieving bogie is also apparent.
London Midland Region, author's collection

Under the direction of the crane supervisor, standing on the carriage, the driver of No RS1038/40 gently handles
ex-LNWR covered goods van No 276370 over the long end of the crane sometime during 1946. Note that conventional
screw jacks have been fitted to the propping-girder ends. Also note the steam-turbine generator immediately behind
the cylinder. *R.S. Carpenter collection*

Ex-MR 40-ton Ransomes & Rapier steam crane as BR No RS1038/40 participates in a bridge-deck renewal at Attenborough Jct on 24 August 1961. This crane looks very smart in black livery, lined in red on the carriage and bogies, or straw on the jib, crab sides and water tank, while the second version of the BR totem has been applied to the water tank. *M.S. Welch*

2
LMS Restocking in 1931

With the grouping in 1923, the London Midland & Scottish Railway took on from its constituent companies twenty-five steam breakdown cranes of varying size, together with a number of small hand cranes allocated to the Motive Power Department for breakdown work. Many of the steam cranes were of low capacity with short jibs, such as Cowans Sheldon 15-tonners dating from the last decade of the previous century. Nonetheless, it did include five relatively modern 35/36-ton-capacity cranes, together with two 25-ton and three 20-ton not quite so up-to-date cranes, only one of which had a long jib.

As the company set about building increasing numbers of larger and heavier engines for use on the system as a whole, the smaller cranes were soon outclassed, resulting in the need to bring in a bigger crane from further afield. For these locomotives supplied up to 31 December 1930, excluding the special case of the Beyer Garratts, the engines alone weighed up to 88 tons.

To meet this challenge, in 1930 the LMS ordered six 36-ton cranes from three different builders. The three from Cowans and two from Craven were capable of lifting their maximum load out to a radius of 25ft and 24ft respectively. The last order was for a single crane from Ransomes & Rapier of Ipswich, but in this case 36 tons could be lifted to a radius of only 20ft, which was no advance on their 1908 design. The reason the LMS spread its favours in this fashion has yet to be established, when one would have expected greater economy and consistency to have been achieved by having one supplier fulfil the entire order.

Supply of 36-ton Cranes
Letters of enquiry were issued to potential suppliers in February 1929, and proposals were submitted by those bidding towards the end of June, after which negotiations would have taken place before firm orders were placed in May 1930. All six of these cranes were delivered in 1931 and allocated in the first instance to Durranhill (Carlisle), Leeds, Motherwell, Rugby, Newton Heath (Manchester) and Kentish Town (London). All had relieving bogies and had a minimum radius of 18ft and maximum of 40ft. The Specification must have called for three pairs of propping girders, when by then two pairs were usually considered satisfactory. As delivered, no jacks were fitted to the ends of the propping girders. The rail clips, buffers, draw gear and some boiler fittings were supplied by the railway company.

The match wagons to all six cranes were built by the LMS Railway Company at their Derby Works. This official photograph was taken of No 299852 when out-shopped in May 1931. In due course it was paired with the first of the Craven cranes. Note the small wheels permitting the lowered solebars to afford easier access for the crew to release and stow the ram's-horn and other lifting equipment. *London Midland Region, author's collection*

A 32-volt, 500W-capacity steam turbine generator, protected from frost, was to be provided for electric floodlighting which was specified to include: jib light; one floodlight either side of crane; lighting in the cabin; one socket either side of crane for a portable lamp, one portable lamp with suitable flexible cable and plug socket.

The match wagons for all six cranes were designed and built by the Company at Derby Works in 1931, to Diagram 1836 to Lot 600, Nos 299850 to 299855, tare 9 tons 3cwt. To ease access and the task of loading the match wagons with tackle, they were mounted on low underframes, the solebars passing below the headstocks. The wagons had particularly short carrying springs, supporting 2ft 8½in-diameter disc wheels with 9 x 4¼in journals. The wagons were fitted with independent lever brakes each side and a through-vacuum brake pipe was provided from the outset. A shackle was mounted on the centreline of the floor, under the jib rest, to draw back the ram's-horn hook and block into their stowage position and to secure them. Later in life, at least two match wagons had a winding mechanism added.

Cowans Sheldon 36-ton Cranes

The LMS Company's order for three cranes was received by Cowans Sheldon on 30 May 1930. These were given Works Nos 5111 to 5113 and delivered the next year at an initial cost of £5,574 each. They were the first cranes built by the company to utilise the relieving-bogie principle. As supplied, these cranes weighed 95 tons in working order, with a maximum axle load of 13 tons, and 6 tons 16cwt of the jib and tackle resting on the match wagon. The total weight of the crane and match wagon was therefore 111 tons 16cwt. Solid-spoked wheels of 3ft diameter, with 12 x 6in-diameter journals were provided on the crane, the journals being reduced to 9 x 5in on the bogies.

The crane had a double-lattice jib formed of four longitudinal angles, with inclined bracing angles riveted inside, and plating only at the outer end and at the foot. The jib was raised by the derricking tackle consisting of ten parts of 4in-circumference steel wire rope, one of which wound round the drum immediately in front of the driver's position. The double hook, or ram's horn, was hoisted by six parts of 3½in-circumference steel wire rope, one of which was taken down to the hoisting drum close by the foot of the jib. The superstructure could be

rotated on the carriage by the slewing gear, while at the site of operations, clutches could be engaged to drive the forward two axles by the travelling gear.

All these motions were driven by a pair of 12 x 8in-diameter cylinders driving a cross-shaft at the centre of the superstructure, acting on trains of gears brought into play by dog clutches for each motion, similar to the machinery of the 35-ton NER cranes described on pp.160–162 of Volume 1. The steam was supplied by a 6ft 8in-high, 4ft 6in-diameter Spencer Hopwood No 14 squat boiler, pressurised to 120psi, mounted at the rear of the superstructure. This was hand coal fired with cold-water feed. A heating surface of 138.7ft^2 and a 12.4ft^2 grate area produced an evaporation rate of 1,055lb/hr, or 1,400lb/hr when worked hard.

This machinery enabled the jib to be raised from the match wagon to minimum radius in 3 minutes. 36 tons could be lifted at the rate of 13ft/min in low gear, or 12 tons at 35ft/min in high gear. One whole revolution of the superstructure with a 36-ton load could be completed in 2 minutes, while with a load of 10 tons, the crane could propel itself at 150ft/min. In addition to the clutch wheels on the carriage side to engage the travelling gear, hand wheels on each end of a common cross-shaft applied the brake to four wheels of the carriage, while the relieving bogies had no brake. The crane, relieving bogies and match wagon were equipped with a through pipe for the train vacuum brake, but were not themselves vacuum braked. The minimum radius the crane could negotiate was 4 chains.

MP2 was initially allocated to Durranhill, but rationalisation of motive power facilities around Carlisle led to its transfer to Kingmoor in 1936. MP4 went to Leeds until after the strengthening described later in this chapter. It also ended up on the West Coast mainline at Crewe. Finally, the Northern Division received Plant No 1250 at Motherwell. The latter movements, following the cranes' increase in capacity, will be discussed in due course.

Right, Figure 10 Elevation of Cowans Sheldon 36/50-ton crane supplied to the LMS in 1931. *Author*

COWANS SHELDON 36/50-TON FOR LMS						
Works No	Running No			Match wagon No	Allocation	Disposal
	MP/ Plant	5/41, BR	BR CEPS			
5112 6637	2	RS1001/50 ADM1001	(ADRC 95202)	299854	Durranhill 2/31, Kingmoor 3/36 to & from ScR 1958–1/10/60, Lostock Hall 7/62–1970, Springs Branch 3/72–9/6/76, Wigan 20/8/77–9/4/81	Withdrawn 8/80 & sold to Midland Rly Trust
5111 6636	4	RS1005/50 ADM1005	(ADRC 95203)	299851	Leeds 1931, Crewe N 12/39, Crewe DD 24/6/72–1/79	K&WVR 5/82
5113 6638	1250	RS1054/50 ADM1054	ADRC 95204	299855	Motherwell 1931–1/10/60, St Margaret's 1962–30/5/66, Haymarket 1966–11/86	GWS, Didcot 9/87
Note: Dates shown in *italics* are spot dates upon which the crane is known to have been at the depot concerned.						

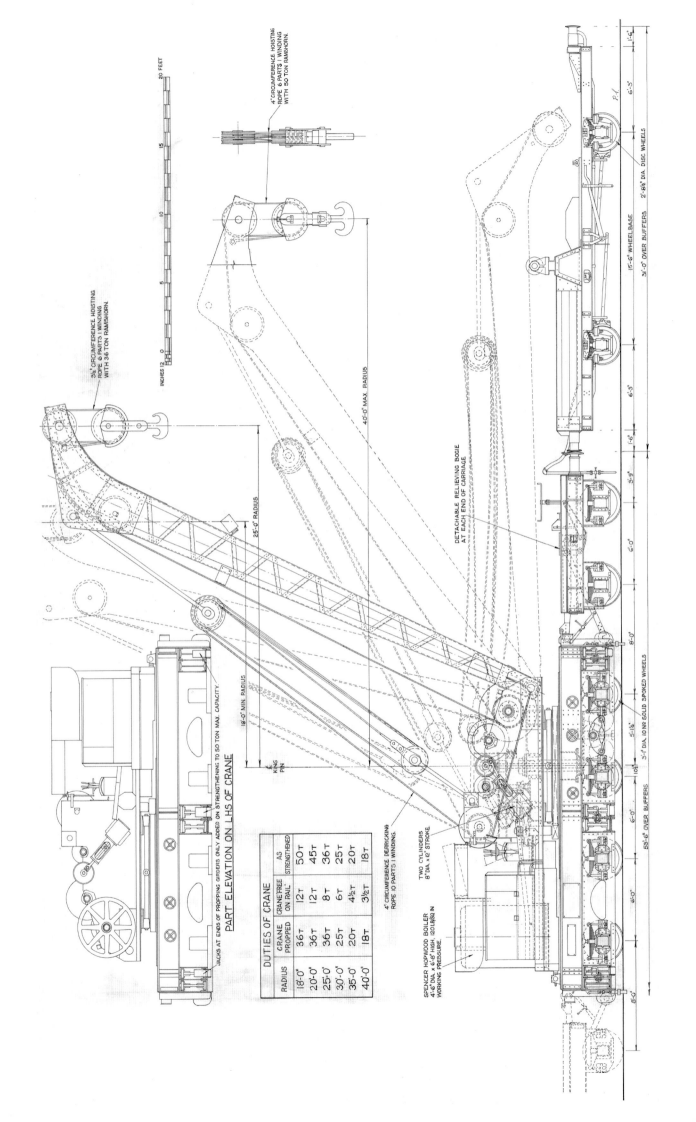

20 FEET

15

10

5

INCHES 12   0

4" CIRCUMFERENCE HOISTING
ROPE 6 PARTS 1 WINDING
WITH 50 TON RAMSHORN.

3½" CIRCUMFERENCE HOISTING
ROPE 6 PARTS 1 WINDING
WITH 36 TON RAMSHORN.

40'-0" MAX. RADIUS

25'-0" RADIUS

18'-0" MIN. RADIUS

C. OF
KING
PIN

JACKS AT ENDS OF PROPPING GIRDERS ONLY ADDED ON STRENGTHENING TO 50 TON MAX. CAPACITY.

PART ELEVATION ON L.H.S. OF CRANE

DUTIES OF CRANE

RADIUS	CRANE PROPPED	CRANE FREE ON RAIL	AS STRENGTHENED
18'-0"	36T	12T	50T
20'-0"	36T	12T	45T
25'-0"	36T	8T	36T
30'-0"	25T	6T	25T
35'-0"	20T	4½T	20T
40'-0"	18T	3½T	18T

4" CIRCUMFERENCE DERRICKING
ROPE 10 PARTS 1 WINDING.

TWO CYLINDERS
8" DIA. x 12" STROKE.

SPENCER HOPWOOD BOILER
4'-6" DIA x 6'-8" HIGH 120 LBS/SQ IN
WORKING PRESSURE.

DETACHABLE RELIEVING BOGIE
AT EACH END OF CARRIAGE

P.L.

1'-6"

6'-3"

2'-8½" DIA. DISC WHEELS

15'-6" WHEEL BASE

31'-0" OVER BUFFERS

6'-3"

1'-6"

3'-9"

6'-0"

8'-0"

5'-1½"

3'-1" DIA. 10 N9 SOLID SPOKED WHEELS

10T

6'-0"

53'-6" OVER BUFFERS

6'-0"

8'-0"

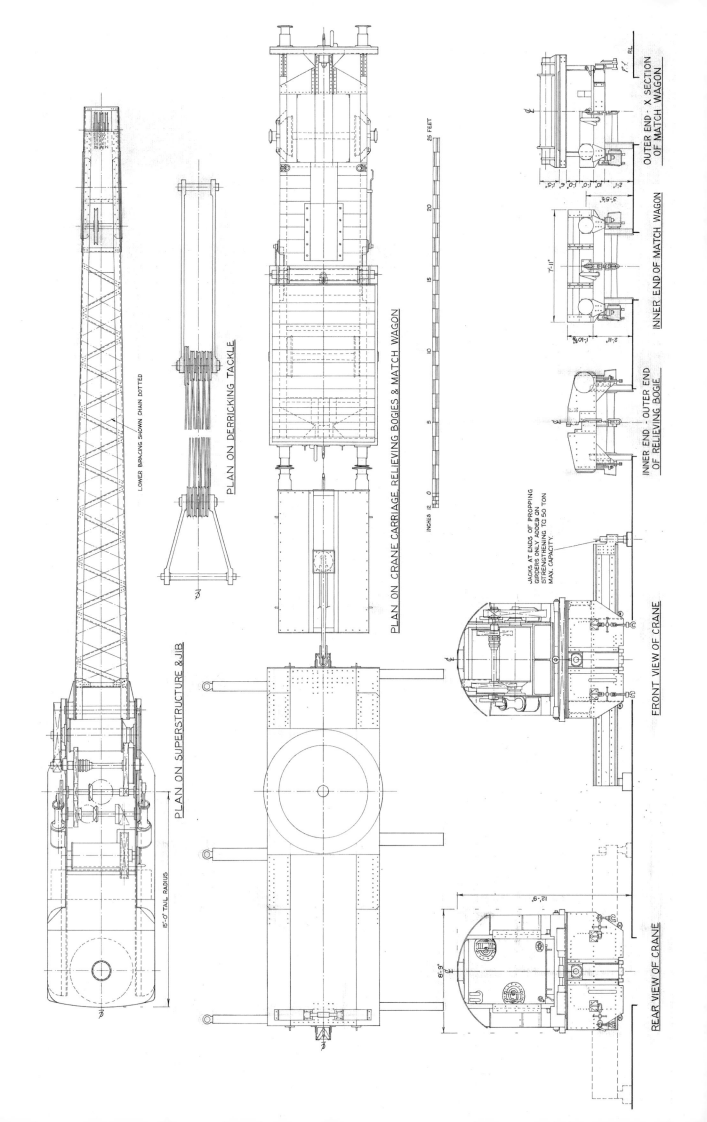

LOWER BRACING SHOWN CHAIN DOTTED

PLAN ON DERRICKING TACKLE

PLAN ON CRANE CARRIAGE RELIEVING BOGIES & MATCH WAGON

PLAN ON SUPERSTRUCTURE & JIB

15'-0" TAIL RADIUS

INCHES 12 0   5   10   15   20   25 FEET

OUTER END - X SECTION OF MATCH WAGON

INNER END OF MATCH WAGON

3'-9⅜"
7'-11"
2'-11"
1'-10⅝"

INNER END - OUTER END OF RELIEVING BOGIE

JACKS AT ENDS OF PROPPING
GIRDERS ONLY ADDED ON
STRENGTHENING TO 50 TON
MAX. CAPACITY.

FRONT VIEW OF CRANE

12'-9"
8'-9"

REAR VIEW OF CRANE

Left, Figure 11 Plan and end views of Cowans Sheldon 36/50-ton crane supplied to the LMS in 1931. *Author*

Ex-LMS 50-ton Cowans Sheldon steam crane at Sedgeley Jct, Dudley Port, on 14 May 1961 during the renewal of the deck of an underbridge. No RS1005/50 looks magnificent in its recently applied bright red livery with black and straw lining. *M.S. Welch*

The relieving bogie to No RS1054/50 undergoing restoration soon after arrival at Didcot. *M. Golder*

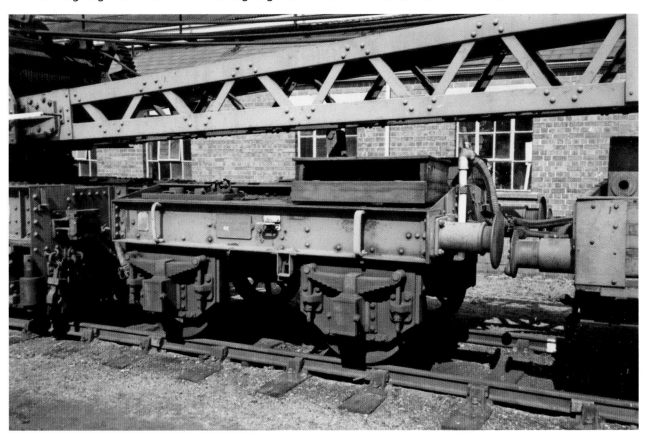

No RS1001/50 from Lostock Hall stands outside Cowans Sheldon's St Nicholas Works, Carlisle, on 19 August 1966 with the rear bogie temporarily removed for attention. At the time, the crane was in a lined-out Carmine/Crimson Lake livery. *Author*

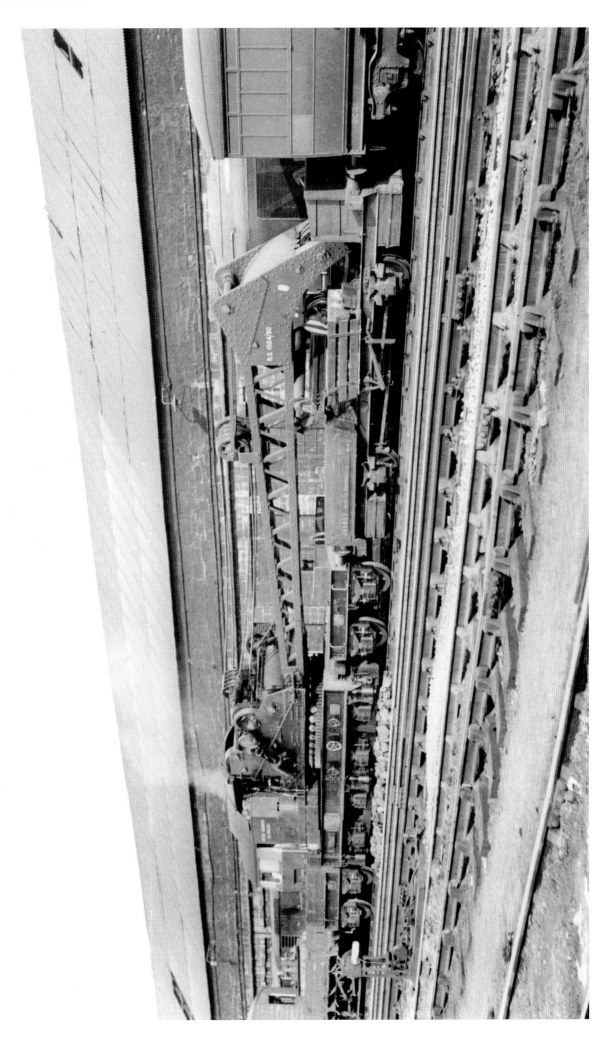

No RS1054/50 was allocated from the outset to Scotland, first to Motherwell and later to first St Margaret's and then Haymarket. Here it is seen still in BR black livery at St Margaret's on 30 May 1966. Note the additional tool and lumber boxes added to the match truck and relieving bogies. *M.S. Welch*

Right This photographs shows TDM1001, formerly RS1001/50, allocated to Wigan works, working with ex-LNER 45-ton Ransomes & Rapier No RS1083/45 from Newton Heath, at Rochdale on 20 August 1977. The cranes are carrying out the awkward operation of turning and lowering to the roadway on the left, below the old metal deck, which will be cut up into smaller pieces before carting away. The three propping girders, now fitted with screw jacks, have been drawn out and the jacks screwed down on timber packing. *M.S. Welch*

Below No M1005, formerly RS1005/50, and by now also based at Wigan Traction Maintenance Depot, together with another Ransomes & Rapier 45-ton crane, No ADRR95214 from Tinsley, undertakes a tricky task on 8 April 1981, hampered by the presence of the over-bridge and overhead electric wires. An anhydrous-ammonia tanker in an Up freight had derailed on a crossover west of Hadfield station while regaining the Up line after proceeding 'wrong line' due to a previous derailment. *M.S. Welch*

Craven Bros 36-ton Cranes

The two Craven Bros cranes were ordered in May 1930, at an initial cost of £5,390 each to Order No 12683, and were delivered in 1931. They were generally to the same performance specification as those provided by Cowans Sheldon, although not quite achieving the same lifting capacities. They were the last steam cranes built at Reddish and last breakdown cranes from Craven.

Craven continued its previous practice of placing the wheel springs outside the carriage side plates with extended hangers, and used the same layout for the relieving bogies. This tended to restrict the width of the frame of the crane, and led to the need for massive gussets to support the propping girder boxes and an external subframe carrying the periphery of the slewing ring and roller path. With the two relieving bogies carrying 10 tons each, the crane's axle loads were brought down to a maximum of 12 tons 17cwt.

Steam at 120psi was supplied by a 4ft 6in-diameter, 6ft 6in-high Spencer Hopwood boiler. The outside inclined 8in-diameter, 14in-stroke cylinders, activated by Walschaert's motion, enabled the crankshaft to achieve a speed of 140rpm.

The jib was of the fully-lattice N truss form, with solid plating only at the jib foot and head. As built, four steel wire ropes formed the hoisting tackle to a ram's horn suspended between a pair of sheaves and taken back up to a small block suspended from the underside of the jib. As with previous Craven practice, by releasing this block and removing the main block, hoisting could be carried out at double the speed. Derricking was by two ropes, each winding in six parts to sheaves mounted on top of the jib head.

One notable development was the adoption of an articulated jib foot. On all the cranes described so far, the crane superstructure and jib had to be considered as a rigid body in plan when travelling round curves. The superstructure was able to rotate about the kingpin, with the jib restrained by the jib rest on the match wagon, often with a limit to which the tail of the crane could move laterally relative to the carriage. As a result, the radius of line curvature that the long-jibbed cranes (introduced during the period under review) were permitted to travel was restricted.

On 8 January 1930, Albert Edward Horrocks of Craven Bros filed a patent application with the United Kingdom Patent Office for articulating the jib of a crane by providing a slot in the jib foot, within which the transverse pin at the front of the crab sides was free to slide when the jib was in a horizontal position. A latch was also included, to ensure that the pin could not move while the jib was raised in its working position. It must have been quickly realised that once strain was taken up on the derricking tackle, the high reaction force down the length of the jib would ensure the jib foot would remain firmly in contact anyway, and an amended specification was submitted on 6 February 1930. British patent No 346,348 was granted for the invention on 8 April 1931.

As-new LMS 36-ton Craven Bros crane No MP9 paired with match wagon No 299853. The tone of this monochrome image suggests that the crane is black, while the match wagon has a slightly lighter hue. Note that the relieving bogies are handed, with the large-diameter hand wheels of both bogies on the right-hand side of the crane. A short man is deliberately stood beside the crane to give an exaggerated sense of the scale of this impressive crane. *Herbert Morris, author's collection*

CRAVEN 5000

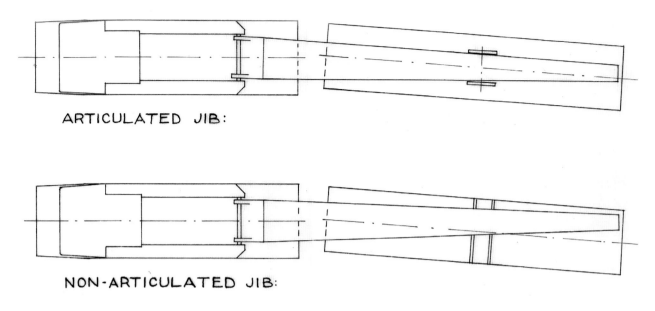

ARTICULATED JIB:

NON-ARTICULATED JIB:

Figure 12 Diagram demonstrating the difference between fixed and articulated jibs when passing round a curve. *Author*

Craven Bros fitted articulated jibs without latches to the two cranes they supplied to the LMS. The foot of the jib was arranged so that, when in the lowered position, a small degree of movement was possible between it and the crane's superstructure. To achieve this, the circular transverse bar, about which the foot of the jib could rotate, was contained on each side within a horizontal elongated slot, part way through the heavy cheeks of the crab sides at the front end. This bar was extended on each side in square section through to the exterior, and

could slide between a pair of horizontal bars mounted on the outside of the front of the crab sides, but was prevented from rotating. When the jib was horizontal and supported by the match wagon, the bar was able to move forward within the slot, and hence small rotations of the jib in relation to the superstructure could take place in plan, thereby permitting lateral movement of the jib head relative to the rest of the crane, so the jib could follow the curve, see drawing on this page (Figure 12).

A photograph taken looking down on a Craven 36-ton crane while standing on a sharp curve to demonstrate the benefit of the articulated jib. Note that, despite the angle of the distant crane carriage to the nearer match wagon, the jib head is still central on the jib rest. The jib is not in line with the crane, but is on the chord between it and the centre of the jib rest. *Barry Lane collection*

CRAVEN BROS 36/50-TON FOR LMS						
Cost	Running No			Match wagon No	Allocation	Disposal
	MP	5/41	BR CEPS			
£5,390/£6,102	8	RS1013/50 ADM1013	(ADRV 95205)	299852	Rugby 1931–45, Crewe Wks (on loan) 6/45–1/7/47, Rugby 1952–5/64, Bescot 1965, Cricklewood 12/68–28/2/69, Bescot 6/9/69, Crewe (spare) 21/9/71, Longsight 11/72–1977, Carlisle 10/77–5/79	Withdrawn 4/82, sold to E Lancs Rly 11/82
£5,390/£6,102	9	RS1015/50 ADM1015	(ADRV 95206)	299853	Newton Heath 1931, Willesden 12/39, Derby 1962, Willesden 13/8/65–4/72, Allerton 1/79	Withdrawn 2/82, sold to Dinting RC 2/82

Note: Dates shown in *italics* are spot dates upon which the crane is known to have been at the depot concerned.

Sent to Rugby on delivery, in 1936 No MP8 was specially fitted out with an extension to the jib to enable it to lift 8 tons at a radius of 23ft up to a height of 55ft above rail level. This was required for erecting structural components in connection with the modernisation of motive power depots and at Birmingham New Street. No MP9 went to Newton Heath at the outset.

A fine scale model of a Craven 36-ton crane was made by the model engineer Sidney J Ward of Northampton. This cup-winning model of an LMS Craven, built at Northampton in 1934 to the maker's drawings, was once displayed in the Great Hall at Euston station. The model was rebuilt in the 1960s and is now in the custody of the University of Northampton, but sadly in storage rather than on display where it might encourage present-day students to pursue a career in hands-on engineering.

A Craven 36-ton crane on delivery to Newton Heath in 1931, showing a close-up of the driver at the controls and with the superstructure slewed across the track. This photograph was taken by William Atherton of Craven Bros on the occasion of handing over the crane to the railway. It was numbered MP9 by the LMS and after strengthening became No RS1015/50 from May 1941. *Herbert Morris, author's collection*

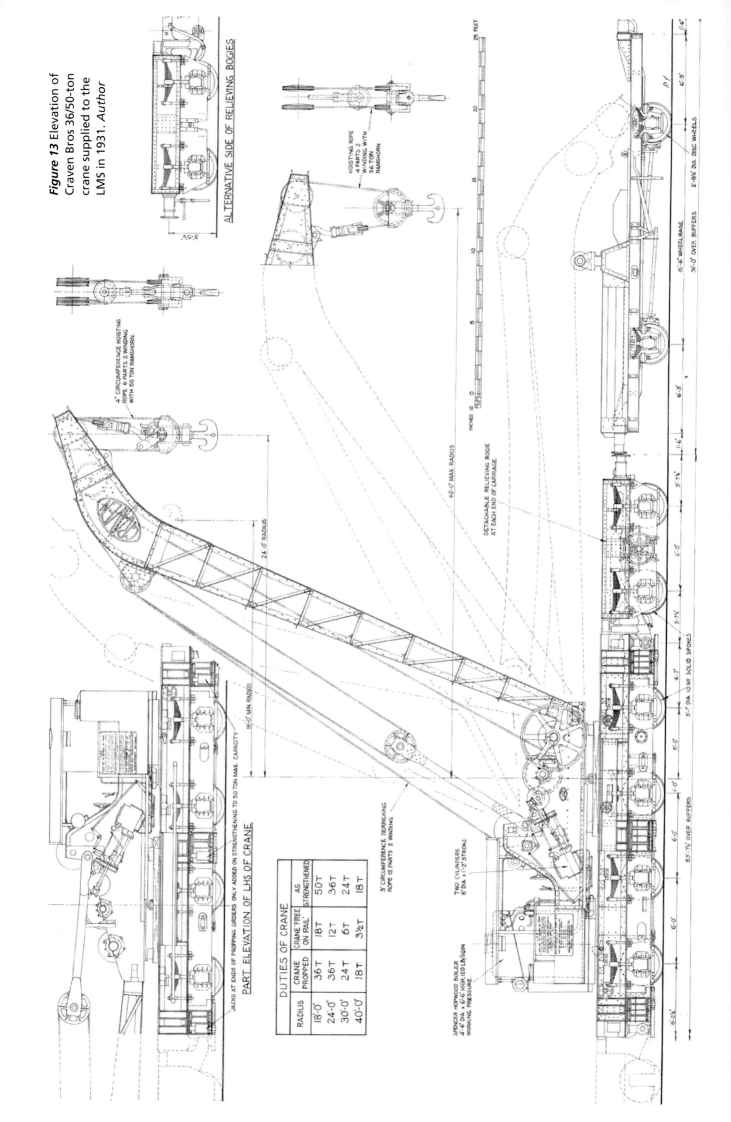

Figure 13 Elevation of Craven Bros 36/50-ton crane supplied to the LMS in 1931. *Author*

ALTERNATIVE SIDE OF RELIEVING BOGIES

HOISTING ROPE
4 PARTS 2
WINDING WITH
36 TON
RAMSHORN

4" CIRCUMFERENCE HOISTING
ROPE. 6 PARTS 2 WINDING
WITH 50 TON RAMSHORN.

40'-0" MAX RADIUS

24'-0" RADIUS

18'-0" MIN RADIUS

DETACHABLE RELIEVING BOGIE
AT EACH END OF CARRIAGE

INCHES 12 0   5   10   15   20   25 FEET

JACKS AT ENDS OF PROPPING GIRDERS ONLY ADDED ON STRENGTHENING TO 50 TON MAX CAPACITY

PART ELEVATION OF LHS OF CRANE

3" CIRCUMFERENCE DERRICKING
ROPE 12 PARTS 2 WINDING

TWO CYLINDERS
8" DIA. x 11'-2" STROKE

SPENCER HOPWOOD BOILER
4'-6" DIA. x 6'-6" HIGH, 120 LB/sqIN
WORKING PRESSURE.

DUTIES OF CRANE		
RADIUS	CRANE PROPPED	CRANE FREE ON RAIL	AS STRENGTHENED
18'-0"	36 T	18 T	50 T
24'-0"	36 T	12 T	36 T
30'-0"	24 T	6 T	24 T
40'-0"	18 T	3½ T	18 T

P1

1'-6"

6'-3"

2'-8½" DIA. DISC WHEELS.

15'-6" WHEEL BASE

36'-0" OVER BUFFERS

6'-3"

1'-6"

3'-7½"

6'-0"

3'-7½"

3'-1" DIA. 10 NR SOLID SPOKES

4'-7"

5'-0"

1'-0"

6'-0"

6'-0"

6'-2½"

53'-7½" OVER BUFFERS

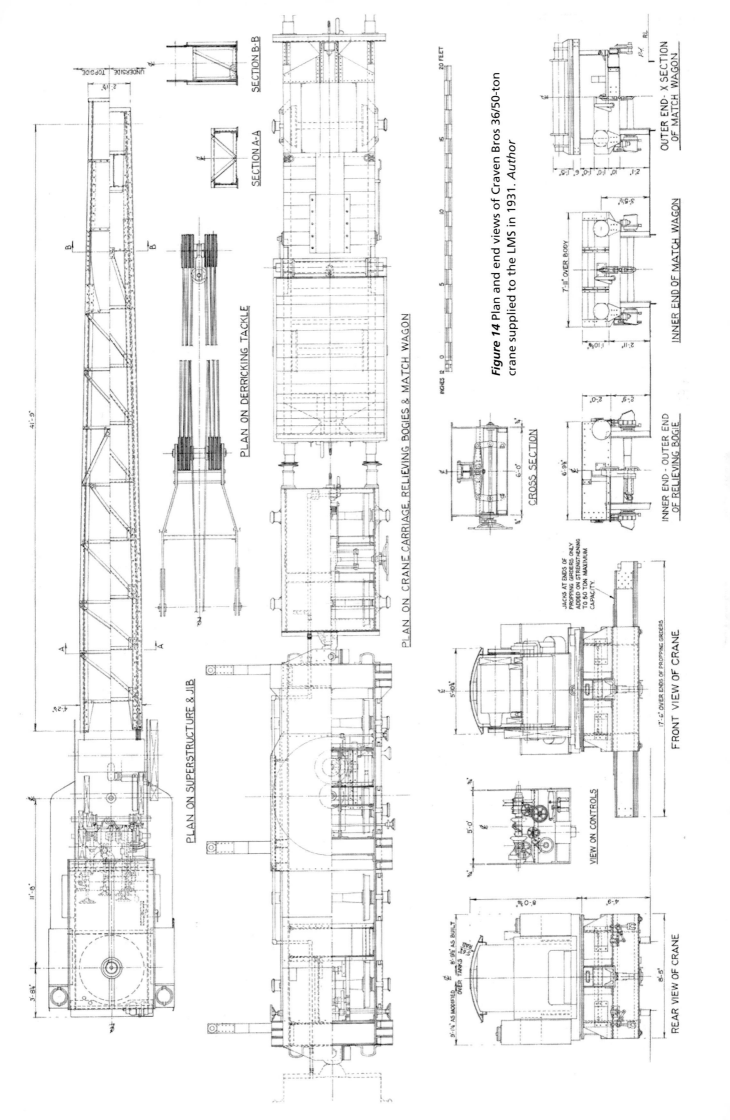

Figure 14 Plan and end views of Craven Bros 36/50-ton crane supplied to the LMS in 1931. *Author*

One of the LMS's Craven 36-ton cranes soon after delivery in 1931. Seen here on a typical minor incident of a few derailed wagons, including a GER five-plank open wagon. As built, these cranes had four falls to the hoisting rope and no jacks at the ends of the three sets of propping girders. *Unattributed*

Rugby's crane fitted with a jib extension to enable it to lift loads of up to 8 tons to a height of 55ft. It is shown here with an LMS 12-ton five-plank open wagon high in the air. The ram's-horn hook has been temporarily discarded and the smaller hook reeved over the jib extension. *London Midland Region, author's collection*

Left On 31 November 1931, LMS 2-6-0 No 13153, built the previous year, was hauling a freight train and ran into some empty coaching stock just north of Tring station. The then nearly-new Craven 36-ton breakdown crane, probably from Rugby, is seen here during the clearing-up operation. *Unattributed*

36-ton Craven Bros crane allocated to the Motive Power Section at Rugby is seen on 10 February 1939 with jib raised and attached to match wagon No 299852. The left-hand relieving bogie has had a wooden box added in which to carry timber packing. *London Midland Region, author's and Paul Bartlett's collections*

Recently out-shopped in 1964, No RS1015/50 at Derby, is pristine in its BR black livery with 'ferret & dartboard' emblem and the first signs of hazard warning in the form of yellow and black wasp stripes. *BR, LMR, author's collection*

Ransomes & Rapier 36-ton Cranes

This crane was originally supplied to the LMS in 1931 by Ransomes & Rapier to Order No D2958, at a cost of £5,578 and was rated at 36-ton capacity at a radius of 20ft when propped. Acquired at the same time were three cranes from Cowans Sheldon and a pair from Craven Bros of Manchester, which could lift 36 tons out to a radius of 24/5ft, the minimum radius being 18ft for all six cranes. Quite why the company should have gone to the bother of ordering a single example with inferior performance is unknown, when in fact Rapier was to match the capacity of the other two makes a year later with the crane it supplied to the LNER.

The design was based on that previously supplied to the Midland Railway 15 years earlier, although the carriage frame was to be 3in deeper, while a more elaborate combined horn guide and spring hanger casting was incorporated in place of separate items. The centres of the derricking and hoisting drums were lowered by 3in as part of an attempt to keep the maximum height down in order to improve route availability. The Specification required the provision of three sets of propping girders. With the front set out of use, the crane could still lift 19 tons at 20ft, 10½ tons at 30ft and 6½ tons at 40ft radius, at any position while supported on the inner propping girders.

Although it was specified that the axle load in travelling condition was limited to 18 tons, the adoption of relieving bogies meant not more than 12½ tons was anticipated. The crane was to pass round a 6-chain curve, for which purpose the tail of the crane was to be left free, but anchored by spring shock absorbers, with lateral movement of the jib restricted to the bolster on the match wagon.

The base casting to the superstructure extended for the length of the roller path and under the crab-side plates, rather than being attached to their sides. It also provided the supports to the jib foot. This foundation was cast in three parts and then welded together. The jib introduced transverse bracing in the form of an N truss, rather than the previous strut and double cross-bracing used by Ransomes & Rapier.

Originally numbered MP3, the Rapier crane was allocated when new to Kentish Town. Following uprating, it was sent to Holbeck at the end of 1939, where it was given the number No RS1004/40 in May 1941. This was changed to No 159 on being transferred to the Eastern Region, then to DE331159, and revised yet again to ADRR95207 when TOPS was introduced.

Healey Mills formally took over Holbeck's area on 31 July 1978, and the crane was transferred to Doncaster where it spent its final days with British Rail until declared surplus to requirements in January 1979. Nonetheless,

as the last steam breakdown crane on the Eastern Region, it stood in for Doncaster's 75-tonner, No ADRC96709, whilst this was at Derby Works being converted from steam to diesel-hydraulic propulsion, and continued to be maintained in working order at Doncaster for another three years, until the diesel conversions became more reliable.

It was then sold for scrapping to Wath Skip Hire of Bolton-on-Dearne in December 1982, from where it was promptly sold on to the Nene Valley Railway (NVR). Having been transported by rail to Peterborough, it was put into immediate use. It remains at the NVR and is in frequent operation for mechanical- and civil-engineering department lifts, as well as educational demonstrations and photographic charters.

The original match wagon, No (DM) 299850, had by 1966, like that of its half-sister crane No RS1038/40, received a more sophisticated jib rest which permitted transverse movement by means of rollers rather than skidding. Around mid-1970 to mid-1971, crane No 330159 was paired with LNER match wagon No DE961652 in lieu of its LMS original wagon. The replacement had formerly been used by LNER 35-ton steam breakdown crane No SB5/961601/ (DE330)131 supplied by Ransomes & Rapier in 1932, but withdrawn in March 1970 (see later). By 1976, the wheel flanges on No DE961652 had worn very thin, so early in May 1976, No DM299850 was reinstated, having been refurbished in 1975, and remained with the crane thereafter.

Further drawings for this crane will also be found on p.58 (R&R 36T, SR etc), while the original match wagon is also depicted on pp.29-30 and 39-40 (LMS CS 36/50T & Craven 36/50T) and the replacement one on pp.68 and 78 (LNER CS 35T).

Figure 15 Ransomes & Rapier's general arrangement drawing for the LMS 36-ton crane. *Author's collection*

LMS RANSOMES & RAPIER 36/40 TON							
Purchased by	Date ordered: delivered	Running No			Match wagon No	Allocation	Disposal
		1st	2nd	CEPS			
LMS	30/5/30: 1931	MP3	RS1004/40 (331)159	(ADRR 95207)	(1) 299850 (2) 961652	Kentish Town 4/31, Holbeck 12/39, to ER 10/56, Doncaster 1/8/78	Withdrawn 12/82

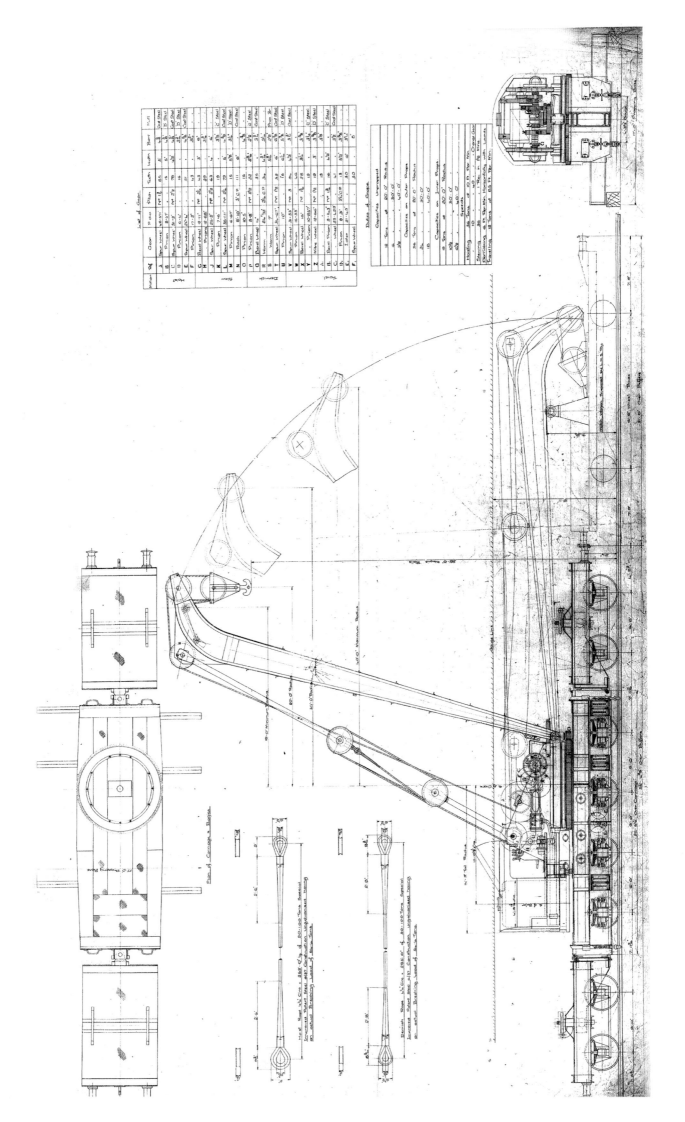

Ransomes & Rapier 36/40-ton crane No RS1004/40 with its match wagon and further relieving bogie shunted clear, together with a 45-ton Cowans Sheldon crane of 1926, probably from Doncaster, have just lifted out a centre girder over Westgate, Wakefield, on 15 April 1951 during the renewal of the bridge deck. The bridge deck has been placed on an LNER 42-ton bogie bolster (Quint D), plus a four-wheel match wagon at each end, which gives some idea of the length of the girder. *BR, NER, author's collection*

No DE331159 awaits the call of duty at Leeds Holbeck around March 1966. The original jib rest on the match wagon has been replaced. This is of a more sophisticated type with roller support on a trolley able to traverse sideways to accommodate movement while rounding a curve. *Unattributed*

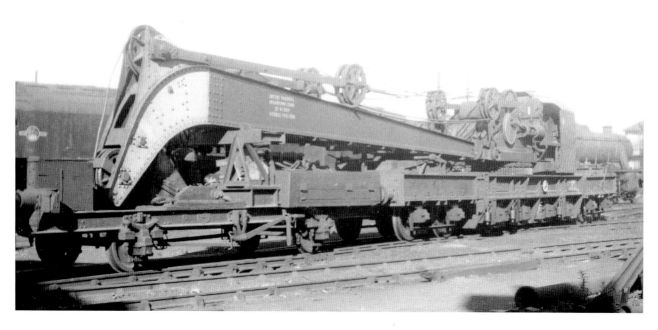

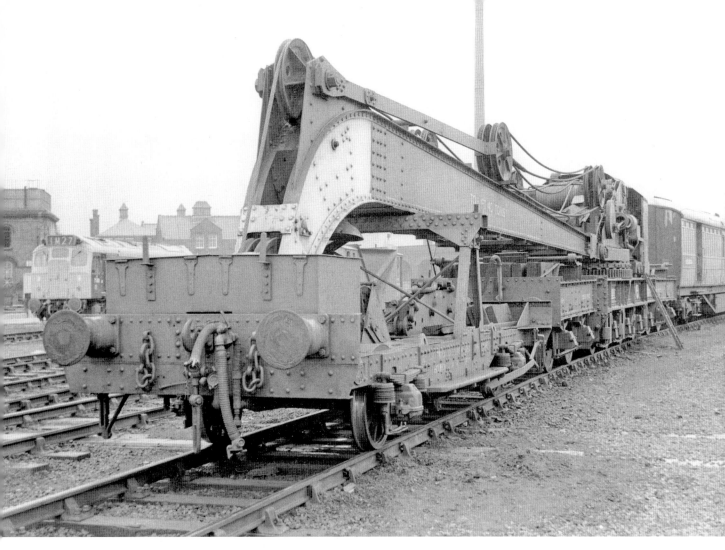

No DE331159 was still at Holbeck on 10 June 1972, in bright red livery. By this time, however, it had received replacement match wagon No DE961652, released for further use by the withdrawal of the next Rapier crane supplied to the LNER in 1932. *Author*

The Ransomes & Rapier maker's plate thought to be unique to this crane. *J.C. Dean*

Left Holbeck's 40-ton crane again, but this time at Neville Hill, on display as part of the open day there on 28 April 1973 with its jib raised and smoke drifting down towards the photographer. *John Bateman, courtesy HMRS*

Above A ladder leans against the carriage of the crane giving access to the driving area. Note the large steel foundation casting to the superstructure. *Author*

Right No DE331159's relieving bogie showing the large four-bar capstan to actuate the screw jack within, to apply and release the transfer of load from the crane for running in train formation. Note the white pointer and quadrant on the frame side used to show the degree to which the relieving load had been transferred from the crane to the bogie. The 'on' and 'off' arrows indicate the direction of rotation to apply or release load. *Author*

A close-up view of an axle box and propping girder on the crane on the same occasion. The screw jacks were fitted during the uprating around 1939. *Author*

Strengthening of Cranes to 50 tons Capacity

The LMS's locomotive building programme continued and, after the arrival of William Stanier in 1933, led to the introduction of even bigger engines. A further 520 engines of over 72 tons were built between the beginning of 1931 and end of 1938, the Princess Coronation Pacifics weighing in at 108 tons without tender, while Turbomotive tipped the scales at 110½ tons!

As with so many of the LMS Motive Power Department's activities during this period, it seems that a review of breakdown arrangements took place around 1937/8. The Cowans and Craven 36-ton cranes were designed to handle a maximum load of 36 tons from the minimum radius of 18ft out to a maximum of 25ft or 24ft. The stability of these cranes was such that actually they could safely lift 50 tons at their minimum radius. In addition, when lifting over the end, as opposed to over the side, even greater loads could be handled. One of the results of the review therefore was that the Cowans and Craven 36-ton cranes were reassessed and strengthened to lift 50 tons at their minimum radius of 18ft. On the other hand, the two Rapier 36-ton cranes with relieving bogies were merely re-rated to a capacity of 40 tons at 18ft, but without strengthening.

All were also fitted with screw jacks at the ends of the propping girders, to obviate the need to place timber folding wedges under the ends of the extended girders, and the girders were converted to extend by ratcheting, rather than by hauling on a rope. The increase in capacity was really only in recognition of what the crane crews were already doing anyway. These now became the highest capacity cranes in mainline use in the country, until the introduction of the 75-ton cranes in 1961 by British Railways.

In the case of the Cowans Sheldon cranes, the order for the strengthening work was placed on 28 August 1938 and carried out to Works Nos 6636 to 6638 at a cost of £468 each. In addition to the provision of propping jacks and ratchet gear to move the girders in and out, the main element of the work was the alteration of the hoisting rope from 3½ to 4in circumference. This required the provision of new sheaves, but still of 2ft 3in diameter, and a slightly larger ram's horn. Additional notice plates were fitted to indicate the increase in capacity. In its revised state, the maximum height of lift for the ram's horn above rail level was 36ft 6in at minimum radius, with a 34ft range – i.e. 2ft 6in above rail level.

The strengthening exercise on the two Craven cranes was undertaken by the new owners Herbert Morris at Loughborough. By providing a new higher-capacity main block, again of the ram's-horn type, re-rigging the ropes to the supplementary block to pass over a pair of additional sheaves in the jib head, and attaching this block to the top of the main block, there were now six parts of rope instead of four. To be able to maintain a similar range of positions for the hook above and below rail level, the 288ft-long hoisting rope was replaced by one 345ft in length. By this means, and by accepting a reduced speed of hoisting, the increase in lifting capacity was achieved. It was still possible to re-rig the blocks to provide for lifts of up to 36 tons on four falls and 18 tons on two falls of rope, with consequential increases in speed and a vast drop of the hook below rail level – up to 73ft! One wonders, however, whether the time and effort required to undertake such an exercise was ever put into practice.

Once completed, the five 50-ton cranes became the frontline plant on the LMS for dealing with derailments, collisions and bridgeworks. This resulted in some adjustment to the allocations, so that the 50-ton-capacity cranes were strategically positioned along the length of the West Coast mainline at Willesden (London), Rugby, Crewe, Kingmoor (Carlisle) and Motherwell. These were then available to deal with Stanier's Pacifics in the event of them being derailed. The uprated Ransomes & Rapier cranes were stationed on the Midland Division at Derby and Holbeck.

Amazingly, upon withdrawal from BR, all six LMS 1931 cranes, but not the 1916 ex-Midland crane, passed into the hands of private owners and can be found on heritage railway lines.

The additional duty plate added to Cowans Sheldon cranes following strengthening in 1938, in this case No RS1005/50. *Author*

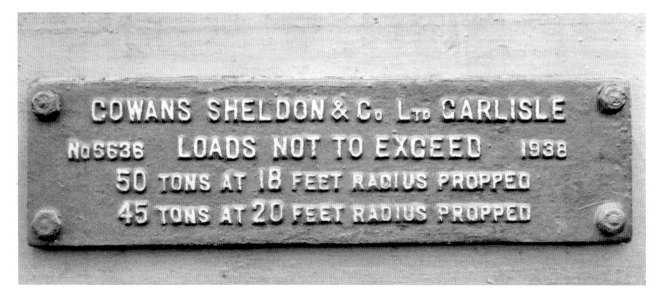

A pair of former LMS 50-ton cranes, both in red livery, in the process of installing a new LMR Standard A Type bridge deck at Kirkby Stephen on 9 July 1978. On the left is Craven crane No RS1013/50, while on the right is Cowans Sheldon No RS1001/50. These examples of cranes supplied to the LMS in 1931, originally of 36-ton capacity to a radius of 25 or 24ft radius, but strengthened in 1939 to lift 50 tons at their minimum radius of 18ft. At the same time, screw jacks were fitted to the ends of the propping girders. *M.S. Welch*

Craven 50-ton crane No RS1013/50, together with ex-GW 45-ton Ransomes & Rapier No 17, at Colwick on 26 February 1961, engaged in lifting precast concrete beams into a bridge span between them. *M.S. Welch*

Sister crane No RS1015/50 and its breakdown train from Willesden at Rugby on 11 November 1963. The overhead gantries await the electric line equipment, which thereafter will severely restrict the activities of breakdown cranes. *M.S. Welch*

Liveries

Monochrome photographs suggest that most of the LMS 36-ton cranes supplied in 1931 were painted black, but equally it is clear that by some time prior to the Second World War, No 1250, later RS1054/50, like other breakdown cranes on the Northern Division, had the Crimson Lake lined locomotive livery applied with coach insignia. Yet the match wagons may have remained in the goods-wagon livery, although slate rather than light- to mid-grey. In the case of the Motherwell crane, this style is evident both before and after strengthening.

By the 1950s, all six 50- and 40-ton cranes seem to have been finished in a black livery, but in July 1959 a general instruction was issued that, as breakdown cranes went through the workshops for overhaul, they were to be repainted bright red. No RS1001/50, however, was painted in Crimson Lake with Black and Straw lining to the coal bunker and solebars of the crane and relieving bogies.

The liveries of these cranes are explored in greater detail in *LMS Journal* No 18 pp 6 to 27.

3

Ransomes & Rapier Pre-war Developments

LNER 35-ton Crane

Having in 1926 equipped itself with the means of handling its largest locomotives, the LNER was content for the time being to rely on a varied selection of a couple of dozen generally short-jib steam breakdown cranes to deal with other tasks. These cranes had various capacities, ranging from five at 35 tons down to eleven at 15 tons, together with a few 15- and 10-ton hand cranes. By the early thirties, however, the LNER appeared to have embarked on a policy of obtaining, finances permitting, one modern long-jibbed crane every year or so. All these subsequent cranes supplied to the company were provided with relieving bogies.

The first delivery was a 35-ton Rapier crane (Order No D4648) for Cambridge in 1932, similar to the MR and LMS 36-ton examples. As noted in Volume 1, the LNER's first acquisition had been two 45-ton cranes from Cowans Sheldon in 1926. Mounted on a pair of two-axle bogies, their axle load averaged 20 tons, a maximum in Great Britain equalled only by the 75-tonne telescopic-jib cranes of 1977, described later, and therefore their route availability was constrained to main lines and such secondary routes as had been upgraded to modern standards.

Matters on the former Great Eastern Railway (GER) network in East Anglia were somewhat different, however, resulting in a need for a much reduced axle load. Whereas the last cranes purchased by the GER had relied on removable counterweights to keep the maximum axle loads within the 14.2 tons specified, in the LNER's new order placed on 1 February 1932, a limit on the axle loads of 15 tons was specified. In the event, by adopting the relieving-bogie system, a maximum axle load of

12 tons 11cwt was attained. Furthermore, this new crane could lift its maximum load of 35 tons out to a radius of 25ft, compared with the 23ft 6in of the previous 45-ton, 23ft of the GER's 35-ton cranes, or 36-tons to a radius of 20ft for the crane it had supplied to the LMS a year previously.

To achieve this, the two sets of telescopic girders were extended to provide a propping base of nearly 18ft, and these were fitted from the outset with screw jacks. The cylinder size was increased to 9½in diameter with a 14in stroke. Other aspects were similar to the LMS crane. The crane was capable of traversing a 5-chain curve and both the crane and match wagon were piped for vacuum braking.

The four-wheeled match wagon was built by the LNER at their Stratford Works. This too was of low construction to aid the handling of heavy lifting gear to and from track level. The jib rest was of the trestle form, with provision for the jib support cradle to move sideways as the crane traversed a curve.

The crane was allocated in the first instance to Cambridge, from where it was well able to reach the territory of the former Great Eastern Railway. The arrival of a 45-ton crane at Cambridge early during the Second World War led to the 35-ton crane being transferred to Stratford, London, in time to be on hand to tackle bomb damage during the Blitz. It was in turn replaced there by a new BR 75-ton crane in early 1962, and the 45-ton crane went instead to Norwich, from where it was retired and scrapped in March 1970.

Drawings for this crane will also be found on pp.58 and 59 (R&R 36T, SR etc).

	Running No		Match wagon No	Allocation	Disposal
Order No	**LNER**	**BR 1st**			
D4648	SB5?, 961601	(330)131	961652	Cambridge 9/32, Stratford 1940–6/11/61, Norwich 8/67–3/70	Withdrawn 3/70

RANSOMES & RAPIER 35-TON FOR LNER

Note: Dates shown in *italics* are spot dates upon which the crane is known to have been at the depot concerned.

Top left Ex-LNER 35-ton Ransomes & Rapier crane No DE131 in the breakdown train including two ex-GN coaches and headed by an ex-GER 0-6-0 at Stratford, London, in August 1955. *L. Seabrook/L. Gibbs, courtesy HMRS*

Bottom left Match wagon No DE 961652 supporting the jib of the crane while at Stratford in March 1957. Note the temporary bogie carried on the wagon. This wagon was later paired with ex-LMS No DE330159. *L. Seabrook/L. Gibbs, courtesy HMRS*

Right The elaborate list of route restrictions and other instructions painted on the crane. *L. Seabrook/L.Gibbs, courtesy HMRS*

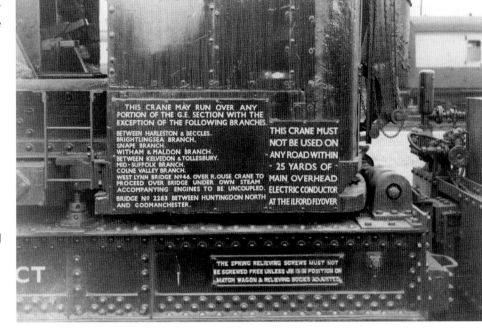

Below No DE330131 at Doncaster Works on 31 August 1963, freshly painted red following probably its last overhaul. The jib of a Grafton steam crane partially obscures the match wagon. *Author*

Southern Railway 36-ton Cranes

Late in 1937, ten years after acquiring its first pair of 36-ton cranes, the smaller Southern Railway took delivery of another two. Whilst of the same lifting performance of 36 tons at 20ft radius, this time the relieving-bogie principle was adopted in preference to the removable counterweight, and a maximum axle-load of 13 tons was achieved. The carriages were similar to the LNER crane of 1932, although with a slightly reduced lifting capacity they had a propping base of 16ft, rather than the 18ft of the LNER crane. The wheels of the relieving bogies were 3ft 2in diameter instead of 3ft 5½in. As well as screw jacks, the girders were fitted with rack gear to aid their extension and withdrawal.

Whilst the superstructure owed much to the two Rapier cranes supplied to the company in 1927, it also had to comply with the SR's very restricted Tonbridge to Hastings via Battle line, with a gauge of 12ft 11in height, and 8ft 4in width, from which the earlier cranes were barred. The tight clearances in tunnels on this line had long been a source of difficulties to the operating authorities and those charged with providing the rolling stock and maintaining the track. This was the reason for the building of special 8ft-wide carriages and the provision of Maunsell's famous 4-4-0 Schools class of locomotive. The implications and probable costs led to the Southern Railway's failure to implement electrification prior to the Second World War.

The slewing rack and live ring were similar to the LNER crane, but reduced in diameter to suit the restricted loading gauge. Circular lookout windows were provided in rear of the housing. The crane and match wagon were fitted with through piping for vacuum braking, while the ensemble was capable of traversing 5-chain curves at slow speed.

The match wagons were built by the SR at Ashford, Kent, at a cost of £429 each. After arriving at the scene of operations, if space permitted, the shorter and lighter four-wheeled match wagons, together with the relieving bogies, could be lifted out of the way by the crane, so that running without a match wagon was unnecessary. It was found with these cranes, and no doubt others, that with the jib lowered sufficiently to clear the loading gauge, the hook trailed on the track, so that great care was necessary if they had to be moved under bridges. Similarly, in due course it must have been found that, without a lowered underframe or articulated jib, on tight curves the tip of the jib fouled the solebar. As a result, a modification was put in hand on No DS3093, with notches being cut in the solebars to allow the jib head to pass over them. One hopes its loss of section was made up elsewhere beneath to maintain strength.

According to Rapier's order book, it was originally intended to post these two cranes, one each to Ashford (Kent) and Fratton (Portsmouth). It the event, other thoughts seem to have prevailed, as they initially went to Nine Elms and Bricklayers Arms. At these depots, both would soon become embroiled in the aftermath of the Blitz two years later, indeed to prevent No 1196S becoming damaged or isolated from the rest of the network by falling bombs, it was temporarily moved to Feltham. Adjustments after the war led to this crane going to Brighton, where sadly 18 years later the supervisor was rash enough to pick up and slew a motor bogie to an EMU without props in place. The crane turned over, following which it was cut up on site, only to be replaced by its sister. After 40 years of service, this crane too was withdrawn and cut up.

Late in 1937, the Southern Railway acquired another two 36-ton cranes from Ransomes & Rapier, this time with relieving bogies, allocating them to Nine Elms and Bricklayers Arms. The sheet-metal covers over the axle boxes of the crane and bogies suggest this is No 1197S, which is thought to be still in SR livery. *Unattributed*

No DS1196 in early BR black livery with white jib head. By this period it had been transferred from Nine Elms to Brighton. The wagon behind the crane indicates that it has been utilised on a bridge renewal. Note the bogie on the match wagon for placing temporarily under loads to be moved. *Lens of Sutton, author's collection*

RANSOMES & RAPIER 36-TON FOR SR									
Date ordered: delivered	Order No	Cost	Running No		Match wagon No		Allocation		Disposal
			Grouping	BR 1st	Grouping	BR			
10/35: 1937	E4334	£7,425	1196S	DS1196	1196SM	DS3092	Nine Elms 11/37, Feltham 10/5/40 (temporary), Nine Elms 10/42, Brighton 6/46, overturned 25/10/64		Cut up 10/64
10/35: 1937	E4334	£7,425	1197S	DS1197	1197SM	DS3093	Bricklayers Arms 12/37, Hither Green 20/2/62, Brighton 25/10/64–1970, Stewart's Lane 30/6/79		Withdrawn 11/78
Note: Dates shown in *italics* are spot dates upon which the crane is known to have been at the depot concerned.									

Overleaf left, Figure 16 Elevation of Ransomes & Rapier 36-ton cranes supplied to the LMS in 1931, the LNER in 1932, the SR in 1937 together with their match wagon, and the WD in 1940. The match wagon for the LMS crane is shown on pp.29-30 [CS 36/50T] or pp.38-39 [Craven 36/50T], while that for the LNER one appears on pp.68 and 77 [CS36T]. *Author*

Overleaf right, Figure 17 Plan and end views of Ransomes & Rapier 36-ton cranes supplied to the LNER in 1932, the SR in 1937 and the WD in 1940. *Author*

Figure 16

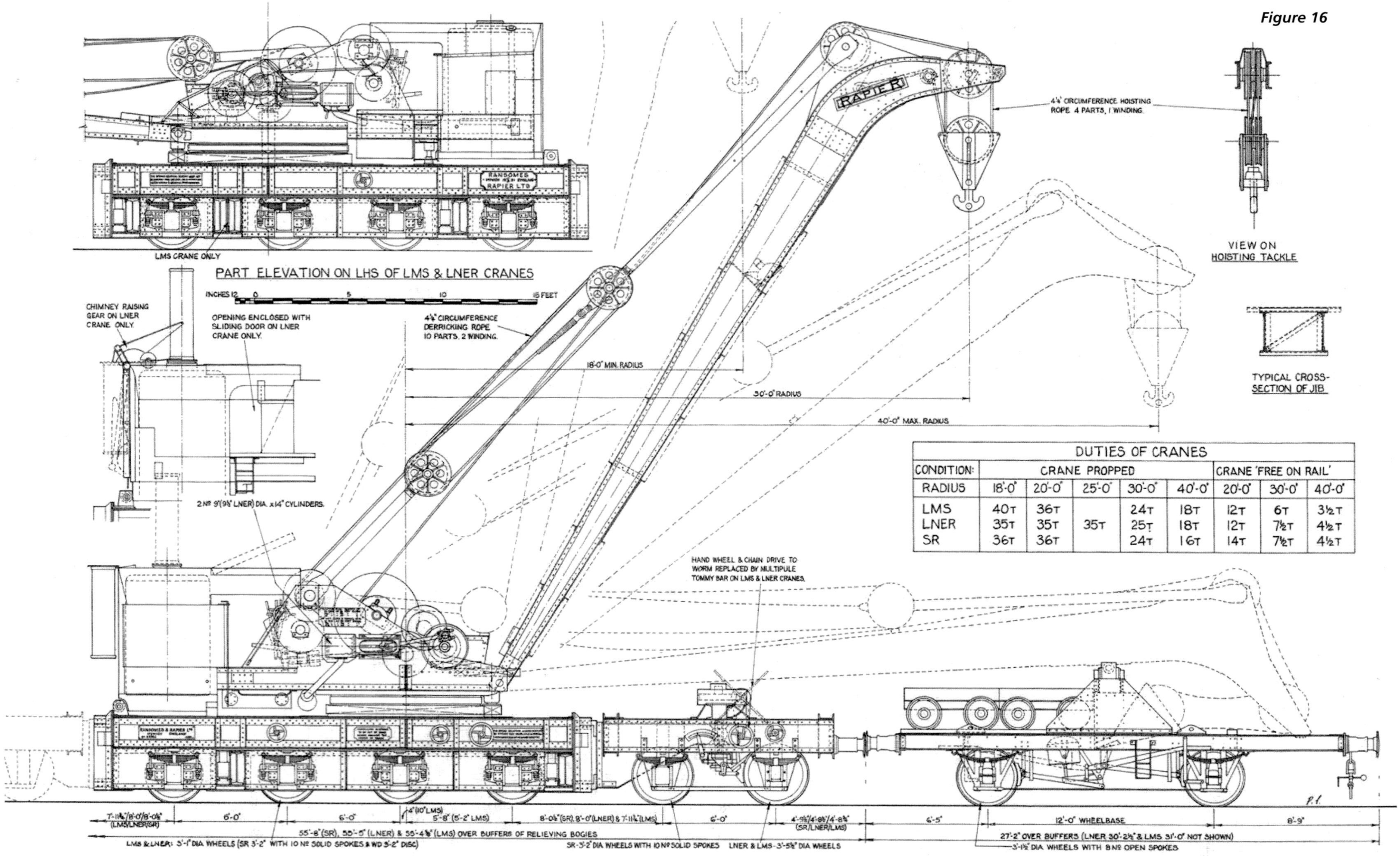

DUTIES OF CRANES

CONDITION: RADIUS	CRANE PROPPED					CRANE 'FREE ON RAIL'		
	18'-0"	20'-0"	25'-0"	30'-0"	40'-0"	20'-0"	30'-0"	40'-0"
LMS	40T	36T	35T	24T	18T	12T	6T	3½T
LNER	35T	35T	35T	25T	18T	12T	7½T	4½T
SR	36T	36T	35T	24T	16T	14T	7½T	4½T

VIEW ON HOISTING TACKLE

4¼" CIRCUMFERENCE HOISTING ROPE, 4 PARTS, 1 WINDING.

TYPICAL CROSS-SECTION OF JIB.

40'-0" MAX. RADIUS.

5'-0" RADIUS

18'-0" MIN RADIUS

RAPIER

RANSOMES & RAPIER LTD.

PART ELEVATION ON LHS OF LMS & LNER CRANES

INCHES 12 6 0 5 10 15 FEET

LMS CRANE ONLY.

4¼" CIRCUMFERENCE DERRICKING ROPE 10 PARTS, 2 WINDING.

OPENING ENCLOSED WITH SLIDING DOOR ON LNER CRANE ONLY.

CHIMNEY RAISING GEAR ON LNER CRANE ONLY.

2 N° 9'/9½' LNER) DIA. x14" CYLINDERS.

HAND WHEEL & CHAIN DRIVE TO WORM REPLACED BY MULTIPLE TOMMY BAR ON LMS & LNER CRANES.

27'-2" OVER BUFFERS (LNER) 30'-10½' & LMS 31'-0" NOT SHOWN)

12'-0" WHEELBASE

3½" DIA. WHEELS WITH 8 N° OPEN SPOKES

8'-9"

6'-5"

6'-0"

4'-4¾"(LNER)/4'-8½' (SR/LNER/LMS)

8'-0"(SR) 8'-0"(LNER) 8'-7-11½'(LMS)

3'-5½" DIA. WHEELS WITH 10N° SOLID SPOKES LINER & LMS 3'-5½" DIA. WHEELS

5'-8" (5'-2" LMS)

5'-8"(SR) 5'-5½'(LNER) & 5'-4¾"(LMS) OVER BUFFERS OF RELIEVING BOGIES

6'-0"

55'-8"(SR) 55'-5½"(LNER) & 55'-4¾"(LMS) OVER BUFFERS OF RELIEVING BOGIES

6'-0"

SR 3'-5½" DIA WHEELS WITH 10 N° SOLID SPOKES & N° 2 DISC

3'-1" DIA WHEELS (SR 3'-2" WITH 10 N° SOLID SPOKES & N° 2 DISC)

7'-11½'/8'-0'/8'-0½" (LMS/LNER/SR)

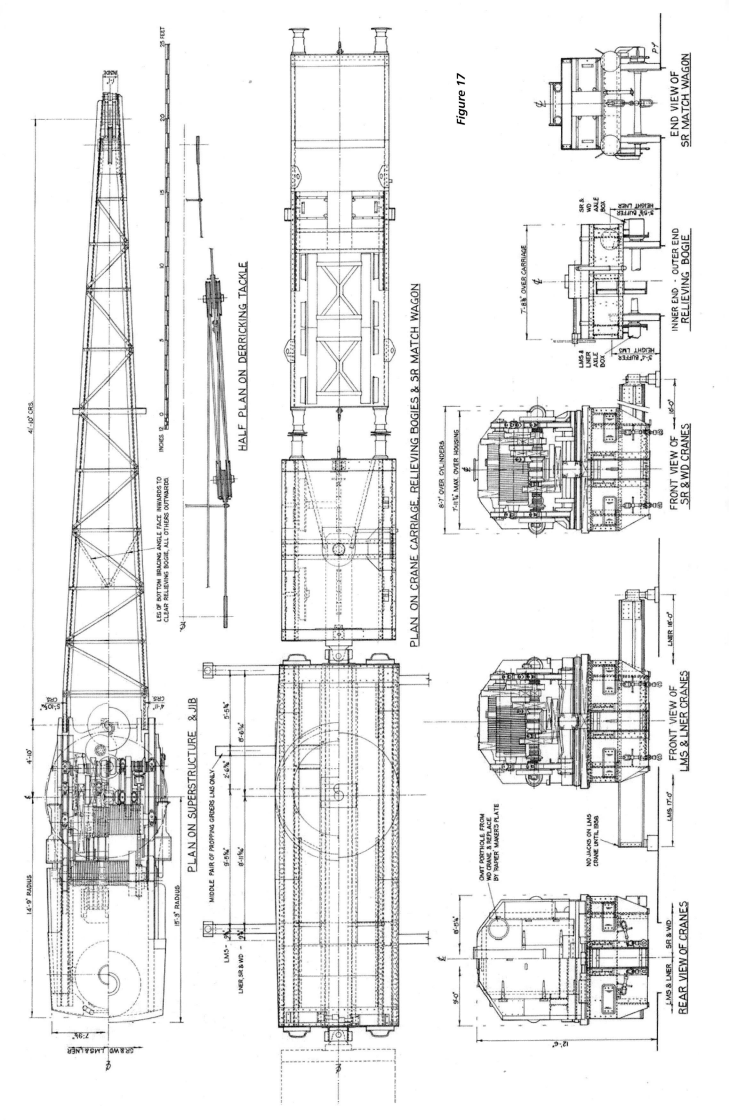

PLAN ON SUPERSTRUCTURE & JIB

HALF PLAN ON DERRICKING TACKLE

PLAN ON CRANE CARRIAGE, RELIEVING BOGIES & SR MATCH WAGON

END VIEW OF SR MATCH WAGON

INNER END - OUTER END RELIEVING BOGIE

FRONT VIEW OF SR & WD CRANES

FRONT VIEW OF LMS & LNER CRANES

REAR VIEW OF CRANES

Figure 17

No DS1197 on 21 February 1960, having just arrived to attend to a Battle of Britain Class 4-6-2, No 34084 *253 Squadron*, derailed by the trap points and partly down the embankment at the exit onto the mainline, while 2-6-0 N class No 31810 waits in the background. Blocks of hardwood timber are being placed on which to support the props, while lifting tackle is being sorted out on the match wagon. *R.C. Riley, courtesy Transport Treasury*

No ADS1197, at the head of the breakdown train, pokes its head out from under the roof of Brighton station on 10 September 1977. Its capacity is now quoted in metric tonnes. Behind it is a tank wagon to provide feed water in the absence of water columns following the withdrawal of all steam locomotives. *Colour-Rail*

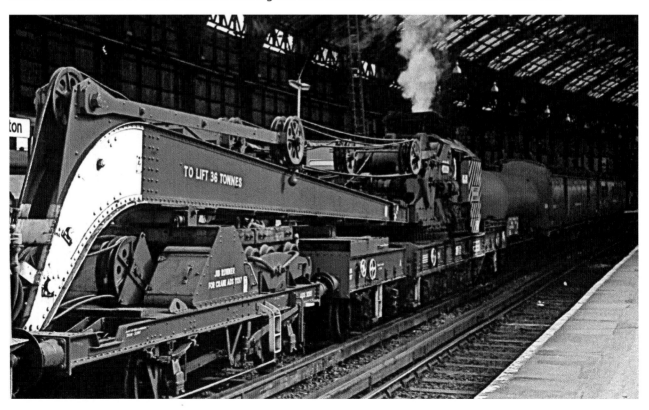

During a visit to Stewarts Lane, Paul Bartlett captured these details, firstly of the relieving bogie A, with additional plank around part of it and fitted with an access ladder. *P. Bartlett*

Next, the jib resting on the match wagon. At some time there must have been a problem while rounding a tight curve when the tip of the jib fouled the solebar of the match wagon, resulting in the notch being formed to allow it to pass through. *P. Bartlett*

War Department 36-ton Cranes

With war having broken out, the War Department, through the Ministry of Supply, placed a provisional order with Ransomes & Rapier on 8 November 1939 for two 36-ton cranes to Order No E9085, similar to those recently supplied to the SR. These were to be through-piped for Westinghouse brakes, and the crane wheels were to feature rolled-steel disc centres instead of cast iron. Frills were to be omitted from the boiler fittings; the lookouts at the rear of the housing deleted and additional slings provided.

Whereas the SR had supplied its own match trucks, in this case their provision was included with the order from Rapier. These were to be similar to those provided for the 45-ton cranes for the GW and SR, then already on order but yet to be specified. Interestingly, these had lowered solebars, perhaps anticipating the possibility that the jib head might foul solebars at conventional height when on particularly sharp curves, as experienced much later by the SR.

The first crane was completed in September 1940, followed a month later by the other. They were sent to the railway training depots on the Longmoor and Melbourne (Derby) Military Railways. One was shipped to Alexandria, sometime in 1941, was in use in Palestine by mid 1942, and eventually ended up on the books of Israel Railways. The other was still with the Melbourne Military Railway in late 1944. It was most probably not one of the cranes to go to Europe, as one was still there in late 1946, before later moving to the Central Ordnance on the Bicester Military Railway where it remained until at least circa 1955.

Left A party of Army officers watch anxiously as one of the War Department's 36-ton Ransomes & Rapier cranes cautiously eases its way across a temporary bridge over the River Trent on the Melbourne Military Railway. This Unit Construction Railway Bridge, the rail equivalent and forerunner of the better known Bailey Bridge, was built by members of the Bridging School at King's Newton as part of an exercise in May 1942. The absence of lookouts in the rear of the housing is confirmed by the cast-iron maker's plates in their place. *Author's collection*

On the assumption that one crane went to the Middle East and did not return, this must be the other, following its move from Melbourne to the Bicester Military Railway. It is seen here at the workshops of the Central Ordnance Depot during the early 1950s. *J. Moss*

Cowans Sheldon Pre-war Developments

Cowans Sheldon 35/36-ton Cranes for the LNER

Following the acquisition of the 35-ton crane from Ransomes & Rapier in 1932, in 1936 the LNER upgraded the specification to a 36-ton crane lifting to a radius of 25ft, and with a 6-ton auxiliary hoist for a further crane, with relieving bogies. This time the crane came from Cowans Sheldon (Works No 5755). Its 40ft jib, measured between jib foot and sheave pin for the main block, enabled it to reach out to a radius of 40ft on the main hoist when, as the table on p.68 (Figure 18) shows, it could lift 18 tons, or 4½ tons when 'free on the rail'. In addition, it was equipped with a 6-ton auxiliary hoist for lighter work, the benefit being that it was faster in

operation. In addition, the diagram suggests that the crane was also equipped with a single 20-ton hook, which by means of a pair of shackles could be hung from the ram's horn.

This crane was paired with a purpose-built well-type match wagon, similar to that provided four years earlier for the 35-ton Ransomes & Rapier crane for Cambridge. The crane spent the first 20 years of its life stationed at Colwick, near Nottingham. Subsequently, in January 1966, it was reassigned to the London Midland Region, where it was renumbered RS1106/36 and allocated to Toton in February 1967, until withdrawn 20 years later. After fifty years of mainline service, it was acquired by Peak Rail at Buxton in December 1987.

The driver of ex-LNER 36-ton Cowans Sheldon steam crane No 124 looks up towards the jib head while at Whetstone on 18 May 1963. The crane is in black livery lined out and with 'ferret and dart-board' totem. *M.S. Welch*

No 124 attends to ex-GE 0-6-0 class J15 No 65475, whose tender had become derailed at Huntingdon East on 3 August 1955. The match wagon is of the same design as that paired with the Ransomes & Rapier 35-ton crane No DE330131. *E. Sawford*

By now transferred to the London Midland Region and renumbered RS1106/36 the crane stands outside the diesel repair shed at Toton on 8 November 1969 during a boiler washout. *Author*

A close-up of the other side on the same occasion. Note the handle for the propping-girder ratchet clipped to the bottom left end plate. *Author*

Nearly a decade later, No ADM1106, still based at Toton, on 25 March 1979, lifts the end of a DMU damaged in a collision at Chinley North Jct. This had occurred much earlier, on 14 February, when a two-car DMU was incorrectly hand-signalled past a signal at danger and collided with the locomotive of a stationary freight train. The damaged unit was moved to an adjacent closed section of line retained as a siding, where later the crane was used to lift one end of the unit while interim repairs were carried out prior to running it to the works. By this time the auxiliary hoist had been dispensed with. *M.S. Welch*

Colwick's crane was followed a year later by a 35-ton crane from Cowans Sheldon (Works No 6080) without auxiliary hoist, for Tweedmouth. The 1-ton reduction in maximum capacity appears to be entirely to suit the specification of the North Eastern Area, which adopted 35 rather than 36 tons, and the design of the crane seems to be otherwise similar. The match wagon for this crane, to LNER wagon diagram 136, was of a simpler design, with conventional solebars and was no doubt cheaper, but equipped with automatic vacuum brake, tare weight 8 tons 12cwt 3qtrs. The crane's arrival at Tweedmouth allowed an ex-NER 15-ton Cowans Sheldon crane of 1893 to be withdrawn. By the mid-1960s, the 35-ton crane had been transferred to Thornaby and was at York by 1970, before being withdrawn in September 1972 and subsequently cut up.

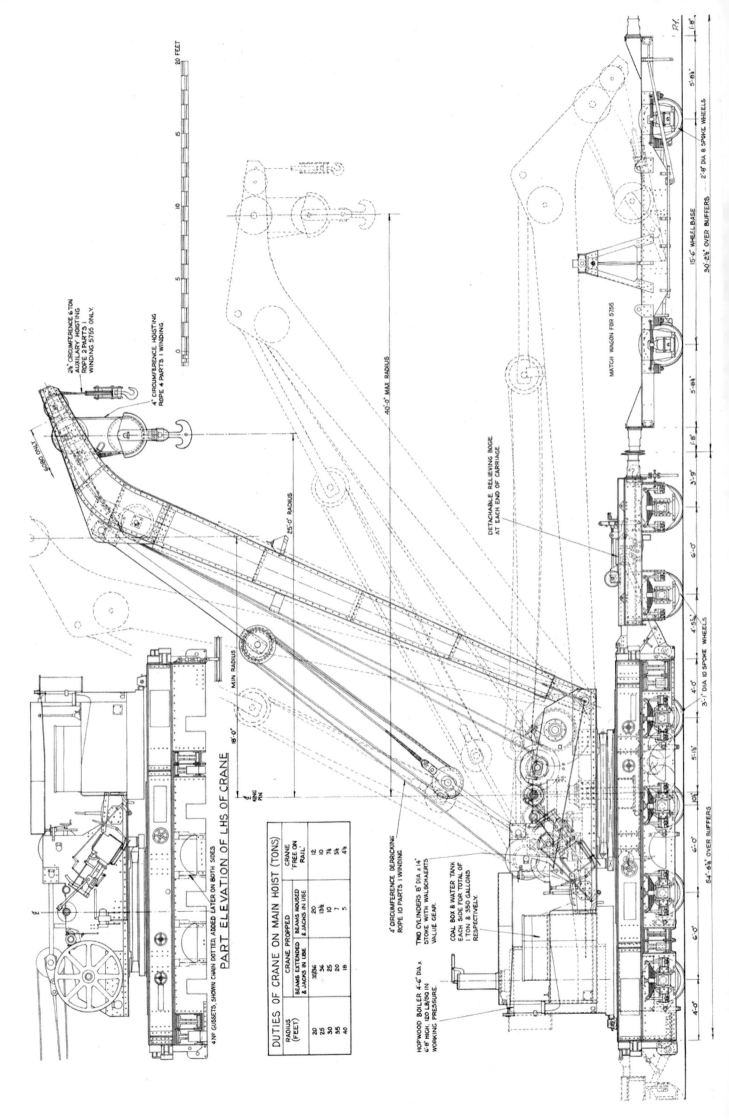

Left, Figure 18 Elevation of Cowans Sheldon 35/36-ton crane supplied to the LNER in 1936/37, together with its match wagon. Plan and end views are reproduced on p.77. Details of the match wagon for the 35-ton crane can be derived from pp.76-77. *Author*

Not long before withdrawal, ex-LNER 35-ton Cowans Sheldon of 1937, No DE331158, with steam up stands on duty at York on 3 October 1970. Note the additional hand rail on the end of the match wagon. *Author*

No DE331158 again at York from the other end on 3 October 1970. *Author*

The last order for a crane to be made prior to nationalisation in 1948 was for a further example of the LNER's preferred type of 36-ton with 6-ton auxiliary hoist and relieving bogies. It was built by Cowans Sheldon and allocated to Immingham in 1948, when it was numbered 941602, and later in the BR series as DB 966103. Here it is re-railing an 08 Class 0-6-0 diesel shunting locomotive at Boston West Junction in 1969. *N.H. Pigott*

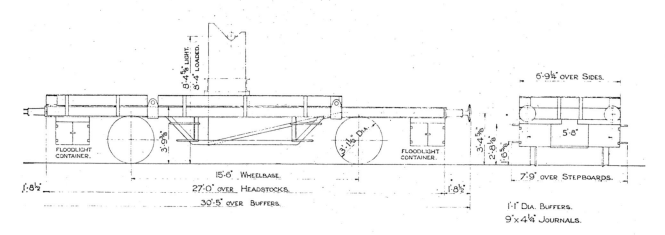

CRANE MATCH WAGON.
(FOR 36 TON BREAKDOWN CRANE.)

630

BR diagram 630 for match wagon to crane No. 103. *BR, author's collection*

LNER COWANS SHELDON 35/36 -TON							
Date ordered: delivered	Works No	Running No			Match wagon No	Allocation	Disposal
		Grouping	1st BR	CEPS			
1/7/35: 1936	5755	941591	124, RS1106/36, TDM1106	ADRC 95223	941753	Colwick 1/11/47–6/11/61, to LMR 1/66, Toton 8/11/69–11/86	Withdrawn 6/87, Peak Rail 12/87
1937	6080	CME 5 901630	(DE331)158	-	901715, (DE)2111	Tweedmouth 1/10/37–1/10/60, Thornaby c1965, Darlington 23/9/64, York 2/4/65–3/10/70, York OOU 11/6/73	Withdrawn 9/72
1948	9017	(941602)	(DB966)103	ADRC 95222	DB998500	Immingham 1948, Stratford 26/3/77, Finsbury Pk 8/78–12/78, Thornaby 3/84–11/86	Dean F Railway 4/86
Note: Dates shown in italics are spot dates upon which the crane is known to have been at the depot concerned.							

As No ADRC95222, the crane is seen here following its upgrading in 1972 to 45-ton capacity, passing under the wires at Stratford in May 1972. Tool boxes have been attached under the frame of the match wagon at each end. *K. Lane*

Looking down on No ADRC95222, while involved in some work on an over-bridge at Bridlington on 9 April 1983. *R. Watson*

On another occasion in Teeside Yard, No ADRC95222
appears to be re-railing an all-steel wagon loaded with
scrap metal. *R. Watson*

By 1946, with the war over, the railways were attempting to restore their infrastructure, facilities and services against the backdrop of likely nationalisation. Although the LNER had acquired six 45-ton cranes during the Second World War, following the conflict it reverted to its pre-war policy, and on 19 December 1946 another 36-ton crane with an auxiliary hoist was ordered from Cowans Sheldon (Works No 9017). This, however, was not delivered until 1948, at a cost of £13,513, by which time the railways had been nationalised. It was generally similar to the Colwick crane, but there are minor differences resulting from experience over the intervening years.

One notable change, however, was the adoption of an articulated jib foot. When lowered onto the match wagon, the articulated jib allowed some rotation at the jib foot and, with the superstructure now locked relative to the carriage, the ability to negotiate curves was improved. In the case of the Cowans cranes, the foot of the jib was made in the form of a crutch which, when horizontal, allowed the jib to be drawn forward and subsequently permitted some movement between the jib and the crab sides. The match-wagon jib support had a pair of inclined faces, which engaged with pins projecting from the jib sides, so that as the jib was lowered through the last stages, it was drawn away from the crane by a small amount. The match wagon, completed in April 1949, was otherwise similar to those paired with the 45-ton cranes, although full vacuum brake equipment was fitted along with the revised jib rest to suit the articulated jib, tare weight 8 tons 16cwt (BR wagon diagram 630).

Having spent its early days in the Immingham area of Lincolnshire, in 1971 the Eastern Region of BR entered into negotiations with Cowans to have No 103 upgraded to lift 45 tons at 20ft radius. By the adoption of a Lebus drum for two-layer winding this was put in hand during 1972. With this system, the continuous groove in the drum is parallel to the flange, except for two crossover points on each revolution where the groove moves across the drum half a pitch to give a full pitch of movement for each revolution. On its return to duty, it found its way to Stratford, on to Finsbury Park and later Thornaby, before being withdrawn and acquired by the Dean Forest Railway in 1986. In 1995 it was resold to the Great Central Railway (North) and is currently operational at Ruddington.

Nos 124 and 103 did not have as good a route availability as the wartime 45-ton cranes discussed in the following chapter, being RA 4 in normal conditions and 3 in an emergency, as against RA 3 and 2 (see Vol 1, p.209 for an explanation of the LNER's route availability scheme).

Résumé Up to 1939

Before going on to consider the impact of the Second World War, and setting aside the last crane described above delivered after the war, perhaps it is opportune to review the cranes built from the grouping at the beginning of 1923 up to the point at which war became inevitable. A summary of the stock of steam breakdown cranes of 15-ton capacity or more at the outbreak of war was as shown in the table below.

Following a period of consolidation as the new management settled in, the LNER was first off the mark, in 1926, with two 45-ton cranes of the highest capacity to date, soon to be followed by the Southern Railway with two 36-ton cranes. While not immediately affected by grouping, the Metropolitan Railway had acquired a 20-ton crane in 1925, later upgraded to 30-ton, and the London Underground a 30-ton unit in 1931. All of these cranes were discussed in Volume 1.

In 1931, the merits of adopting relieving bogies for high-capacity cranes was taken up in earnest by the LMS, successor of course to the pioneering Midland Railway, with six examples of 36-ton cranes. These were soon to be followed by the LNER with three cranes over the next six years, and a pair by the Southern in 1938, the last before the war. In addition, towards the end of the 1930s, the LMS had reviewed its breakdown arrangements resulting, among other things, in the upgrading of five cranes of 36-ton capacity to a maximum of 50 tons, all of which have been considered previously.

Absent from the acquisitions of breakdown cranes by the mainline companies during this period was the Great Western. Although it gained two 35/36-ton and a pair of 20-ton cranes from its Welsh constituent companies, one of which had in the interval been scrapped, it had purchased no new cranes since 1912.

Coy/Capacity	50/45T	36/35T	30T	25T	20T	15T	Totals
BRITISH STEAM BREAKDOWN CRANES AT OUTBREAK OF THE SECOND WORLD WAR							
LMS	5	6$	2	-	4 + 1*	14#	31 + 1*
LNER	2	9	-	3 + 1*	4	12	30 + 1*
GW	-	5	-	-	4	3	12
SR	-	6	-	-	2	4	12
LPTB	-	-	2	-	-	-	2
Totals	7	26	4	3 + 1*	14 + 1*	33	87 + 2*

Notes:
1. * Allocated to Workshops
2. $ Including 2 No. 40T.
3. # Ignoring ex-FR 15T.

5

Wartime 45-ton Cranes

The rapidly deteriorating political situation in Europe during the latter part of the 1930s led the government and the railway companies to consider the consequences of the outbreak of war and to take precautions against aerial bombardment of our cities, industries and transport infrastructure. At the time, the belief in high circles was that the enemy's 'bombers will always get through'. Aerial onslaught on internal communications, therefore, might be so shattering and extensive in its effect that the distribution of adequate resources, centred at strategic points, would be vital for the purpose of restoring severed lines of transport in the shortest possible time, reducing the impact to a minimum. On land, this of course still largely meant the railways, and various measures were put in hand to prepare for such an assault.

As a consequence, the Railway Technical Committee on Air Raid Precautions was set up in December 1937. It was foreseen that under concentrated hostile attacks, it would be necessary to rapidly clear the lines, to erect emergency structures in place of collapsed bridges and to undertake the prompt repair of damaged track.

Among the numerous matters considered by the Committee was the need for adequate lifting power in the form of railway breakdown cranes. The recommendations therefore included the provision, at government expense, of a number of high-capacity steam breakdown cranes. To meet the envisaged work of dealing with disruptions to the rail network as a consequence of enemy bombing raids, cranes of 45-ton capacity were called for and these were to be provided to three of the railway companies to supplement the existing stock of cranes. The wide range of operations throughout British railways called for the adoption of composite loading gauge No 2, 12ft 11in tall, whilst the maximum axle load was restricted to 13¾ tons and that all cranes should be fitted with a through-vacuum pipe.

The load-performance requirement specified for these cranes was in the order of that of the LNER 45-ton cranes of 1926 for the upper loads, but applied to the longer jib featured in the original Rapier 36-ton cranes of 1908. However, a much wider route availability was required

for the new 45-ton cranes, resulting in the need for relieving bogies, as used on the 35/36-ton cranes supplied to the LMS, LNER and Southern between 1931 and 1938. The six new cranes supplied by Cowans went to the LNER, whilst four by Rapier were delivered to the GW and another two were sent to the Southern.

The solution from the Cowans stable was 10 tons lighter in total weight than Rapier's. As a result, the lifting performance of the former at larger radii and free on rail was not quite as good as the latter. Nonetheless, both designs achieved a good route availability of RA 3 or 2 in an emergency, at the reduced speed of 15mph. These cranes were considered additional to the existing stock of breakdown cranes and, once delivered, no old cranes were withdrawn, but were retained in order to strengthen the breakdown resources and deal with possible emergencies arising out of enemy action.

The LMS received no allocation of 45-tonners, due no doubt to the availability of their five recently strengthened 50-ton cranes. Instead, perhaps somewhat surprisingly, they later persuaded the authorities to permit the construction of a prototype 30-ton-capacity crane on a 0-6-4 carriage intended as a replacement for the now outdated short-jibbed 15- and 20-ton cranes. Following delivery of this prototype in 1941, ten more were constructed at the height of the war, the order being split equally between Cowans and Rapier. Two more from the first stable were also supplied to the Ministry of Supply at about the same time.

As we have seen in Volume 1, cranes are a useful asset to military authorities and as the government had paid for the latest ones, it was recognised that such cranes were, from time to time, going to be diverted for military purposes, as discussed later.

In particular, two of the LNER's new 45-ton cranes were requisitioned by the War Department and shipped to Persia (now Iran) in 1942, from where they did not return. By 1943, these had been replaced on the LNER by another pair, but this time from the Rapier stable. Further cranes to this specification were built new by both suppliers for the Ministry of Supply, ready for the invasion of Europe in 1944. These were operated by peripatetic units as the front advanced across Europe. Afterwards, some cranes were sold out of military service. One oil-fired Cowans example was subsequently acquired second-hand in 1960 by the London Midland Region's Chief Civil Engineer's Department, for use on bridgeworks as part of the modernisation programme and was later taken over by the Motive Power Department.

Cowans Sheldon 45-ton Cranes for the LNER

The six cranes supplied by Cowans Sheldon were ordered on 28 April 1939 at a cost of £9,482 each and allocated Works Nos 6870 to 6875. The previous two cranes from the Cowans Sheldon stable could lift 36 tons to a radius of 25ft when propped, whilst the minimum radius was 18ft. By recognising that at reduced radius the stability of the crane permitted the lifting of even greater loads, the capacity of these cranes was increased to a maximum of 45 tons at 20ft radius. For this purpose, the strength of the hoisting tackle and winding gear was increased and the auxiliary hoist was dispensed with. Otherwise, the design was much as before, although the height of the relieving bogies was reduced, and hydraulic jacks were used in lieu of screw jacks to transfer load from the crane to the bogie in running condition. The length of the jib appears to have been increased by 1ft. The match wagons were similar to those provided for the 35-ton crane of 1937, although the jib rest was repositioned and through-vacuum brake piping only was provided, resulting in a tare weight of 8

tons 18cwt (LNER wagon diagram 160). The match wagons for the LNER were built by Hurst Nelson of Motherwell at the end of 1939.

Delivery of the six cranes from Cowans Sheldon is believed to have started in late 1939 with Works No 6870 for Thornton, followed in the new year by the rest, posted to New England (Peterborough), Darlington, Cambridge, Gorton and King's Cross. As a consequence of their arrival, existing cranes were released to be cascaded to other less-strategic depots. In turn, other smaller cranes were reallocated, sometimes to depots previously without steam cranes. An example is that the previously mentioned Rapier 35-ton crane at Cambridge was moved to Stratford, releasing a medium-length jib ex-GER 35-ton Rapier crane of 1919 to be sent to Norwich Thorpe, and in turn its ex-GN 15-ton Cowans Sheldon of 1899 to Colchester.

In 1968, following its transfer from Peterborough to March, No DE330110, formerly 941599, suffered a buckling failure of the jib while making a heavy lift. As a result, its jib was replaced by an all-welded one similar to those fitted to the 30- and 75-ton cranes supplied to BR between 1959 and 1964, including the provision of an articulated jib foot and necessary alterations to the match wagon to accommodate this.

Like many high-capacity breakdown cranes, all these 45-ton Cowans Sheldon cranes survived the demise of steam traction on British Railways in 1968 by a number of years and, as will be related later, the four remaining in Britain, together with a sister MoS crane went on to be converted to diesel power.

COWANS SHELDON 45-TON FOR LNER							
Works No	Running No				Match No	Allocation	Disposal/ converted
	Grouping	1st BR	CEPS	Converted			
6870	971588	RS1058/45 TDM1058	ADRC 95220	ADRC 96717	971589	Thornton Jct 1/40, Eastfield *10/42–9/80*, Derby Wks *10/84–11/86*	Converted 10/85
6871	941599	(330)110	ADRC 95218	ADRC 96719	941765	Peterborough N 2/40–*6/11/61*, March 2/68–*12/78*, Healey Mills 9/80, Derby Wks 10/84–11/86	Converted 8/86
6872	901719	(331)156	ADRC 95217	ADRC 96716	901720	Darlington 1940, Thornaby 1/10/65–*9/80*, Derby Wks *10/84–11/86*	Converted 10/85
6873	961606	(330)133	ADRC 95219	ADRC 96720	961665	Cambridge 1940–*3/70*, Stratford (temporarily) *12/78*, Inverness *9/80*, Derby Wks *10/84–11/86*	Converted 1/87
6874	951515	WD 150	-	-	951675	Gorton 1940, requisitioned by WO 1942, Tehran 5/42	-
6875	941600	-	-	-	941766	King's Cross 1940, requisitioned by WO 1942, Ahwaz 5/42	-

Notes:
1. The movements of the cranes converted to diesel-hydraulic will be considered on p.190 onwards.
2. Dates shown in *italics* are spot dates upon which the crane is known to have been at the depot concerned.

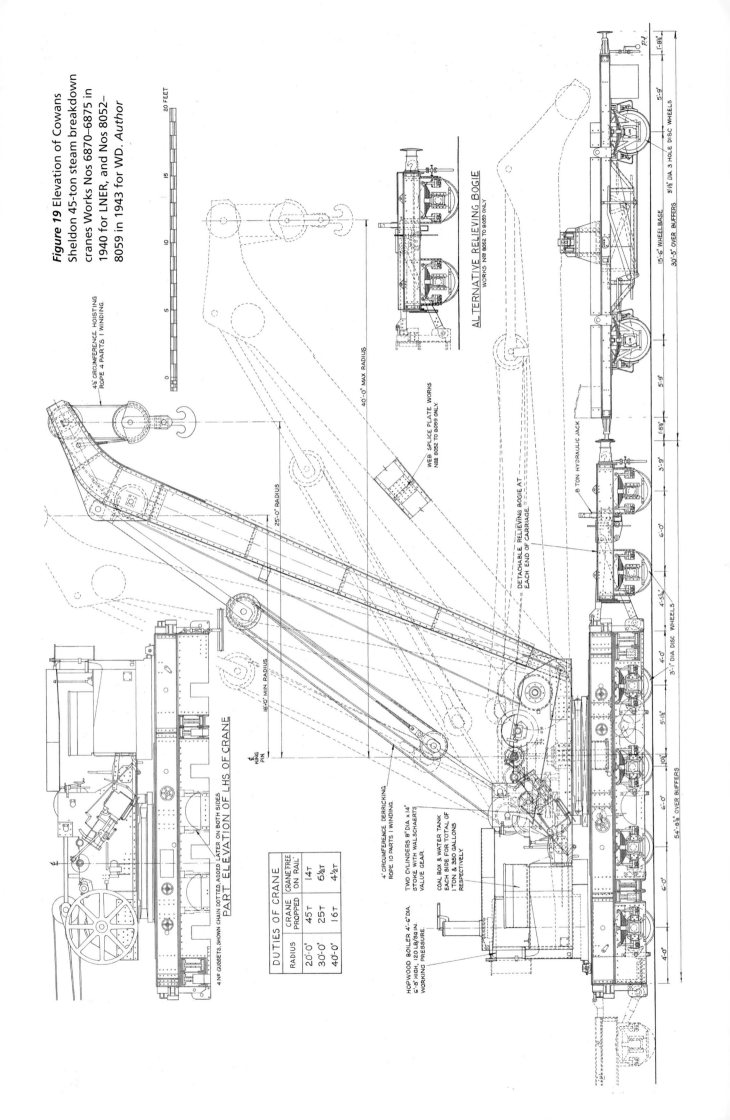

Figure 19 Elevation of Cowans Sheldon 45-ton steam breakdown cranes Works Nos 6870–6875 in 1940 for LNER, and Nos 8052–8059 in 1943 for WD. *Author*

20 FEET

4½" CIRCUMFERENCE HOISTING ROPE 4 PARTS 1 WINDING

25'-0" RADIUS

40'-0" MAX RADIUS

WEB SPLICE PLATE WORKS Nos 8052 TO 8059 ONLY

ALTERNATIVE RELIEVING BOGIE
WORKS Nos 8052 TO 8059 ONLY

DETACHABLE RELIEVING BOGIE AT EACH END OF CARRIAGE.

8 TON HYDRAULIC JACK

3'-1" DIA DISC WHEELS

3'-1½" DIA 3 HOLE DISC WHEELS

15'-6" WHEELBASE

30'-5" OVER BUFFERS

54'-6⅝" OVER BUFFERS

1'-8½"

5'-9"

5'-9"

6'-8½"

3'-9"

6'-0"

4'-5½"

5'-1½"

10½"

6'-0"

6'-0"

4'-0"

18'-0" MIN RADIUS

¢ KING PIN

4" CIRCUMFERENCE DERRICKING ROPE 10 PARTS 1 WINDING.

TWO CYLINDERS 8"DIA x 14" STROKE WITH WALSCHAERTS VALVE GEAR

COAL BOX & WATER TANK EACH SIDE FOR TOTAL OF 1 TON & 350 GALLONS RESPECTIVELY.

HOPWOOD BOILER 4'-6"DIA 6'-8" HIGH, 120 LB/SQ IN. WORKING PRESSURE.

4 Nº GUSSETS, SHOWN CHAIN DOTTED, ADDED LATER ON BOTH SIDES
PART ELEVATION OF LHS OF CRANE

DUTIES OF CRANE		
RADIUS	CRANE PROPPED	CRANE FREE ON RAIL
20'-0"	45T	14T
30'-0"	25T	6½T
40'-0"	16T	4½T

Figure 20 Plan and end views of Cowans Sheldon 36/45-ton steam breakdown cranes Works Nos 5755, 6080, 6870–5 and Nos 8052–9. *Author*

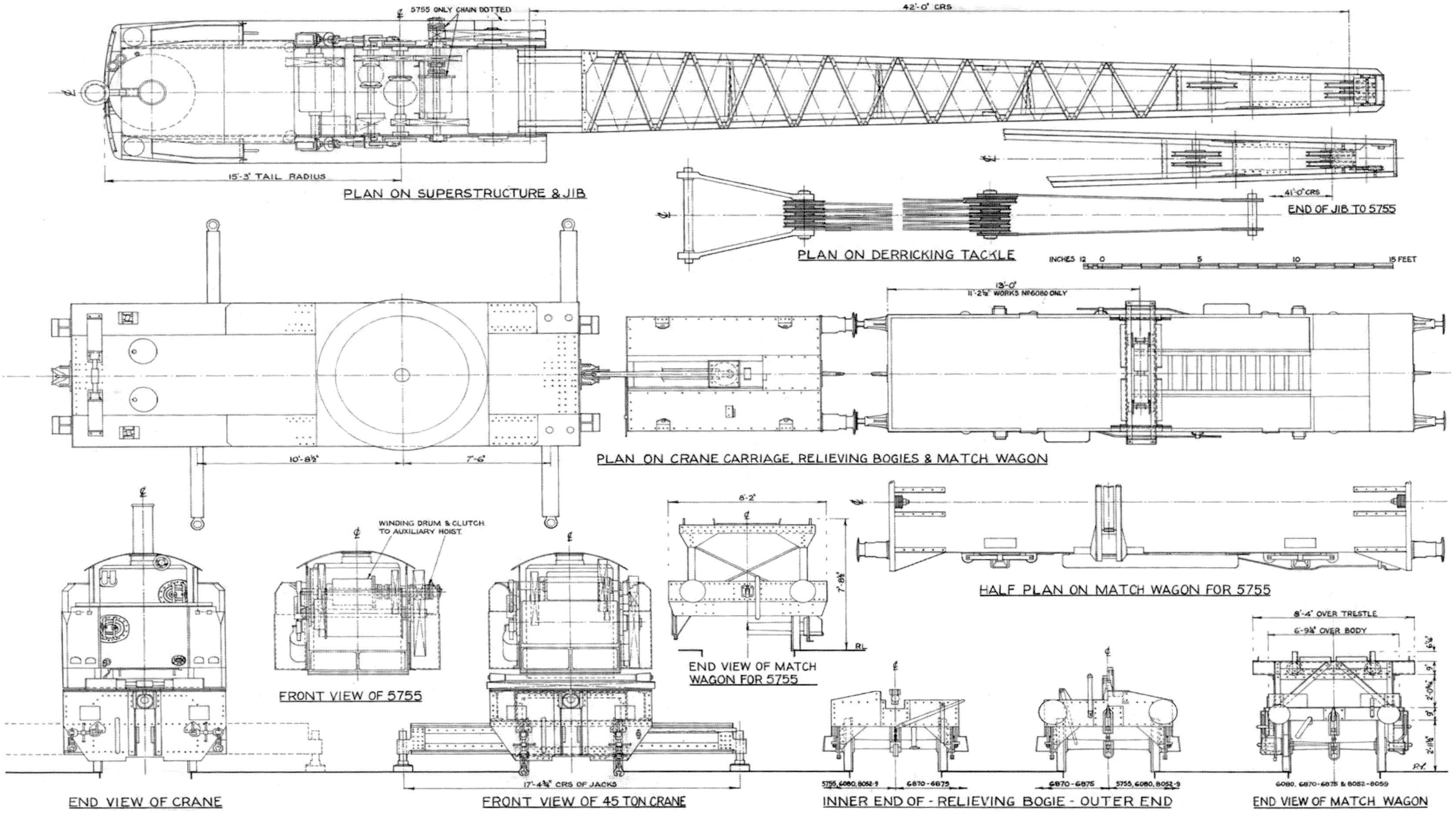

5755 ONLY CHAIN DOTTED
42'-0" CRS
15'-3" TAIL RADIUS
PLAN ON SUPERSTRUCTURE & JIB
41'-0" CRS
END OF JIB TO 5755
PLAN ON DERRICKING TACKLE
INCHES 12 0 5 10 15 FEET
13'-0"
11'-2½" WORKS Nº6080 ONLY
10'-8½"
7'-6"
PLAN ON CRANE CARRIAGE, RELIEVING BOGIES & MATCH WAGON
8'-2"
7'-8⅜"
RL
END VIEW OF MATCH WAGON FOR 5755
HALF PLAN ON MATCH WAGON FOR 5755
WINDING DRUM & CLUTCH TO AUXILIARY HOIST
FRONT VIEW OF 5755
8'-4" OVER TRESTLE
6'-9¾" OVER BODY
17'-4¾" CRS OF JACKS
END VIEW OF CRANE
FRONT VIEW OF 45 TON CRANE
5755, 6080, 8052-9
6870-6875
INNER END OF - RELIEVING BOGIE - OUTER END
6080, 6870-6875 & 8052-8059
END VIEW OF MATCH WAGON

One of the six Cowans Sheldon 45-ton cranes supplied under the ARP arrangements in 1940 to the LNER. This time crane No RS1058/45 awaits the call of duty outside Eastfield motive-power depot on 11 June 1978. The match wagon No DE971589 was built by Hurst Nelson. *Colour-Rail*

Another view of No RS1058/25 at Eatfield on 28th May 1967. *Martin Welsh*

Sister crane No ADE330110 at March on 3 March 1976. This crane became unique, when following an accident, its jib was replaced by a welded one with an articulated foot and consequential alterations to the jib rest on the match wagon. *Colour-Rail*

Peterborough's 45-ton crane No 941599 stands ready for duty on 26 August 1952. Note the artistic touch to the white jib head. Instead of being kept some distance out at New England shed, it was stabled close to the Peterborough North station to enable it to be on its way more quickly once called out. *A.E. West, courtesy M.S. King*

A closer view of No 941599 on the same occasion, with the chimney raised and a wisp of smoke emanating. *A.E. West, courtesy M.S. King*

Looking down on the machinery of No RS1058/45 during the dismantling of the former Caledonian Railway viaduct at Stevenson in 1949. Compare this with Figure 42 in Volume 1, p.161. *J. Templeton, author's collection*

Call to Arms

Matters were not to be left undisturbed for long however, as by 14 January 1942 Sir Alan Mount was reporting to the Railway Executive Committee that the Ministry of Supply, on behalf of the War Office, required six breakdown cranes of 35/45-ton capacity, two for urgent shipment to the Middle East. Two days later, the LNER offered to release the 45-ton cranes from Gorton and King's Cross. The Committee recommended that the remaining four be obtained from crane manufacturers and replacements for the two LNER cranes were also requested. The Ministry of Supply contracted the LNER to refurbish their two cranes, to convert them to Westinghouse air brake and oil firing, and to dismantle and pack them for shipping, which

was achieved by 28 February 1942, after which they were shipped to the Middle East. From May 1942, they were based at Tehran, No 951515 as WD 210, and the other at Ahwaz locomotive depot, Persia (now Iran). The Ahwaz crane toppled over during the first year and had to be recovered, after dismantling, by the Tehran crane.

The two replacement cranes for the LNER were received from Ransomes & Rapier in 1943 (Order No F4991/3) and duly took up duty at Gorton and King's Cross, enabling the temporary reversal of the cascading of 1940 to be finally implemented. In the meantime, Topping, a member of the breakdown gang at Gorton, having been called up for military service, found himself put in charge of his own crane, now WD210 stationed at Tehran. Vigorous use of scouring powder soon revealed its original identity: 'LNER, LOCO RUNNING DEPT, GORTON, 951515' between Farsi script and its new WD number. These two cranes never returned to the United Kingdom and are believed to have remained in the Middle East; one being photographed in October 2005 preserved at Tehran Station in the company of a Vulcan Foundry 2-10-0.

Requisitioned LNER 45-ton Cowans Sheldon crane, now No WD 210, at Tehran, Persia (now Iran). Its top layer of paint, hastily applied in preparation for military service, has been scoured back to reveal its previous identity as No 951515 from Gorton by its previous driver, now on active service. Note also the Farsi script. *D. Green collection*

Liveries

The livery worn by the pre-war LNER cranes is unknown. Although originally specified to be grey, the 45-tonners supplied at the beginning of the Second World War were turned out black with lettering in white or straw, either then or later lined out in red. The maker's name was applied along the jib sides in large cut-out aluminium letters. The first decade of nationalisation saw a continuation of black with straw lettering, while clutch wheels and the background of notice plates were red. A radical change in appearance took place following the issue of instructions in July 1959 that breakdown cranes were to be painted bright red with white lettering. The instructions allowed for black and straw lining, but no evidence has come to light that this was ever applied to an ex-LNER crane, and the practice ceased from 1965. At the same time, the first stirring of safety considerations began to appear, with the painting of jib heads white and the application of warning notices and ever-increasing amounts of yellow and black diagonal hazard striping. For those cranes repainted after 1977, which apart from the diesel conversions may have been few if any, an all-over unlined yellow livery with black lettering was applied.

Cowans Sheldon 45-ton Cranes for MoS

On 12 October 1942, the Ministry of Supply placed a contract with Cowans Sheldon for 45-ton cranes (Works Nos 8052 to 8059). Apart from a reversion to the earlier deeper design of relieving bogies, but operated by hydraulic jacks, and oil-fired boilers, these were the same as the LNER's 45-ton cranes. They were delivered in 1943 and all found their way to continental Europe in 1944.

The above batch included WD Nos 222, 223 and 226. Later numbers were in the Tn84XX series. Three of this batch were transferred to the SNCF in 1947 – one of which was ex WD No 222. All were converted to diesel propulsion in the early 1970s. These are believed to include: Nos GD243 at Ternier, GD447 at Bordeaux and GD644 at Marseille, all in 1973. No 8056 was sold circa 1947 to the Hungarian State Railways (MAV), becoming No LD223 at Tapolca, and by the millennium was installed in the new Budapest Railway Museum, while one was in Suez in 1956 and remained to be handed over to the Egyptian State Railways.

COWANS SHELDON 45-TON FOR MOS					
Works No.	Running No.			Allocation	Disposal
	Army/1st BR	CEPS	Converted		
8052				To Steel Co Wales	
8053	RS1085/45	ADRC 95221	ADRC 96718	Overhauled CS 6/60, CCE Dept, Crewe 1962–5/64, CMEE Dept Crewe, Bescot 11/11/69–9/80	Converted 5/86
8054					
8055					
8056				MAV No 223 Tapolea	Museum Budapest
8057					
8058					
8059	62001			Eskmeals 1981	Converted 1970s
Note: Dates shown in *italics* are spot dates upon which the crane is known to have been at the depot concerned.					

The London Midland Region Chief Civil Engineer's ex-WD 45-ton Cowans Sheldon steam breakdown crane No RS1087/45 in grey livery at Whetstone in May 1963. *M.S. Welch*

No RS1085/45 stands on a bridge at South Hampstead on 15 November 1964, when working with a 75-ton crane, out of view on the right, during the reconstruction of an ex-GC bridge on the Marylebone to Neasden line over the Slow lines of the West Coast main line, see Volume 1, p.216. *M.S. Welch*

Further north, on 5 January 1969, the CCE's crane loads a life-expired girder removed from Windsor Street in Salford, on the Liverpool to Manchester line, onto a 50-ton bogie wagon. With only an estimated weight of the load at the near limit of the crane's capacity, a man, bending down, has been posted to the rear of the crane to alert the supervisor as soon as the wheels start to lift! Note the temporary footbridge in the background to maintain pedestrian access from one side to the other, and temporary diversion of the public utilities. *M.S. Welch*

Cowans Sheldon 45-ton crane No SSIVBTN53g, ex-WD226, was photographed at Hengelo, the Netherlands, on 24 June 1945 on its way to Germany. *Cramer Driehergen*

At least three other WD cranes, however, returned to Britain, because Works Order No 8052 was acquired by the Steel Company of Wales in 1966 and No 8059 was still in government service at Eskmeals in 1981, having been converted to diesel propulsion in the 1970s. Works Order No 8053 was in due course sold as surplus to the Chief Civil Engineer's Department of the London Midland Region of British Railways in June 1960, and following an overhaul by Cowans Sheldon, was numbered RS1085/45, becoming the only oil-fired steam breakdown crane ever to operate on a British railway. It was put to work on bridge works as part of the implementation of the electrification of the West Coast main line under the Modernisation Plan. It was based at Basford Hall, Crewe, until taken on by the CME&E in November 1969 as regional spare at Bescot, where in due course it became No ADRC95221. As an engineer's crane it was initially painted grey, but had yellow applied long before this became normal for breakdown cranes. This crane then joined the four surviving cranes supplied to the LNER in 1940 and was converted to diesel propulsion, after which it received the No ADRC96718. It is now preserved at the Llangollen Railway.

Ransomes & Rapier 45-ton Cranes for GW and SR

The second tranche of 45-ton cranes provided by the government under the Air Raid Precaution preparations was supplied by Ransomes & Rapier. The initial order for this design for six was placed on 28 April 1939 (Order No E8136/8), of which two went to the Southern Railway and four to the Great Western Railway in 1940. It is known that the GW cranes, including the match wagons, cost £9,425 each and it is presumed the SR's were similar.

The design of the carriage was based on the SR 36-ton of 1937, modified to suit the enhanced capacity. The relieving bogies were redesigned in more skeletal form and in train formation these assisted in distributing the crane's total weight of about 107 tons, yet achieved a maximum axle load of 14 tons and could negotiate a 5-chain curve. Like their predecessors, these cranes were able to travel along the Hastings line between Tonbridge and Battle. 12 by 7-inch axle boxes, to SR pattern, were fitted to the carriage and 10 by 6-inch axle boxes to the bogies. The buffers, couplings, and relieving bogie axle boxes were GW standard. They had a water-feed tank fitted under one end of the carriage, from which the tanks alongside the boiler and the belly tank under the crab could be replenished.

To achieve the increase in capacity from 36 to 45 tons, the counter-balance took the form of vertical cast-iron weights across the rear of the superstructure, which precluded the provision of any rear-facing lookouts, instead of which the maker's name 'Rapier' was twice cast in the end on the diagonal. Nonetheless, openings had to been included to give access for washing out the boiler. A Stones turbo-generator and a lighting system were fitted. GW boiler fittings were mounted on a 6ft 11in high, 4ft 6in-diameter Cochran Hopwood boiler, pressurised to 120psi and lagged with an asbestos mattress enclosed by steel sheet. One of these boilers is illustrated on p.17 of Volume 1. Hoisting gear was fitted to assist in raising and lowering the chimney. As well as the hinged section of the roof to the housing, which could be raised once at site, on the left-hand side, beside the driver's position, was a fold-down platform, which the driver could also use to observe proceedings.

The jib followed previous practice and was equipped with a 14in electric floodlight on a swivel within the structure at about two-thirds the way up.

There were minor differences in the cranes supplied to various users. For instance the GW cranes did not have chimney-raising gear, although where provided, this equipment was often removed during the lives of the other cranes, either to eliminate the risk of colliding with overhead structures, or to reduce the tail radius when working in constricted sites.

Details of four-wheeled match wagons, to be built by RY Pickering of Wishaw, were confirmed in August 1939 and were to have GW-style 10 x 6in split axle boxes. The match wagons for both companies were to be fitted with an extensive range of tool boxes, with outside-falling doors, but the wagons for the SR had one set of lockers removed very shortly after delivery, in order to allow the stowage of a pair of temporary bogies on the match wagon.

There seems to have been some confusion as to whether these cranes belonged to the government, who paid for them, or the railway and the SR's at least were not formally taken into stock until 23 December 1942. They were, nonetheless, from the outset manned by railwaymen and in the early days the cranes were employed extensively on war work.

RANSOMES & RAPIER 45-TON FOR GW & SR							
Purchased by	Date delivered	Running No			Match wagon No	Allocation	Disposal
		Grouping	1st BR	CEPS			
SR	11/7/40	1560S	DS1560	ADRR 95209	1560SM DS3094	Feltham 8/40, Nine Elms 6/46, Eastleigh 1964–4/1/66, Hither Green 11/86, Stewart's Lane OOU 4/88,	Preserved at Swindon 6/89, Tyseley 1/06, cut up 2010 at Halesowen
SR	23/7/40	1561S	DS1561	ADRR 95210	1561SM DS3095	Guildford 8/40, Ashford (K) 6/62, Chart Leacon 31/10/67–16/7/77, Brighton 5/78–, Stewart's Lane late 1986–10/4/88	Preserved at Swindon 6/89, Southall 1/10, Swanage Railway 4/12
GW	13/8/40	16	ADW16	ADRR 95211		Old Oak Common c8/40–1/79, Swindon OOU 10/84–11/86	Withdrawn 3/82, scrapped 9/86 at Swindon
GW	2/9/40	17	RS1097/45 ADM1097	(ADRR 95208)		Stafford Rd c9/40, to LMR 1963, Tyseley 1/1/68, Saltley 19/1/69–6/3/76, Willesden 1/77–23/6/77, Crewe 9/78–1/79	GCR 2/82
GW	10.40	18	ADW18	ADRR 95212		Canton c10/40–15/11/56, Laira 1963, Landore 1965–12/79, Old Oak Common 1983	Carnforth 2/84
GW	12.40	19	ADW19	ADRR 95213		Bristol c12/40, Swindon 26/10/42–1948–10/60, Bristol 11/64–1/79, Laira 10/84–11/86	Swindon Works Ltd 12/87, Flour Mill Works, Forest of Dean 4/12
Note: Dates shown in *italics* are spot dates upon which the crane is known to have been at the depot concerned.							

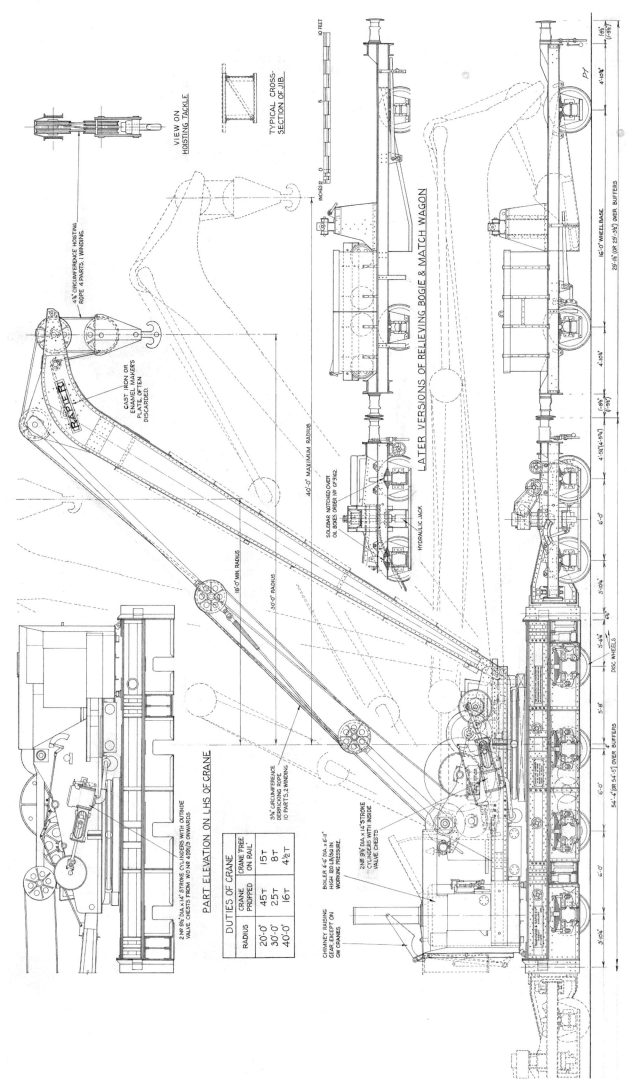

VIEW ON
HOISTING TACKLE

TYPICAL CROSS-
SECTION OF JIB

4¾" CIRCUMFERENCE HOISTING
ROPE 4 PARTS, 1 WINDING.

RAPIER

CAST IRON OR
ENAMEL MAKER'S
PLATE, OFTEN
DISCARDED.

40'-0" MAXIMUM RADIUS

18'-0" MIN. RADIUS

30'-0" RADIUS

3¾" CIRCUMFERENCE
DERRICKING ROPE
10 PARTS, 2 WINDING.

PART ELEVATION ON LHS OF CRANE

2 N⁰ 9¾" DIA x 14" STROKE CYLINDERS WITH OUTSIDE
VALVE CHESTS FROM W.O. N⁰ 4599/3 ONWARDS

DUTIES OF CRANE		
RADIUS	CRANE PROPPED	CRANE FREE ON RAIL
20'-0"	45T	15T
30'-0"	25T	8T
40'-0"	16T	4½T

CHIMNEY RAISING
GEAR, EXCEPT ON
GW CRANES.

BOILER 4'-6" DIA x 6'-11"
HIGH 120 LB/SQ IN.
WORKING PRESSURE.

2 N⁰ 9¾" DIA x 14" STROKE
CYLINDERS WITH INSIDE
VALVE CHESTS

SOLEBAR NOTCHED OVER
OIL BOXES ORDER N⁰ GF9162.

HYDRAULIC JACK

LATER VERSIONS OF RELIEVING BOGIE & MATCH WAGON

10 FEET

5

INCHES 12   0

6'-8"
(-9½")

4'-10¼"

16'-0" WHEELBASE

29'-1½" (OR 29'-3¾") OVER BUFFERS

4'-10¼"

1'-8½"
(1'-9½")

4'-5¾"(4'-5¾")

6'-0"

3'-10¼"

6¾"

3'-4½"

DISC WHEELS

5'-8"

6'-0"

6'-0"

54'-4" (OR 54'-5") OVER BUFFERS

3'-10¼"

Figure 21 Elevation of Ransomes & Rapier 45-ton cranes supplied to SR, GW, LNER & MoS. *Author*

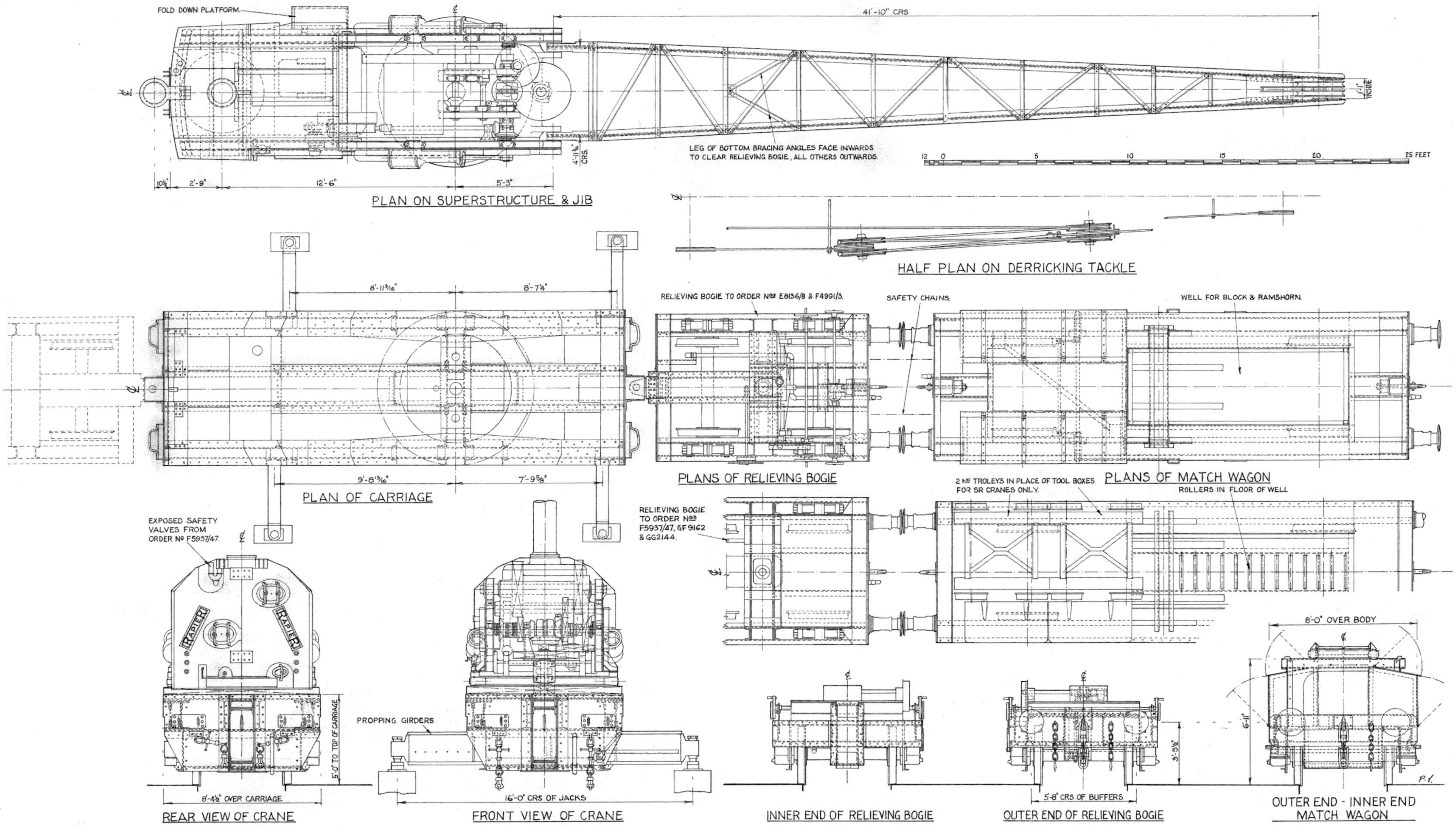

Figure 22 Plan and end views of Ransomes & Rapier 45-ton cranes supplied to SR, GW, LNER & MoS. *Author*

INSIDE

25 FEET

20

15

10

5

0

12

41'-10" CRS

LEG OF BOTTOM BRACING ANGLES FACE INWARDS
TO CLEAR RELIEVING BOGIE, ALL OTHERS OUTWARDS.

CRS.

4'-11⅞"

PLAN ON SUPERSTRUCTURE & JIB

5'-3"

12'-6"

2'-9"

10"

FOLD DOWN PLATFORM.

HALF PLAN ON DERRICKING TACKLE

WELL FOR BLOCK & RAMSHORN

SAFETY CHAINS.

RELIEVING BOGIE TO ORDER Nos E8136/8 & F4901/3.

PLANS OF MATCH WAGON

ROLLERS IN FLOOR OF WELL

2 No TROLLEYS IN PLACE OF TOOL BOXES
FOR SR CRANES ONLY.

PLANS OF RELIEVING BOGIE

RELIEVING BOGIE
TO ORDER No3
F5957/47, 6F 9162
& G6214/4.

OUTER END - INNER END
MATCH WAGON

8'-0" OVER BODY

6'-11"

OUTER END OF RELIEVING BOGIE

5'-8" CRS OF BUFFERS

3'-5⅞"

INNER END OF RELIEVING BOGIE

PLAN OF CARRIAGE

8'-7¼"

7'-9⅝"

8'-11⅜"

9'-6⅝"

FRONT VIEW OF CRANE

16'-0 CRS OF JACKS

PROPPING GIRDERS

REAR VIEW OF CRANE

RAPIER

RAPIER

EXPOSED SAFETY
VALVES FROM
ORDER No F5957/47

5'-0" TO TOP OF CARRIAGE

8'-4½" OVER CARRIAGE

The Crane's Motions

By this time Ransomes & Rapier had a well-honed design for the machinery and gearing of their high-capacity steam breakdown cranes and these are drawn and scheduled on the drawing below (Figure 23).

Derricking the jib

Bevel wheel P was engaged by a dog-clutch on the crankshaft, which then drove the bevel pinion on a longitudinal shaft at the end of which the worm R imparted motion to the worm wheel S above. This then rotated the spur pinion T acting on the spur wheel U, itself attached to the derricking drum.

Hoisting a load

Unlike the arrangement adopted by Cowans Sheldon, Rapier placed the hoisting drum behind the crankshaft. Two speeds of hoisting were obtained by means of a two-way dog-clutch which engaged either spur pinion A with spur wheel B for light loads at high speed, or spur pinion C with spur wheel D for full load at lower speed. B or D drove spur pinion E, all on the same layshaft, which turned spur wheel F on the hoisting drum.

Slewing the superstructure

A double-cone clutch at the mid-point along the crankshaft could be used to engage either bevel wheels G or G1, depending on which direction was required, and in both cases bevel wheel H on a vertical shaft was activated. At the foot of this shaft, spur wheel H drove a string of spur pinions (K & M) and spur wheels (L & N) all at the front end of the superstructure, the last of which acted upon the spur rack O mounted on the carriage.

Self-propelled travel

Finally, a dog-clutch was used to engage spur pinion V, which acted on spur wheel W and in turn on spur wheel X, which was attached by means of a short shaft to bevel wheel Y. This drove bevel wheel Z at the top of a vertical shaft running down through the centre of the king pin. Not shown on the drawing is the arrangement of the gears in the carriage, which started with spur pinion A1 at the foot of the vertical shaft driving spur wheel B1 behind the second axle. Then, by a series of bevel wheels B1/C1 and D1/E1, the centre of the carriage was reached, from where spur wheel G1 could be engaged by means of a clutch with pairs of spur wheels H1 and J1, the last being on the second and third axles.

Figure 23 Ransomes & Rapier drawing No 72512 illustrating the arrangement of the superstructure of a 45-ton crane and showing the gear trains. *Ransomes & Rapier, author's collection*

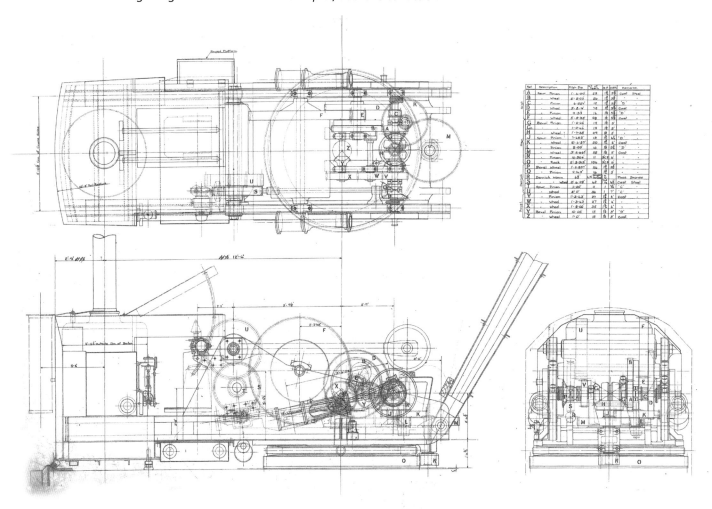

Allocation

The Southern's cranes were initially sent to sheds close to, but outside, London, at Feltham and Guildford, from where they could quickly be sent in to cope with air-raid damage without being exposed to undue risk themselves. Guildford had been without a crane for some years, while Feltham was temporary host to No 1196S, taking refuge from Nine Elms from the bombing, but to which, nonetheless, it shortly returned. A 'General Post' took place after the war, resulting in No 1560S transferring to Nine Elms, while No 1561S remained at Guildford. The arrival of two 75-ton diesel cranes in 1964 led to Nos DS1560 and DS1561 going to Eastleigh and Ashford (Kent), only for the former to swap cranes with Hither Green a few years later. No ADRR95210, alias DS1561, went to Brighton in 1978, both ending up at Stewart's Lane prior to withdrawal ten years later, ADRR95210 becoming the last steam-powered breakdown crane to remain in service with BR.

The four GW cranes were allocated to the main depots of Old Oak Common, Wolverhampton, Canton and Swindon, where some remained much of their lives. Their arrival allowed 36-ton crane No 1 to be transferred to Bristol and 15-ton No 3 to Worcester, while Canton graduated from a 6-ton hand crane to a 45-ton monster. The arrival of two new 75-ton steam cranes in 1962, together with a pair of new 30-ton cranes, caused some cascading of the existing cranes to other less important depots, and so on down the line, culminating in the withdrawal of a number of the old small-capacity cranes. Subsequent adjustment of the regional boundaries resulted in the transfer of No 17 to the London Midland Region.

Remarkably, three out of the four GW 45-ton cranes, plus the two Southern cranes were purchased for use on heritage railways, although sadly 1560S was cut up in April 2010.

Above The order for ARP cranes on the GW and Southern railways to the same specification was fulfilled in 1939/40 by Ransomes & Rapier, and here is the SR's 45-ton crane No 1561S, at Ransomes & Rapier's in grey livery in train formation awaiting delivery. *Author's collection*

Left One of the GW's four 45-ton Ransomes & Rapier cranes, with chimney raised and relieving bogies removed, lifting a wagon at Swindon Works on 6 September 1940 soon after delivery. In the background is a Cowans Sheldon 20-ton crane. *BR, WR, author's collection*

Above One of the Southern Region's 45-ton cranes on 27 April 1954, attending to Drummond 0-6-0 No 30346 at Shortwood Crossing near Staines, having overshot the buffers while shunting. Nobody was hurt, but apparently pedestrians wishing to use the crossing had to walk round the locomotive. One cannot see Health & Safety approving today! Note the spreader beam with a pair of brothers hanging from each end. *Unattributed*

Left The right-hand side of the superstructure of ex-GW 45-ton crane No 17 at Saltley on 1 February 1969, by then transferred to the London Midland Region and renumbered No RS1097/45, showing the feed pump, boiler fittings and turbo-generator. *Author*

Opposite top The driver of No DS1560 concentrates on handling the off-loading of some pre-tensioned concrete beams at Havant on 4 January 1966. *Author*

Opposite bottom One of the relieving bogies of ex-SR No DS1560 at Havant on 4 January 1966. The load on the bogie on this batch of cranes was taken up by screw jack, operated by turning the larger hand wheel which activated a chain drive. Note the lowered solebars and the inner headstock passing through a slot in the cantilever beam. *Author*

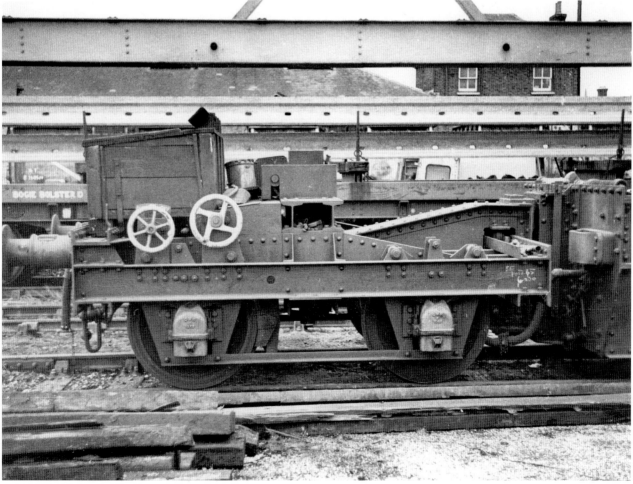

On 6 May 1977, the rear motor bogie of the eighth car of a ten-car EMU, the 04.14 from Addiscombe to Cannon Street, derailed on a crossover at Borough Market Junction, causing a coupling to fail. Here, 45-ton crane No ADS1560 has arrived and is getting ready to restore to order. *Unattributed*

Above Ex-GW 45-ton crane No 19 stands ready to respond to being called out on 6 October 1963 at Old Oak Common, still in black livery. Note the profusion of tool boxes on the match wagon and the addition of steps. *M.S. Welch*

Right Ex-SR 45-ton crane No ADS1561, with its jib slightly raised above its match wagon as it is repainted on 3 March 1979 following an overhaul. *Colour-Rail*

Right The two large apertures in the counterweight on the rear of the superstructure allow access to the rear tube door, and the man-hole door. Below these, the large aperture bottom right permits access to the blow-down valve and a mud-hole lid, the smaller hole above the ash-pan to another mud-hole lid. The vertical slot bottom left is where the damper linkage emerges. *Colour-Rail*

Ransomes & Rapier 45-ton Cranes for LNER, MoS and SR

As noted previously, in January 1942 the War Department had requisitioned two of the LNER's 45-ton Cowans Sheldon cranes and despatched them to Persia (now Iran). Two replacements were immediately ordered on 12 February 1942, but were built instead by Ransomes & Rapier (Order No F4991/3). This order was followed on 23 September 1942 by another for six more for the Ministry of Supply (MoS), at a total cost of £72,789, to meet the anticipated needs in Europe following the allied invasion in June 1944 (Order No F5937). In 1945, the Southern Railway acquired an additional crane on its own account to handle Bulleid's Pacifics in the West Country, while a year later a further example was supplied to the MoS at Shoeburyness.

Although generally similar to the 1940 cranes, variations included the following:

a) The initial batch to the SR and GW had internal valve chests. Cylinders with outside valves actuated by rocker arms passing through the crab sides from the eccentrics inside were introduced in 1943.

b) The method of loading the relieving bogies was changed from mechanical to hydraulic, open-fronted axle boxes were provided instead of split axle boxes, and other changes were made to the bogies from Order No F5937/47 in 1943 for the MoS.

c) As a result of moving away from the use of standard GW boiler fittings on the MoS cranes, the boiler safety valves were repositioned to pass through cut-outs in the counterweights at the tail of the crane.

Ransomes & Rapier, having fulfilled the order for ARP cranes in 1939/40, went on to provide more cranes to the same specification with only small differences. The first examples, in 1943, were two for the LNER as replacements for the requisitioned cranes mentioned previously. This ex-LNER 45-ton Ransomes & Rapier crane, now transferred to the London Midland Region as No RS1083/45 and stationed at Newton Heath, was photographed at Penrith in June 1967 placing its forward relieving bogie on the recently-laid adjacent track. *M.S. Welch*

RANSOMES & RAPIER 45-TON FOR LNER, MOS & SR									
Purchased by	Date Delivered	Order No	Cost	Running No			Match wagon No	Allocation	Disposal
				Grouping	1st BR	CEPS			
MoS for LNER	4/43	F4991/2/3	£9,481	941601	(330)102	ADRR 95214	941767	King's Cross c5/43–6/11/61, Grimesthorpe 1961, Tinsley 10/65	Withdrawn 27/11/85. NYMR 7/86
MoS for LNER	5/43	F4991/2/3	£9,481	951516	122, RS1083/45, ADM1083	ADRR 95215	951676	Gorton c6/43–6/11/61, to LMR 1/2/58, Newton Heath 13/6/65–1/79	Bluebell Rly 11/81
MoS	c11.43	F5937	£12,131	62003?				c11/43, converted to diesel '76	
MoS	c12.43	F5937	£12,131					c12/43	
MoS	c1.44	F5937	£12,131	62005?				c1/44, Bicester, Shoeburyness 1978, converted to diesel 1983/4	
MoS	c2.44	F5937	£12,131	WD214, 62006?				c2/44, Shoeburyness, Longmoor 1964–5/7/69, Marchwood, converted to diesel, Long Marston 10/72–1982,	Preserved G&WR Toddington
MoS	c4.44	F5937	£12,131					c4/44	
MoS	c5.44	F5937	£12,131	63008				c5/44, 'Effingham', Shoeburyness	1971
SR	c11.45	F9162	£14,062	1580S	DS1580, WR 151	ADRR 95216	1580SM/ DS3096	Exmouth Jct 11/45–11/64, to WR 1/1/63, Newton Abbot 8/65–7/69, Laira 1/72–1/79, Old Oak Common	Preserved, on G&WR 9/4/83, Llangollen Railway 1989, transferred to Mid-Hants Railway 24/7/92
WO	1946	G2144	£15,000	63013				c8/46 'Montgomery', Shoeburyness	Withdrawn pre-1985

Note: Dates shown in *italics* are spot dates upon which the crane is known to have been at the depot concerned.

The design of the headstock for later match wagons was revised, as was the jib support to the SR's crane of 1945. This and the subsequent crane for the MoS also had the solebars to the relieving bogies notched over the axle boxes to provide additional space for oil boxes. The location of the steam turbo-generator for the lighting varied considerably between different batches of cranes, although they were usually somewhere on the right-hand crab side.

The cranes supplied to the LNER were fitted with that company's buffers, draw hooks, vacuum-pipe hose couplings, etc., and boiler fittings. The large axle boxes on the crane carriage were of LNER pattern, while those of the relieving bogies and match wagon continued the GW style. In addition to the main floodlight on the jib, wander plugs and inspection lamps, cab light and jib-head spotlights were provided, necessitating collector gear inside the roller path to enable lighting points to be arranged on the carriage. The relieving bogies were fitted with trays for tools etc. The match wagons were supplied by Rapier, but it is not known whether or not their construction was let out to a sub-contractor. The tool boxes on the match wagon to Gorton's crane seem to have been removed by the early 1950s.

A close-up of the carriage and superstructure of No RS1083/45 on the same occasion. The driver is positioned well up to be able to see forward over the machinery. Note the pointer and sector plate to indicate the degree of load transferred to the relieving bogie. *M.S. Welch*

The detached match wagon and one of the relieving bogies from ex-LNER 45-ton crane No DE330107 at Chesterfield on 22 August 1976; see the frontispiece. *53A Models of Hull collection*

The six cranes for the MoS were practically duplicates of the LNER cranes, but were also piped for both vacuum and Westinghouse brakes and had hydraulic operation of the relieving bogies. The British composite loading gauge was considered suitable for the Middle East and Continental 'Passé partout'. The boilers were coal fired, but suitable for conversion if required to oil firing at a later date. They are recorded as having been tested by Rapier between October 1943 and April 1944, and four were included in the twelve cranes having crossed the Channel by December 1944. One, however, was under repair at the LMS Derby Works until December 1944 and could not have travelled to Europe until later. Another was at Shoeburyness and apparently did not leave there until its disposal in 1971. Two remained in Germany until circa 1951 (Tn8410 and 8413), while another was sold in 1946, for £11,000 to the Netherlands State Railways and was still in use there in 1955. One of this batch of Rapier 45-ton cranes was in Suez from 1948 to 1956 and remained to be handed over to the Egyptian State Railways. A few of both Cowans- and Rapier-type 45-ton cranes still in British military hands were converted to diesel power during the 1970s.

Six more Ransomes & Rapier 45-ton cranes were supplied to the Ministry of Supply for War Department use and, after the war, one more to the Southern. One of the WD cranes was used at the Longmoor Military Railway for training railway troops and is seen there on the last open day on 5 July 1969. *Author*

A close-up of the crane at Longmoor on the same occasion. *Author*

Rear view of the crane superstructure, showing the holes in the counterweight to afford access to the mud-holes used to wash out the boiler. *Author*

The introduction of Bulleid's Pacific locomotives and the assembling of the invasion forces in the West of England prior to D-Day had shown up the inadequacy of the Southern Railway's breakdown-crane capacity in the area. As an interim measure, Salisbury's 36-ton crane was loaned to Exmouth Jct and a WD 45-ton crane was stationed at Salisbury during the build-up to D-Day. As a consequence, an order was placed on 1 June 1944 for a further 45-ton crane, similar to the ARP and MoS version from Rapier, but this was not delivered until late in 1945 to Exmouth Jct (Order No F9162), becoming the last breakdown crane supplied by Ransomes & Rapier to a British railway. This crane was made more unusual since, in line with normal practice, the wheel sets, axle boxes etc. were supplied by the customer to the manufacturer, and in this case Bullied Firth Brown cast disc wheels were provided. This crane was fitted with a Cochran Hopwood boiler with standard SR boiler fittings.

It is difficult to be specific about the liveries worn by breakdown cranes, particularly in pre-BR days. In general terms, however, it is believed that GW and probably LNER cranes were black and SR ones dark grey with red buffer beams. Not surprisingly, the Army's cranes were painted khaki. Starting from the military cranes, the name 'Rapier' was applied in the curve of the upper jib sides on large enamel plates.

A close-up of the modified cylinder arrangement, with outside valve chest actuated by the rocking lever at the rear projecting through the crab side. *Author*

Exmouth Jct's Ransomes & Rapier 45-ton crane, the last delivered in November 1945 to the Southern Railway, poses in the sunlight in what appears to be newly-applied, BR's first, black livery as No DS1580. With regional boundary changes, this crane found its way to the Western Region as No 151 and was posted successively to Newton Abbot, Laira (Plymouth) and Old Oak Common, before being acquired by the Gloucestershire Warwickshire Railway. It is now operational at the Mid Hants Railway. *Colour-Rail*

The driver of Exmouth Jct's crane steps out onto the fold-down platform. *Author's collection*

6

LMS 30-ton Cranes

During the 1930s, the LMS reorganised its Motive Power Department, setting up districts with principal depots and a number of sub-depots. In most cases a steam crane was allocated to each district and this was generally kept at the main shed, although it was not unknown for the crane to be based at another large shed within the district. In 1937, there were 29 districts and 30 cranes, but that is not to say that each district had one crane, with one to spare, as a few districts in England and Wales had to make do with hand cranes, while the then geographically larger Scottish districts sometimes had two cranes each. In passing, it should be mentioned that during the Second World War some of the Scottish districts were sub-divided. Thus-equipped, each district was expected to tackle any derailment within its area, only calling for outside assistance in the event of a serious incident beyond its capability.

Before the Second World War, out of the LMS's stock of 31 steam breakdown cranes, just less than half were of 15-ton capacity, dating from the end of the 19th century, but nonetheless handy machines for the more common incidents. The company therefore set about developing a more modern counterpart of 30-ton capacity, long jib and yet uninhibited by limitations on route availability and without the encumbrance of relieving bogies or removable counterweights, etc.

In the preparations for anticipated aerial bombardment at the outbreak of war, as mentioned in Chapter 5, the LMS received no allocation from the government of 45-tonners. Instead, the LMS persuaded the authorities in early 1940 to permit the construction of a prototype 20/30-ton-capacity crane on a 0-6-4 underframe, intended as a replacement to the now outdated short-jibbed 15- and 20-ton cranes. This prototype appears to have been used as a demonstrator and as a result may have moved round a number of depots before settling down in the far north at Inverness. Following delivery of this in 1941, ten more were constructed at the height of the war, the order being split equally between Cowans and Rapier. As well as the new cranes and match wagons, the provision of additional staff-riding and tool vans, with

associated equipment, was sanctioned, although at the time some of the equipment was in short supply and was added only as it became available. Two more cranes from the first stable were also supplied to the Ministry of Supply at about the same time.

Although usually referred to as 30-ton cranes, this was only at the cranes' minimum radius of 16ft, the more useful capacity of 20 tons was available out to a radius of 24ft and therefore more comparable with the old short-jib cranes they were intended to replace. Neither relieving bogies, nor detachable counterweights and the removal of the propping girders were necessary on a 0-6-4 carriage to achieve a maximum axle-load of 13 tons 3cwt, thereby affording a wide route availability. Once the new cranes were delivered, the old cranes they were intended to replace were nonetheless retained in order to strengthen the breakdown resources and deal with possible emergencies arising out of enemy action.

Craven Bros also tendered a proposal for a crane, with four axles spaced at 7ft 6in centres, capable of lifting 36 tons at 14ft radius, 30 tons at 16ft, 22 tons at 22ft and 18 tons at 25ft 6in, together with an auxiliary hoist reaching out to 30ft. This, however, was not accepted by the LMS to fulfil their specification for a 30-ton crane.

Both types of crane were of 0-6-4 wheel arrangement with 3ft 1in-diameter wheels. They were fitted with through-vacuum brake pipe and hinged buffers. Dual control to the steam regulator, hoisting and slewing brake levers was provided, one control on each side of the footplate. Simply-constructed load indicators were provided on both sides and in the driver's cab. The cranes were equipped with Stones turbo-generators and lighting gear. Water was supplied from tanks below the coal bunker, under the footplate and in the carriage. Hopwood No 14 squat boilers were used, 4ft 6in-diameter x 6ft 8in and pressurised to 120psi.

Eleven six-wheel match wagons were ordered, to diagram 2081 for the Cowans cranes Nos 770006–770011 and diagram 2082 for Rapier Nos 770001–770005. These match wagons were ordered in 1942 to Lot 1336 (1 No, see Chapter 8) and Lot 1324 (5 + 5 No)

LMS match wagon No 770011 built by Wolverton in 1942 for the contemporary 30-ton cranes. This one was for RS1066/30. Note the lifting beam and other tackle loaded on the crane end of the wagon. The livery appears to be black sides and bolster on a wagon-grey underframe with white lettering. *BR, LMR, author's collection*

and built at Wolverton in 1942. These were 33ft over the headstock, had 3ft 2in wheels and a tare weight of 10 tons 13cwt which, even allowing for some gear left on it, was within the capacity of the crane to lift from in front of the crane. The longitudinal position of the jib rest was slightly different to suit the two makers' cranes. Those for the non-articulated-jib cranes were fitted with rollers to accommodate any longitudinal movement of the jib due to the taking up of slack in the couplings, whilst in turn these rollers were mounted on a small carriage which could move across the bolster, thus permitting lateral movement of the jib caused by end throw on curves. A similar arrangement was applied as a modification to the match wagons paired with the LMS 36/40-ton Ransomes & Rapier cranes Nos RS1004/40 and RS1038/40. The last two match wagons for the Cowans were different still, to suit the articulated jib, as discussed later.

The match wagons coupled to the cranes provided by the Ministry of Supply for the War Department were long four-wheeled vehicles, perhaps an extended version of those provided for the 45-ton Cowans Sheldon cranes, but with Continental fittings.

Looking down on the same wagon from the other end, showing the well into which the main block and hook fitted. The pair of rollers to accommodate longitudinal movement of the jib relative to the match wagon can be seen mounted within a small carriage, itself within the transverse bolster. This carriage was able to move laterally across the bolster as the jib head swung when rounding curves. *BR, LMR, author's collection*

Cowans Sheldon 30-ton Cranes for LMS and MoS

The LMS had been developing plans for a modern 30-ton crane since before the outbreak of the Second World War as a replacement for its old cranes. A contract for the construction of the prototype was placed with Cowans Sheldon on 9 March 1940 for the price of £5,963 and this was delivered in 1941. The purchase of a further ten cranes of the type was authorised, and an order for half of these production cranes was placed with Cowans Sheldon on 23 May 1941 at a cost of £6,765 each.

Two further 30-ton cranes were ordered from Cowans Sheldon on 4 February 1942 by the Ministry of Supply (Works Nos 7869 and 7870) and these were delivered in 1944. Both are said to have been at Marchwood on Southampton Water in 1944, one of which was reported still to be in the Solent area in December 1944. One then spent time at Longmoor and later at Shoeburyness, during which time it was converted to diesel power. The other found its way to the Continent ending up on the Austrian railways and subsequently preserved at the Das Heizhaus Railway Museum, Strasshof, near Vienna, Austria.

The Cowans cranes were capable of negotiating a 4-chain curve and had a 17ft propping base.

The general arrangement drawing shows the crane with a pair of short-wheelbase four-wheeled wagons attached under the jib, but it is more likely that at the outset the first crane was coupled to ex-Midland Railway 30-ton bogie rail wagon No 117148, probably to diagram

D330, with which it was photographed. However, with a tare weight in the order of 17 or 18 tons and a length of 41ft over headstocks, it would have been beyond the capacity of the crane to lift it clear from in front and this, therefore, was the likely reason for its replacement a year later by the dedicated design of match wagon for the subsequent 30-ton cranes described previously.

This prototype crane, No RS1066/30, was initially sent to Wellingborough for a period of appraisal. Following the delivery of the initial examples of the remaining 30-ton cranes, No RS1066/30 moved on to Inverness, where it stayed until its withdrawal in the late 1970s. With the exception perhaps of No RS1073/30 at Hurlford/Ayr, other cranes of the type spent a more unsettled existence moving from shed to shed and in some cases to other regions, as shown in the table below.

It is reported that on 5 January 1973, No DE331160 from York, together with the assistance of the Holbeck gang and their crane No DE331159, was called out to Garforth near Leeds to a derailment involving four 100-tonne loaded oil tankers. Despite protests from York's foreman, the two cranes were instructed to lift a tanker, as a result of which No DE331160 was damaged beyond economic repair, having suffered a bent king-pin, and Holbeck gained York's area for crane work.

A decade later, however, all the rest had met their end and no British examples have survived.

COWANS & SHELDON 30-TON FOR LMS & MOS							
Purchased by	Date delivered	Works No	Running No		Match wagon No	Allocation	Disposal
			5/41	BR/WD No			
LMS	1941	7117	RS1066/30		(1) 117148 (2) 770011	Wellingborough 1941, Inverness 7/42–30/8/76	Scrapped 24/7/78
LMS	22/6/43	7519	RS1072/30	(331)160	770006	Wakefield 6/43–22/2/66, to ER 10/56, Sunderland 5/66, Dairycoates 1/68–3/70, Botanic Gdns 10/70, York 10/6/72	Withdrawn 1973
LMS	28/8/43	7520	RS1073/30		770010	Hurlford 7/10/43–3/10/66, Ayr 4/10/66–12/78	Withdrawn 11/83
LMS	23/9/43	7521	RS1074/30		770007	Perth 9/43–1/10/60, Thornton 1962, Ferryhill 1966–4/75, Inverness 12/78–22/8/79	Withdrawn 7/83
LMS	1943	7522	RS1075/30	330115	770009	Carnforth 11/43, Rugby 30/5/45–5/2/53, Newton Heath 4/54, Bescot 1/5/64, Chester 11/64, Bescot 2/65, to ER 1/8/68, Shirebrook (spare) 10/68–4/72	Sold for scrap to Arnott Young 11/76
LMS	1944	7523	RS1076/30	WR 11	770008	Llandudno Jct 4/44, Shrewsbury 2/46–10/60, to LMR 1/1/63, Rugby 4/67	Withdrawn 7/69
MoS	1944	7869/70		966 300		Marchwood 1944, Continent 5/45, OBB, Austria No. 966 300	Preserved at Strasshof, 1998.
MoS	1944	7870/69		62007		Marchwood 1944, Continent 5/45, Longmoor 1955–65, Shoeburyness mid-1980s, converted to diesel	

Note: Dates shown in *italics* are spot dates upon which the crane is known to have been at the depot concerned.

Having missed out on the delivery of 45-ton cranes at the beginning of the Second World War, the LMS subsequently received a total of eleven modern 30-ton cranes to replace outdated cranes on its system. The prototype, showing no signs yet of having been numbered RS1066/30, still paired with its first match wagon, ex-MR 30-ton bogie rail wagon No 117148. Some remnants of lining are visible on the crane. *BR, LMR, author's collection*

Overleaf, Figure 24 Elevation of Cowans Sheldon 30-ton crane supplied to LMS and MoS from 1941 to 1944. *Author*

Overleaf, Figure 25 Plan and end views of Cowans Sheldon 30-ton crane supplied to LMS and MoS from 1941 to 1944. *Author*

Figure 24

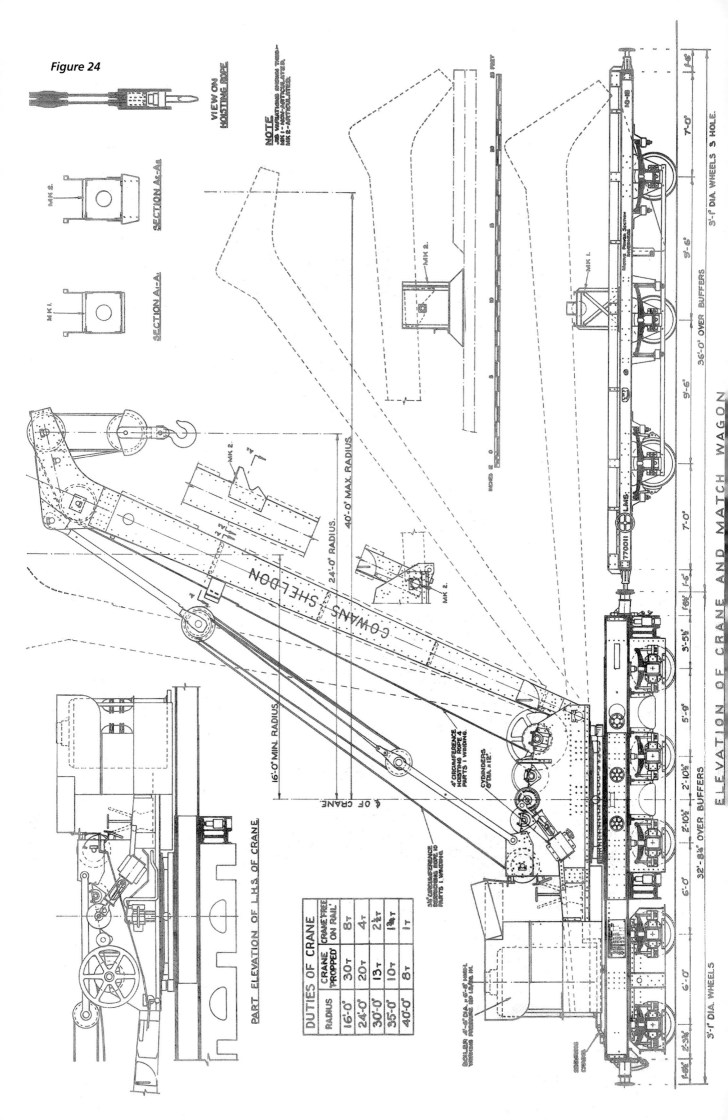

VIEW ON HOISTING ROPE

SECTION A₂-A₂ MK 2.

SECTION A₁-A₁ MK 1.

NOTE
JIB VARIATIONS SHOWN THUS—
MK 1 - NON-ARTICULATED.
MK 2 - ARTICULATED.

PART ELEVATION OF L.H.S. OF CRANE.

40'-0" MAX. RADIUS.

24'-0" RADIUS.

16'-0" MIN. RADIUS.

₵ OF CRANE.

GOWANS SHELDON

MK 2.

MK 2.

4" CIRCUMFERENCE HOISTING ROPE 4 PARTS 1 WINDING.

CYLINDERS 8" DIA. ×12".

3½" CIRCUMFERENCE DERRICKING ROPE 10 PARTS 1 WINDING.

BOILER 4'-6" DIA. ×6'-6" HIGH. WORKING PRESSURE 120 LB./SQ. IN.

DERRICKING CHAINS.

DUTIES OF CRANE		
RADIUS	CRANE 'PROPPED'	CRANE FREE ON RAIL
16'-0"	30ᴛ	8ᴛ
24'-0"	20ᴛ	4ᴛ
30'-0"	13ᴛ	2½ᴛ
35'-0"	10ᴛ	1¾ᴛ
40'-0"	8ᴛ	1ᴛ

MK 2.

MK 1.

1770011

L.M.S.

10-11B

25 FEET

INCHES 12 0

3'-1" DIA. WHEELS 3 HOLE.

3'-1" DIA. WHEELS

32'-8¼" OVER BUFFERS

36'-0" OVER BUFFERS

ELEVATION OF CRANE AND MATCH WAGON

2'-3¾" | 6'-0" | 6'-0" | 2'-10½" | 2'-10½" | 5'-9" | 3'-5½" | 6¾" | 1'-6" | 7'-0" | 9'-6" | 9'-6" | 7'-0" | 1'-6½"

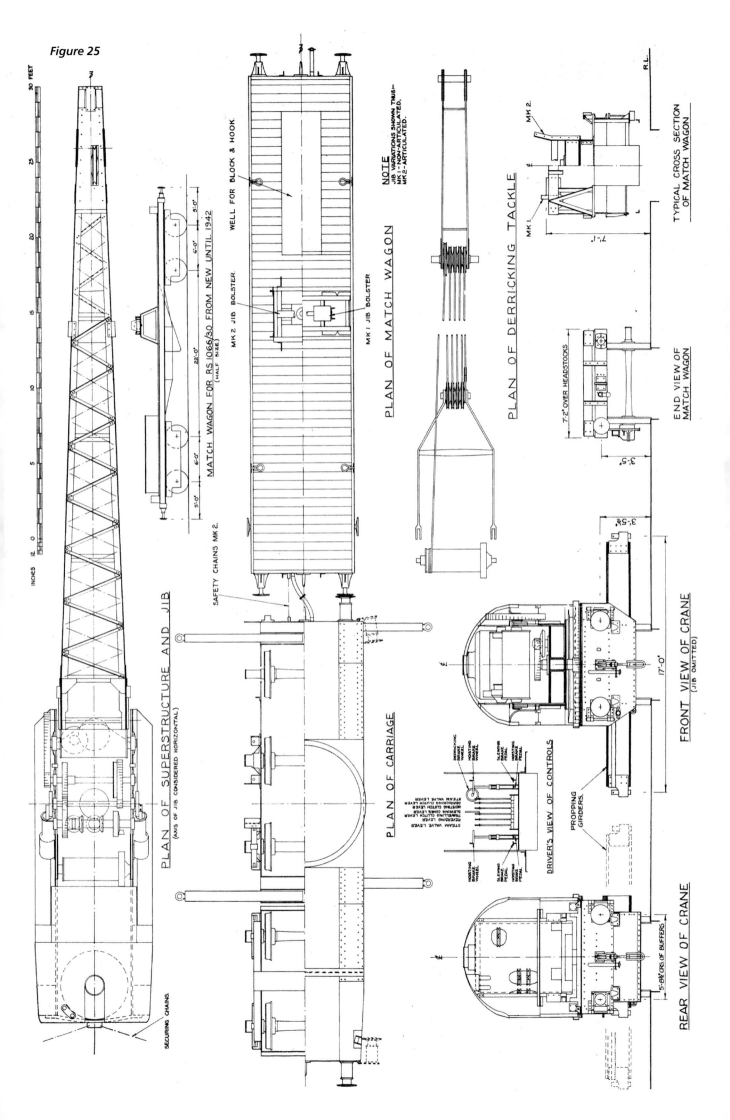

Figure 25

30 FEET
25
20
15
10
5
0

INCHES 5 0

PLAN OF SUPERSTRUCTURE AND JIB
(AXIS OF JIB CONSIDERED HORIZONTAL)

SECURING CHAINS.

MATCH WAGON FOR RS 1066/30 FROM NEW UNTIL 1942
(HALF SIZE)

5'-0" 6'-0" 22'-0" 6'-0" 5'-0"

WELL FOR BLOCK & HOOK.

MK 2 JIB BOLSTER.

MK 1 JIB BOLSTER.

SAFETY CHAINS MK 2.

PLAN OF MATCH WAGON

NOTE
JIB VARIATIONS SHOWN THUS:—
MK 1 - NON-ARTICULATED.
MK 2 - ARTICULATED.

PLAN OF CARRIAGE

PLAN OF DERRICKING TACKLE

MK 2.
MK 1.

7'-1"

TYPICAL CROSS SECTION
OF MATCH WAGON

R.L.

7'-2" OVER HEADSTOCKS

3'-5"

END VIEW OF
MATCH WAGON

DERRICKING
BRAKE
WHEEL
HOISTING
BRAKE
WHEEL
SLEWING
BRAKE
PEDAL
STEAM VALVE LEVER
DERRICKING CLUTCH LEVER
HOISTING CLUTCH LEVER
SLEWING CLUTCH LEVER
TRAVELLING CLUTCH LEVER
REVERSING LEVER
STEAM VALVE LEVER
HOISTING
BRAKE
WHEEL
SLEWING
BRAKE
PEDAL
HOISTING
BRAKE
PEDAL

DRIVER'S VIEW OF CONTROLS

3'-5½"

17'-0"

FRONT VIEW OF CRANE
(JIB OMITTED)

PROPPING
GIRDERS.

5'-8½" C/RS OF BUFFERS

REAR VIEW OF CRANE

No RS1073/30 attends at Largs on 21 July 1957, following the derailment of 2-6-4T No 42122. Steam issues from the drain cock as the crane raises its jib. *J. Templeton, Author's collection*

The cast-iron safe-load plate attached to the carriage frame. *Author's collection*

The axle box, the leaf springs, long spring hangers and reinforcing gussets of a Cowans Sheldon 30-ton crane. Note the spring-relieving screws screwed down on top of the spring buckle. *Author*

Looking at the gearing of a 30-ton crane. With the jib down, the lower bridle gear rests on the crab sides. To the rear is the derricking drum with most of the steel rope extended. Nearer is the crankshaft with the spur and bevel gears for the various motions. *Author*

Livery of LMS 30-ton Cranes

The livery of the LMS 30-ton cranes was black all over. In addition, Nos 1066/30 and RS1067/30 (see below) had ½in-wide red lining 2in in from the edges applied to the coal bunkers, water tanks, crab sides, cylinder wrappers and jib. The solebar of the carriage and bogie were each lined in three panels, while the carriage lower platework was lined in one panel and also round lightening holes. The brake wheel, ends of buffer housings, spring hangers and binding bands were picked out with red lines, except that the brake and clutch wheels on the Rapier crane were white. There is no evidence to indicate that others in the series were likewise lined, although the later ones were definitely not lined out. The control levers were colour coded and the handles chromium plated. These were of varying profiles to assist in identification by touch in the darkness.

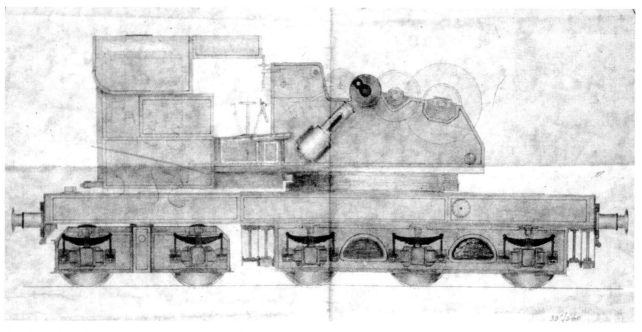

A colour-tinted drawing unearthed in the files at Derby in 1971, showing the proposed livery for the Cowans Sheldon 30-ton cranes. *Author*

Ex-LMS 30-ton Cowans Sheldon steam crane No RS1066/30 at Grantown-on-Spey with snow on the ground in February 1963. Off the picture to the left, Class 2 diesel locomotive No D5335 heads the breakdown train from Inverness, thought to be returning from rerailing two diesel locomotives and a snow-plough off the rails in a snow drift at Dava Summit. The train consists of an ex-MR twelve-wheel clerestory coach as a tool van; an ex-LNWR coach converted into a riding van, see later; a four-wheel sheeted wagon containing timber packing; and the crane. *Norris Forrest, courtesy GNSRA*

Left Following the derailment of a freight train at Lugton, No RS1073/30 from Hurlford loads up some damaged oil-tank wagons on 17 July 1966. Note the debris on the platform and the remainder of the breakdown train well back down the track.
J. Templeton, author's collection

Below The long, flush-sided jib is apparent as the gang feed the block back into the well in the match wagon, while others set about returning the propping girders into their place.
J. Templeton, author's collection

The last two production cranes for the LMS were modified to incorporate an articulated jib, also necessitating a revised form of jib rest. This was the first venture by Cowans to adopt this principle and differed from Craven's example; in that the foot of the jib had an open crutch which, when raised, seated on a large-diameter transverse pin to transmit the strut load. As the jib was lowered and the load came off, however, the sloping plates attached to the underside the jib engaged with the transverse member on the jib rest and drew the jib forward a few inches, so as to provide a small amount of play and thus allow the jib to rotate marginally in plan as the crane traversed a curve. By the same token, the jib-rest on the match wagon was able to rotate a small amount. Because the consequences of a broken coupling would be so serious – with the likelihood that the unrestrained jib would separate from the crane and probably collide with any line side obstruction or train on an adjacent track – a pair of safety chains was provided between the crane carriage, or relieving bogie, and the match wagon.

One of the two 30-ton Cowans Sheldon examples with an articulated jib, No RS1075/30, at Newton Heath on 16 March 1961 in lined BR black livery with white jib head. *M.S. Welch*

No RS1075/30, from Shirebrook, has recently arrived at Ripple Lane as the Eastern Region's relief crane to stand in for the home team's ex-LMS Rapier 30-ton contemporary crane (see later), which is about to be sent to Doncaster for overhaul. On 30 August 1969, it was in the process of being checked out by the breakdown gang one Saturday morning. Note the inclined, shaped plates on the underside of the jib, which when lowered engages on the crossbar on the match-wagon jib-rest, thereby drawing the jib forward and permitting the necessary movement at the articulated jib foot. *Author*

With the driver in the cab and jib raised, the crane is prepared for duty. Unbeknown to him and the rest of the gang they are about to receive a call to deal with a derailed wagon at Purfleet. *Author*

A close-up of the left-hand side, as W.J. Barker, the shed-master of Ripple Lane, fusses around the recent arrival. *Author*

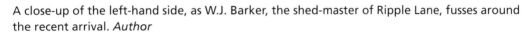

The jib foot of an articulated version of a 30-ton Cowans Sheldon crane. As depicted, the crutch of the jib is drawn forward from the main load-bearing crossmember and the bottom flange rests on a roller. This allows the jib to flex in plan relative to the crane's superstructure as the crane and match wagon traverse a curve. *Author*

The leading corner of a 30-ton Cowans Sheldon crane, showing the buffer mounted on hinges to enable it to be folded back when it is necessary to approach closer to the load or other obstruction. Note also the propping girders tucked in the girder box under the carriage frame. The nearer one draws out on this side and is fitted with a jack to be screwed down on timber packing to spread and support the reaction as the crane lifts the load. The rollers supporting the underside of the articulated jib can also be seen. *Author*

On the match wagon, as the jib is lowered between the inclined side pieces, the tapered piece on the underside engages with the transverse pin and draws the jib forward. The upper half of the jib rest is able to rotate slightly to accommodate the small angular movement of the jib relative to the match wagon when rounding curves. *Author*

Ransomes & Rapier 30-ton Cranes

The order for the construction of five cranes, the other half of the LMS production batch, was placed on 23 May 1941 with Ransomes & Rapier to Order No F3878/81 and a cost of £6,770 each. Although a maximum of a 12½-ton axle load was called for, by efficient design 11 tons 14cwt was achieved, but only a 5-chain curve. The propping base was 15ft 6in. Ransomes & Rapier's patented chimney lowering and raising gear was fitted.

These cranes were originally intended for Birkenhead, Edge Hill, Llandudno Jct, Plaistow and Wakefield, but in fact Wellingborough and Chester received deliveries instead of Llandudno and Birkenhead. The latter crane, however, seems to have wandered between the two until moved to Edge Hill, where it ended its days as a replacement to its sister which had suffered an accident, as discussed later. No RS1067/30 remained at Wellingborough, probably until 1960, when displaced by a new 75-ton steam crane, after which it made its way to Accrington and Spring's Branch. The Eastern Region renumbered RS1068/30 as 136 in February 1956, before moving it to Ripple Lane and adding the prefix of (DE)330 in February 1965. After a short sojourn at Wakefield, No RS1071/30 was transferred to Polmadie, later going to Motherwell.

RANSOMES & RAPIER 30-TON FOR LMS						
Date delivered	Running No		Match wagon No	Allocation	Disposal	
	5/41	BR No			Withdrawn	Scrapped
6/42	RS1067/30		770001	Wellingborough 8/42-4/58, Accrington 10/60, Wellingborough 4/58–29/4/62, Spring's Branch 6/65	7/69	8/69
23/9/42	RS1068/30	(330)136	770002	Plaistow 9/42, to ER 27/2/49, Ripple Lane 12/60	11/76	Sold for scrap to Arnott Young 11/76
10/42	RS1069/30		770003	Edge Hill 10/42, accident 23/10/66	10/66	31/12/67
12/42	RS1070/30		770004	Chester 1/43, Birkenhead 1/44, Chester 1/7/47–5/64, Edge Hill 11/66	7/69	10/69
9/2/43	RS1071/30		770005	Wakefield 2/43, Polmadie 7/43–1/10/60, Motherwell 1962–3/72		15/10/74
Note: Dates shown in *italics* are spot dates upon which the crane is known to have been at the depot concerned.						

LMS 30-ton Ransomes & Rapier crane No RS 1067/30, the first of the batch, soon after delivery when based at Wellingborough. The carriage framework and elements of the superstructure, but not the jib, are lined out. This was omitted before the delivery of other cranes in the order was complete. *BR, LMR, author's collection*

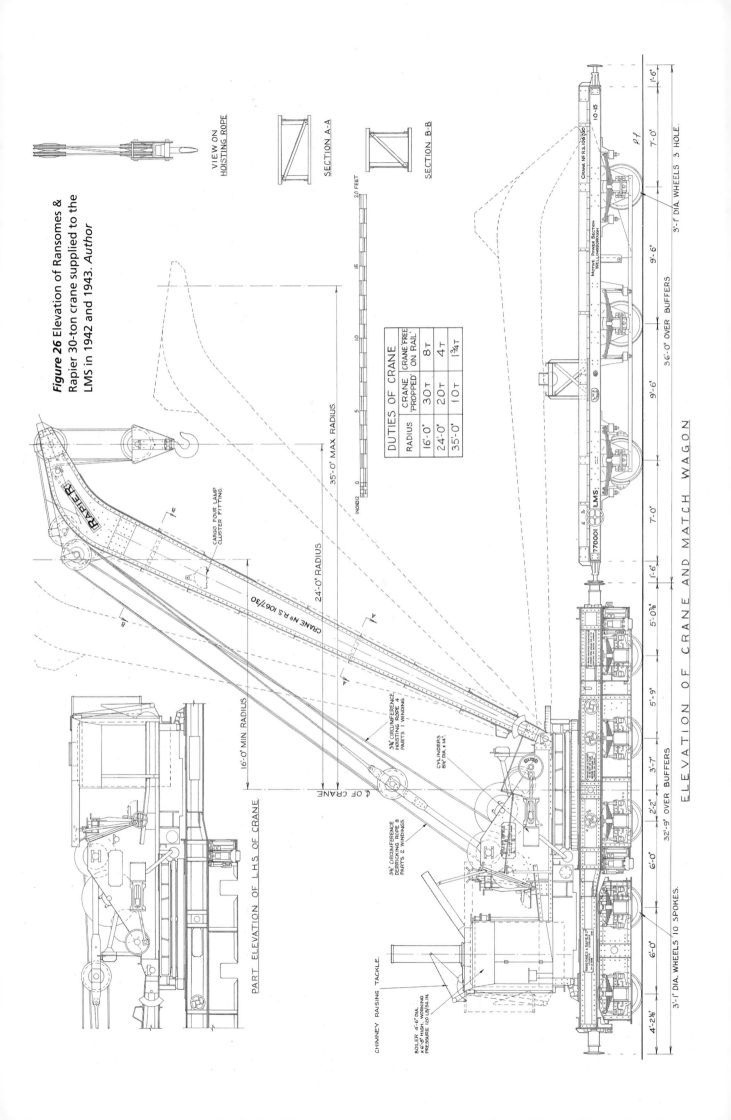

Figure 26 Elevation of Ransomes & Rapier 30-ton crane supplied to the LMS in 1942 and 1943. *Author*

VIEW ON HOISTING ROPE

SECTION A-A

SECTION B-B

PART ELEVATION OF L.H.S. OF CRANE

CHIMNEY RAISING TACKLE.

BOILER 4'-6" DIA.
x 6'-8" HIGH. WORKING
PRESSURE 120 LB/SQ.IN.

3¾" CIRCUMFERENCE
DERRICKING ROPE 8
PARTS 2 WINDINGS.

3¾" CIRCUMFERENCE
HOISTING ROPE 4
PARTS 1 WINDING.

CYLINDERS
8½" DIA. x 14".

CARGO FOUR LAMP
CLUSTER FITTING.

RAPIER

CRANE Nº R.S. 1067/30

35'-0" MAX RADIUS.

24'-0" RADIUS

16'-0" MIN RADIUS

₵ OF CRANE

DUTIES OF CRANE		
RADIUS	CRANE 'PROPPED'	CRANE FREE ON RAIL'
16'-0"	30 T	8 T
24'-0"	20 T	4 T
35'-0"	10 T	1¾ T

CRANE Nº R.S. 1067/30

MOTIVE POWER SECTION
WELLINGBOROUGH

10-15

LMS

770001

RANSOMES & RAPIER LTD
ENGLAND

ELEVATION OF CRANE AND MATCH WAGON

3'-1" DIA. WHEELS 3 HOLE.

3'-1" DIA. WHEELS 10 SPOKES.

1'-6"   7'-0"   1'-6"

9'-6"

36'-0" OVER BUFFERS

9'-6"

7'-0"   1'-6"   5'-0"⅜   5'-9"   3'-7"   2'-2"   6'-0"   6'-0"   4'-2"⅝

32'-9" OVER BUFFERS

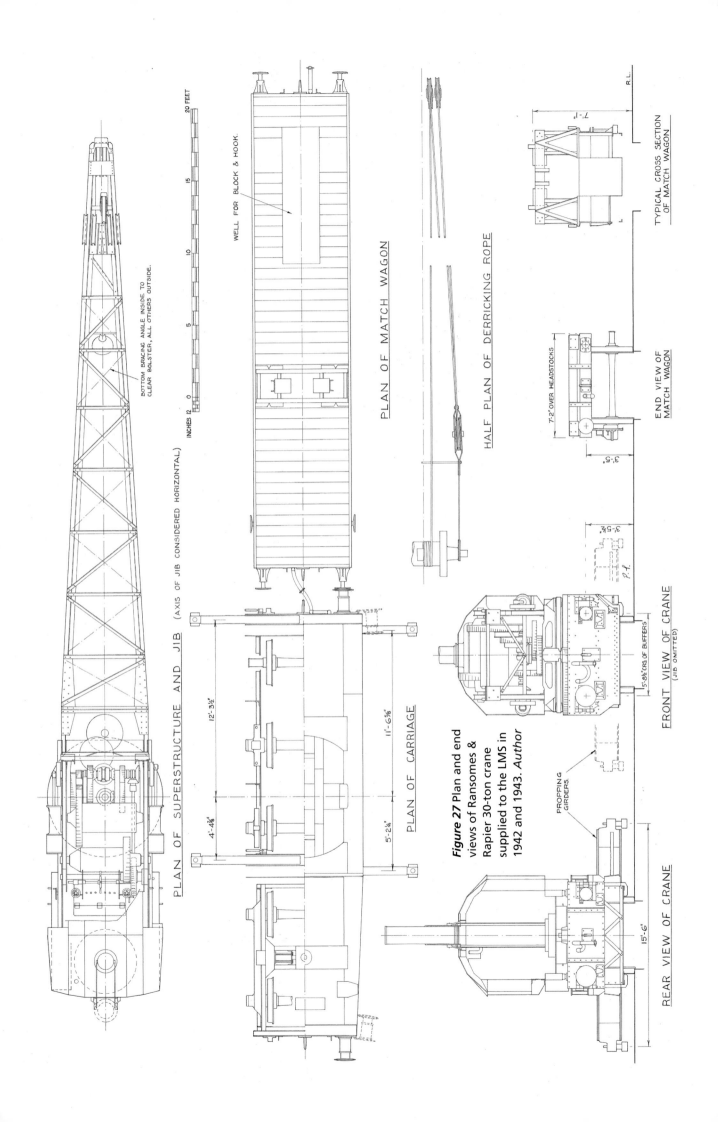

BOTTOM BRACING ANGLE INSIDE TO
CLEAR BOLSTER, ALL OTHERS OUTSIDE.

PLAN OF SUPERSTRUCTURE AND JIB (AXIS OF JIB CONSIDERED HORIZONTAL)

20 FEET

15

10

5

0

12

INCHES

WELL FOR BLOCK & HOOK.

PLAN OF MATCH WAGON

HALF PLAN OF DERRICKING ROPE

TYPICAL CROSS SECTION
OF MATCH WAGON

7'-1"

7'-2" OVER HEADSTOCKS

END VIEW OF
MATCH WAGON

3'-5"

R.L.

12'- 3½"

4'- 4⅛"

11'- 6⅝"

5'- 2¼"

PLAN OF CARRIAGE

3'-5¼"

P.L.

5'-8¼" CRS OF BUFFERS

FRONT VIEW OF CRANE
(JIB OMITTED)

Figure 27 Plan and end
views of Ransomes &
Rapier 30-ton crane
supplied to the LMS in
1942 and 1943. *Author*

PROPPING
GIRDERS

15'-6"

REAR VIEW OF CRANE

An example of the matching 30-ton crane from Ransomes & Rapier, this is No RS1071/30 at Eastfield on 29 May 1966, almost certainly standing in for the regular 45-ton crane, presumably away for an overhaul at the Works. *M. Welch*

No RS1067/30, labelled 'Spring's Branch' later in life, decked out in red with straw and black lining, but still with a black match wagon, No DM770001. *Colour-Rail*

Ripple Lane's regular crane, No DE330136, is seen here on 19 July 1969. It received this number in February 1965, having previously been simply No 136 on being transferred to the Eastern Region sixteen years earlier when it was still at Plaistow (LTSR). Under the auspices of the LMS, it had been No RS1068/30. Its grimy state suggests it is due an overhaul, which shortly it received. *Author*

A close-up view of the crane on the same occasion. Note that the base casting to the superstructure extends under the crab sides and has gussets to project over the rollers of the live ring. *Author*

No DE330136 on 17 April 1970, having returned to Ripple Lane in pristine condition following its visit to Doncaster Works. *Author*

North of the Border, the supervisor in regulation black mackintosh watches as No RS1071/30, based at Polmadie, Glasgow, sets about raising its jib before re-railing ex-LMS 2-6-0 No 42806, which had come to grief at Parkhouse on 19 May 1956. *J. Templeton, author's collection*

The driver looks up as the same crane prepares to assist No RS1058/45 in the dismantling of the redundant flyover at Stevenson in 1949. The machinery and gearing should be compared with the drawing on p.88 (Figure 23) [R&R 45T gearing]. *J. Templeton, author's collection*

During June 1960, No RS1069/30 from Edge Hill stood in for the resident 50-ton crane at Willesden while it was away at works for an overhaul. *M.S. Welch*

7
Nationalisation

The Need for Improvement

When the nationalised British Railways commenced operations on 1 January 1948, there can be little doubt that it inherited a very disparate and potentially run-down collection of assets. Yet the one unifying factor in all the railways absorbed into BR, was that they were all in urgent need of restoration to pre-war standards of maintenance and operation, followed by modernisation, or at best substantial improvement. Though two years had elapsed since the end of the Second World War, the railways as a whole were still suffering desperately from the six years of over-use and lack of priority routine maintenance due to alternative pressing priorities during the hostilities. Locomotives and rolling stock were far from being in the best order, and many of the examples still in service had been earmarked for disposal a full decade earlier, only gaining a reprieve because of the wartime stock shortages. Worse still, in many places the permanent way was in an appalling condition and in the post-war years this situation became more than abundantly evident.

Even before the war, typical of the more mundane incidents to which the breakdown train would be called was a freight-train derailment on an unidentified length of quadruple track on Midland territory. Some wagons appear to have become derailed on a trailing turnout and as a result were fouling both adjacent tracks and in effect blocking the whole line. Soon after delivery, the Ransomes & Rapier 36-ton steam breakdown crane No MP3, then stationed at Kentish Town, has arrived at the site and is getting ready, while a 15-ton Cowans Sheldon in the background is already at work. Note the wagons placed on the ballast beyond the larger crane and another down the bank behind the signal post on the right-hand side. *Author's collection*

On 17 June 1932, the driver of the 7.23pm Up express passenger train from Crewe to Birmingham failed to reduce speed while crossing from the Up Slow to the Up Fast line at the south end of Great Bridgeford Station. As a result, the train was completely derailed immediately after passing through the crossover. The ex-LNWR 4-4-0 engine and tender overturned, the first coach was wrecked and came to rest at right-angles across all four running lines. The remaining three coaches were derailed and partly overturned, while the carriage truck at the rear of the train was also derailed. As a result, four passengers in the train lost their lives and nine passengers, together with the footplate crew, were detained in hospital. Examples of both the recently-acquired Craven and Rapier 36-ton cranes are seen in action, while men stand around and officers of the company examine the engine. *Author's collection*

On 5 January 1946, a collision occurred
at Browney Signal Box on the LNER,
when the 11.15pm Down express
passenger train from King's Cross to
Newcastle, running under clear signals
at about 50mph, collided with the
wreckage of an Up goods train. This
had become divided, and on a falling
gradient, the following portion had
overtaken and run violently into the
leading portion. This resulted in some
of the debris fouling the Down track
into which the express then ploughed.
As a consequence, ten passengers
were killed and eighteen had to be
taken to hospital. In addition, seven
others and four railway employees
suffered from minor injuries or shock.
Soldiers gather round as two 45-ton
Cowans Sheldon cranes hoist an LNER
coach above the debris.
Author's collection

A spate of serious accidents had occurred during the latter years of the 'Big Four', with several notable incidents. The first of these was at Bourne End (LMS) on 30 September 1945, culminating in a bleak week at the turn of the New Year of 1945/6, with Northwood (LNER) 31 December, Lichfield (LMS) on 1 January and Browney (LNER) on 5 January, soon to be followed by Potters Bar (LNER) on 11 February. These highlighted the serious situation that was to face the newly nationalised railways.

A very serious accident occurred on 30 September 1945 at Bourne End on the LMS, when the overnight fifteen-coach express passenger train from Perth to London, running under clear signals, traversed the crossover from the Up Fast to the Up Slow at excessive speed. The engine became derailed and overturned into an adjacent field a little below the line, leading to six of the leading seven coaches piling up behind and being destroyed. Forty-three people lost their lives, while sixty-four suffered serious injuries. An American serviceman looks on in horror at the ensuing carnage, with the smokebox of the un-rebuilt Royal Scot Class No 6157 *The Royal Artilleryman* poking out of the wreckage. *H.C. Casserley*

The Southern Railway was not past giving their passengers a fright, as was demonstrated on 27 December 1946 when the 2.20pm twelve-coach train from Bournemouth to Waterloo was completely derailed at Byfleet (now West Byfleet). The buckeye couplings adopted by the SR, however, maintained all the coaches more or less upright and in line, although the adjacent Up Local and Down Through tracks were both obstructed. Mercifully, only three passengers received injuries and two were taken to hospital. Three or four Ransomes & Rapier 36- and 45-ton cranes were involved in clearing up. *S.C. Townroe*

In the first eighteen months of BR, derailments at New Southgate and Blea Moor continued to demonstrate the problems of bad maintenance as a legacy the strains of the war, but these were not isolated incidents, as a spate of other accidents occurred throughout the length and breadth of the land. In May 1951 the Railway Executive identified a specific problem with recovery operations, as delays in clearing the line were noted in many of these incidents.

A little over a year later, British Railways was to receive its greatest-ever test of rescue and recovery work with the multiple collision at Harrow and Wealdstone on 8 October 1952. More than any other accident, this disaster, which claimed 112 lives that foggy autumn morning and which took four and half days to clear up, set into progress a chain of events which would entirely re-shape BR's breakdown-train policy. On 26 June 1953, within ten months of the accident, the Motive Power Committee resolved to form an Ad-Hoc Committee to look into breakdown-train and crane arrangements.

One may well ask why it took so long to reach such an urgent decision, but it took such a major event to stir the railway's senior management and in turn by implication their political masters, for by this stage, a perilous mental attitude had developed within BR

management. It is clear from the opinions expressed by many railway men that they all came to one conclusion; that there was a lack of confidence to make a decision for fear of being criticised. Such a cause for concern was usually on the grounds of cost or failure if things went wrong and it was therefore 'easier to take no action at all'. With this attitude becoming increasingly prevalent in the early 1950s, it was less trouble to keep on doing exactly what had been done before.

Another big problem for the nationalised railways was the lack of competent staff, not helped by the loss of young men during the period of conflict between 1939 and 1945. Manpower was at a premium in post-war Britain, and anyone with the least motivation could secure themselves a well-paid job in industries with far better working conditions than on the railways. This is not intended to disparage the dedication or intelligence of those who worked on the railways, far from it, but it can be seen that within the industry the more menial jobs became harder and harder to fill. Such competition frequently led to the loss of trained and experienced manpower seeking to broaden their careers moving from the railways to outside industry and not being replaced.

One notable area that was discovered to have significant staffing problems was the breakdown gangs.

The disastrous double collision which occurred during the morning rush hour at Harrow and Wealdstone station on 8 October 1952 shocked the country. The two trains concerned in the primary rear-end collision were the 7.31am Up Local passenger train from Tring to Euston, comprising nine non-corridor bogie coaches hauled by a 2-6-4 tank engine, and again the 8.15pm Up overnight-express passenger train from Perth to Euston, which consisted of eleven bogie vehicles hauled by a Stanier Pacific. By great misfortune a third train ran into the wreckage of the first collision. This was the 8.00am Down express from Euston to Liverpool and Manchester, consisting of fifteen bogie vehicles double-headed, with a 4-6-0 Jubilee class piloting the recently-rebuilt former Turbo locomotive. By early afternoon, the 30-ton Cowans Sheldon crane from Rugby reaches over the mountain of debris as rescuers continue to search for bodies and hopefully a last remaining survivor. Locomotives Nos 45637 and 46202 of the Liverpool train lie on their sides in the foreground. *Metropolitan Police Museum*

Normally, a breakdown gang would be drawn from various grades of artisan staff at a motive power depot, who would be called out in the same way as retained firefighters or lifeboat crewmen, when an emergency took place. Nonetheless, regular training sessions were also organised. For this task the men got an additional allowance, for which they became eligible when the breakdown train passed a recognised marker, normally the starting signal of the train's home yard or depot.

Prior to the Second World War, the financial situation of many railway workers meant that there was always a queue or waiting list to join the breakdown gang, whether the train included a crane or not. The extra allowance was a welcome addition to the weekly pay packet, even if the working conditions the men endured, and occasionally the carnage the men encountered, were often quite atrocious.

During the late 1940s and early 1950s, it was becoming increasingly difficult to recruit men for artisan grades generally, and for breakdown work in particular. Turnout pay was nowhere near as good (or as desperately needed) as it had been prior to the war, even though the pay had increased in real terms. In due course, men became more selective about what overtime they wanted to work, particularly as the average weekly wage had significantly increased as living standards rose. Therefore, even prior to Harrow, the personnel welfare department had considered that working conditions and safety standards would have to be improved to recruit the right quality of men. One obvious inducement would of course be an increase in the rate of remuneration. However, the psychological element was a major point of consideration that was later put forward by a panel of railway doctors.

Actually, the problem of low morale was more acute in some areas than others, indeed at several depots the team spirit was very high, yet on a national basis there no longer seemed to be the pride once associated with being a member of the breakdown gang. One obvious way to improve the situation was the introduction of better conditions, and this could only be achieved by the provision of new service vehicles and cranes. Good kitchen and mess facilities, provision for an hour or two's 'kip' and better tools were all essential elements in the transformation that was to follow.

After Harrow and Wealdstone, the railway's textile research department was asked to design new protective clothing, and this ranged from waterproof leggings, sou'westers and waders of the type supplied to lifeboat crews, to protective gloves of a superior quality that had first been issued to the National Fire Service. It was also decided that the railways needed to provide riding vans that had heating, private lockers (which actually locked) and stores of tinned food in the kitchens. Meanwhile, with regard to safety, improved jacking and lifting equipment, better site illumination, and more thoughtful stowage of heavy equipment and packing all helped to minimise injury.

Finally, the psychological element was another reason why the new, distinctive livery was to be applied to breakdown trains after the report into the Harrow and Wealdstone clear-up operation. To detail all the improvements that were noted in the months that followed would be extremely difficult, but suffice it to say that the formation of the Ad-Hoc Committee on Breakdown Trains was eventually to lead to the major improvements that will be detailed in the following paragraphs.

With the nationalisation of the railways, the British Transport Commission's Railway Executive took over 107 steam breakdown cranes from the grouping companies. The numbers of each capacity contributed by each of the companies were as given in the table below:

STEAM BREAKDOWN CRANES INHERITED BY BRITISH RAILWAYS ON 1 JANUARY 1948					
Max Capacity (tons)	LMS	LNER	GW	SR	Totals
50	5	0	0	0	5
45	0	8	4	3	15
40	2	0	0	0	2
35/36	4	9	5	6	24
30	13	0	0	0	13
25	0	3	1	0	4
20	3	4	4	2	13
15	14	11	3	3	31
Totals	41	35	17	14	107

This represents about 85% of all the steam breakdown cranes ever supplied to British mainline railway companies, because only a handful of old small cranes had been withdrawn and scrapped prior to nationalisation, while four or five had failed to return following requisition by the War Department during one or other of the two world wars. Most cranes of 30 tons capacity and above were of relatively modern design, with a long jib, and represented the pre-nationalisation companies' frontline equipment for dealing with accidents and derailments, and for carrying out bridge works. The lower-capacity cranes were likely to be much older, with short jibs, dating from the turn of the century or before. These tended to be allocated to districts responsible for less-important routes, but were nonetheless still useful for re-railing errant wagons and, only if necessary, would a larger crane be summoned from an adjacent district.

In conclusion, it can be seen that the general trend of the grouping era was towards high-capacity cranes with relieving bogies capable of lifting 36 tons at 24ft radius. The possibility that greater loads at reduced radii would be lifted under emergency conditions was acknowledged by the LMS in their strengthening of this type to 50 tons, and subsequently by the introduction of 45-ton cranes by the other three companies. The LMS also recognised the need for a handy, modern intermediate-capacity crane with a long jib, whereas the other companies merely cascaded their older, lower-capacity cranes, to less-important districts. Older cranes were usually limited to a speed of 25mph in train formation, which clearly restricted their ability to reach the site of any derailment or accident promptly, but perhaps this did not matter when there was always a crane based not too far away. More-modern cranes of the era were usually allowed to run at up to 40 or 45mph.

Ad Hoc Committee on Breakdown Trains and Cranes

The first meeting of the Railway Executive's Motive Power Ad Hoc Committee was on 8 October 1953, the actual first anniversary of the accident at Harrow. This was chaired by Geoffrey HK Lund, Assistant District Motive Power Superintendent, Edinburgh, Scottish Region and the author of a paper entitled *Railway Breakdown and Re-railing Equipment* presented to the Institution of Locomotive Engineers and reproduced in the May/June 1950 issue of their Journal. He was assisted by a committee composed of G Shears (ADMPS Stewart's Lane), Roscoe W Taylor (ADMPS Darlington), WG Thornley (ADMPS Camden), WD Dixon (DMPS Lincoln), GW Robson (DMPS Bristol), AR Stubley (Asst. Outdoor C&W Engineer E & NE Regions), with David Weir of Glasgow as Secretary.

Perhaps because it was a Motive Power committee, it did not include a representative from the Civil Engineer's Department. This was regrettable for several reasons. Firstly, breakdown work naturally impinges on the Civil Engineer's infrastructure and secondly, because the most important item of breakdown equipment, the crane, is constrained by civil engineering factors, such as axle load, loading gauge and bridge loading, both when working and in train formation. Had the Civil Engineer's Department been represented, it would have been more involved in the deliberations and hence committed to a successful outcome. It might also have prevented the Committee from making recommendations which were unacceptable from a civil engineering point of view. Finally, as we have already seen in Volume 1, the Civil Engineering Department was a heavy user of breakdown cranes for bridge works.

The next obstacle was dealing with the fiercely independent Western Region, one member of the LM region involved with the programme commented: 'I fervently believed that Brunel was still alive and only in partial retirement at Torquay!' Those problems aside, the report of the Ad Hoc Committee was to be of immense interest, and, though its recommendations were not fully implemented, they did form the basis for all subsequent breakdown and recovery work. More importantly, they were instrumental in establishing the criteria for ordering the BTC breakdown cranes of 1959.

The Committee's remit was broadly to determine a standard pattern for breakdown trains, and to examine the various proposals from the different regions as to their 'conception of standard requirements'. They were to consider the types of equipment currently carried on the trains, and then submit a recommendation for a uniform list of items needed for each type of vehicle. In respect of the various breakdown vehicles, they were to suggest the types needed to form the various patterns of train and show their internal layout and the storage of equipment. Finally, their remit included the consideration of all the current types of breakdown crane in use, and then to make a recommendation for a general standard crane(s) for procurement in the future.

The whole idea was to provide a uniform arrangement, so that in the event of a major incident like Harrow and Wealdstone in the future, crews from one depot could work another gang's crane without any major difficulties or delays being encountered. Though such incidents were likely to be rare, the additional advantages would be clearly demonstrated if a depot had to borrow a breakdown train from elsewhere if theirs was unavailable. In theory it was a sensible proposal, but as with all innovative ideas, its progenitors were to have their fair share of difficulties in its conception. The main obstacles that would be encountered were the strongly entrenched 'regional' (in reality pre-nationalisation) viewpoints that were still held by some of the Committee's members.

As will be appreciated, the needs of all the various depots and regions differed greatly with respect to breakdown and recovery trains. Some, mostly sub-depots and small sheds, needed only the simplest items of equipment. Their work was largely concerned with minor blockages on running lines or in goods yards, and the only urgency laid upon them was to restore running in the quickest possible time. Other work, such as in times of a major accident or emergency, would be passed on to one of the larger depots. Therefore, the Motive Power Committee decided to classify each depot's needs within one of the following four standard patterns:

1. With a steam crane of 20 tons or over, packing wagon/van, tool van, and riding van.
2. With steam or hand crane under 20 tons, packing wagon/van and a combined tool/riding van
3. Without crane, for larger sub-depots, with tool van and riding van
4. Without crane, for smaller sub-depots, with a combined tool/riding van

This then was the general position, which should have evolved during the first years of BR's existence, however regional variations created so many anomalies that it is difficult to give a concise account of what formed a standard breakdown train. It was that problem which the Ad Hoc Committee was established to investigate and, where necessary, to make recommendations for improvement. Following the Committee's first meeting, members visited eighteen motive power depots, some on each region, together with London Transport at Neasden, to inspect the breakdown equipment and discuss with experienced staff the nature of their work.

Visits were also made to, and consultation meetings took place with, the crane manufacturers Cowans Sheldon at Carlisle and Ransomes & Rapier at Ipswich, meeting with their management and technical staff to explore feasible improvements and developments in crane design. Craven Bros, by then part of Herbert Morris Cranes, had ceased to produce breakdown cranes and hence was not approached. As events were to turn out, it is perhaps a pity they did not also meet with Coles Cranes, but this company was at that time more usually associated with smaller rail and road-mobile cranes. In addition to the leading crane makers, contact was made with a wide range of suppliers of equipment used in breakdown work, such as: British Oxygen, Consolidated Pneumatic Tools, Tangye, Westinghouse and Wild Colliery Equipment.

The BR Research Department's Information Division made enquiries, by means of a questionnaire, of a large number of overseas railway administrations regarding their breakdown arrangements. In view of the very isolationist stance of many British railway enthusiasts, it might seem to be unpalatable to discuss the possibility that those peculiar foreign railways (especially where locomotives have 'outside plumbing') could have had anything to contribute towards our railway development. Be that as it may, many foreign railways did have a much better breakdown system, particularly those countries where the railways had needed to be virtually rebuilt after the war. This was noticeably so in Denmark, Germany and Japan, where BR learned valuable lessons, but also in the 'under-developed' lands such as Africa.

Whilst in many of these cases it is true that it was British engineering companies that had been supplying both the expertise and the equipment, it was more the way in which these foreign railways appraised their requirements and thus prompted their suppliers to produce exactly what was required which most impressed the researchers. This was particularly so in the case of the Danske Statsbaner report on *Railway Re-organisation of Breakdown Equipment*, and its far-sighted recommendations for specialist recovery vehicles.

In its report of 1955, the Committee addressed the general matters of breakdown work. Of particular interest to railway modellers is the recommendation that a move away from black, as the colour for breakdown equipment, should be made to a more distinctive colour, which led to the cranes and vehicles being repainted bright red from July 1959. Electric lighting in tool and riding vans was preferred to propane gas, as a more convenient, cleaner and safer means of illumination. Separate packing vans were considered unnecessary, as it was concluded that

A demonstration of re-railing an ex-LNER B17 locomotive at Stratford MPD with a 120/60-ton power jack under the buffer beam and a heavy re-railing bridge on 24 July 1953. Note the motor pump supplying pressurised fluid to the jack. *BR, ER, author's collection*

Whereas experience of incidents in the past had usually been with steam locomotives, which were sufficiently robust in construction to permit them being lifted at the closest most convenient point, this is not always so on vehicles propelled by diesel and electric motive power, which are usually of stressed-skin construction, especially those of the multiple-unit type. Special consideration was therefore given to the means of re-railing these, and the requirement for special lifting tackle to be able to attach to the appropriate points on the vehicles' structure. Of significance to the outreach requirement for cranes was that these lifting points almost inevitably were some way back from the buffer beam, usually at the centreline of the bogies. This was not a problem in the Works when maintenance was carried out, but was a different matter for the breakdown crew.

Jacks and timber packing, and re-railing ramps have long been the tools of the breakdown trade and these were reviewed. The merits of screw and hydraulic jacks were debated and a standard range proposed. The Western Region representative, one might say almost predictably, could not agree with this, submitting his own minority report proposing the inclusion of a 40-ton hydraulic jack weighing 292lb (132kg) and requiring four men to handle it!

Also used for re-railing vehicles which remained upright and close to the rails was a range of ramps to be placed over the rail head. These were of a variety of shapes and sizes to suit a variety of different situations. The errant vehicle could then be hauled by locomotive along the track on to the ramps and, with luck, it would end up on the rails without too much damage to the permanent way. A 12ft re-railing bridge capable of carrying 60 tons was recommended. These could be used with one or two jacks to traverse a locomotive or other type of heavy vehicle back onto the track without resorting to a crane.

Three types of van on four-wheeled bogies were proposed:

a) Combined tool/packing van
b) Riding van
c) Composite tool, packing and riding van.

The last was for small depots and the first two could be included in breakdown trains with and without cranes. The majority of the Committee deplored the sending of the crane for a simple lifting job without any vans, apparently practised on one or two regions; the reason being that whilst away, the breakdown train might be sent on directly to another incident requiring the equipment in the vans. It was recommended that the vehicles should be capable of being used as brake vans, with the provision of windows in both ends, vacuum brake valves and screw handbrake. The riding van should have a well-heated mess room; toilet, arrangements for cooking, lockers, drying facilities and a separate compartment for the supervisor. Sleeping facilities were not considered necessary, except in the remoter areas of Scotland. Tool vans carrying a wide range of tools, lifting tackle, re-railing equipment and hardwood timber packing were proposed. Four sliding doors on the tool vans, two per side, with lifting davits were called for. The composite

there was sufficient room in the bogie tool vans recommended. Well-type tool vans, to ease the task of handling heavy equipment on and off, were considered, but rejected as too costly, although well-type crane match wagons, similar to those used on the NER/LNER, were strongly advocated. With vacuum braking being almost universal by that time on the railways, the lack of a supply of compressed air from the train braking system, to power various tools and items of equipment on site, was particularly regretted by the Chairman who had been trained on the NER and hence brought up with the Westinghouse air-braking system. Based on London Transport's experience, the provision of specially-equipped road vehicles to attend breakdowns accessible by road was advocated as a speedy means of reaching the site of incidents in certain large conurbations, such as London, Glasgow and Manchester. Turnout times for these vehicles were less than four minutes, compared with perhaps half an hour for a railway breakdown train.

Two men inserting the pin between the block of the haulage tackle and the heavy-duty cable – the ends of which were clamped to the two rail heads – of the Kelbus gear. *Unattributed*

vehicle for use at smaller depots was an amalgam of these facilities, but scaled down in quantity and size to fit into a single vehicle.

As an alternative to the use of cranes for some kinds of breakdown work, power-operated re-railing apparatus had been developed in France and Germany and was assessed by the Committee. This equipment consisted of a power-driven hydraulic pump, which pressurised fluid to operate jacks and traversers in conjunction with re-railing bridges and small bogies. Such equipment had been obtained by the Eastern Region from Maschinenfabrik Deutschland (MFD) for trial at Stratford and Gorton. Its use was particularly recommended by the Committee for allocation to the then few areas electrified on the overhead system.

Sometimes, derailed vehicles end up too far from the track to be reached by cranes and, as an alternative to laying in a temporary length of track, or even in addition, rope hauling gear may be used. The Kelbus equipment advocated could be clamped to the rail head and block-and-tackle strung out to the load to be drawn back. A locomotive could then be attached to the rope of the tackle and used to haul the errant vehicle back close enough to the track to enable it to be dealt with by conventional means, such as jacking and packing, or lifting by crane.

Consideration was given to the means of illuminating the general area of work during the hours of darkness. Paraffin lamps were advocated for general work, supplemented by small hand-held paraffin or miners' battery lamps for supervisors, and paraffin or bottled acetylene for flood lighting.

Other matters considered included fire-fighting and first-aid equipment, protective clothing and stores.

The Committee sought information from overseas railway administrations on the breakdown cranes they used, and included amongst the information received

Slightly the worse for wear and marred by chalk stains, 4-6-0-type Lord Nelson Class locomotive, No 30854 *Howard of Effingham*, having previously been righted, now awaits being hauled up the incline prepared for it, after which it will be towed away to Eastleigh Works for repair, following an accident on 20 July 1952. *S.C. Townroe, courtesy Colour-Rail*

RECOMMENDED TYPES OF CRANE					
Ref	Max Capacity (tons)	To Radius When propped (ft)	Loading Gauge	Max Axle Load (tons)	Max Radius (ft)
1	65	25	L1	20	max achievable
2	35	18	L2	14	36
3	Specifically designed to operate under overhead electrical equipment				

were details of specially designed cranes to work under overhead electric traction equipment. In considering the future requirements for cranes, the Committee had to take into account that there were still a million small, four-wheeled wagons and hundreds of marshalling yards scattered all over the country and most derailments occurred in yards to just such wagons. It was recognised at the time that, whereas there was a need for some cranes to be able to handle the heaviest likely loads, equally the vast majority of incidents were minor events for which a crane that could be set up quickly would be advantageous. Great emphasis was placed on reliability and stability in both the forward and backward directions while slewing when 'free on rail'. In conclusion, therefore, they recommended three types of crane, tabulated above.

The first two types were to have the king post positioned centrally on the carriage to permit equal portée at each end. They were also to be capable of use for bridging operations. The adoption of relieving bogies was assumed to be necessary, to reduce the overall length of the crane in working condition, and a preference was expressed for the system employed by Cravens.

At the time, the concept of the last-proposed type to work under overhead wires was probably ahead of the industry's technical ability to provide such a crane, at least of sufficient capacity for breakdown duties. An attempt at a 6½-ton diesel-electric crane of this form, for permanent way work was, however, fulfilled by Taylor Hubbard in March 1960 at a cost of £18,450. It was described as having a horizontal racking jib capable of extending to a radius of 40ft, at which it could lift 1 ton. When propped it could lift its maximum load to a radius of 18ft. Without the hydraulic rams that were to become commonplace within a decade or so, however, the mechanism appears to have relied on rack-and-pinion gearing and no further examples were ordered.

It is interesting to note that the moment – the load to be lifted multiplied by the lever arm (the distance from the front support to the load) – applied to the largest crane was nearly twice that of any previous crane. In its discussions with crane manufacturers, the Committee had been told that it was doubtful if such high-capacity cranes could be built within the British loading-gauge and axle-load limitations.

Steam propulsion with two cylinders was recommended. Diesel, petrol and electricity were all considered, but rejected on the grounds that steam was simpler, more reliable and flexible in operation, quieter, capable of acting as a brake and, of course, cheaper. Transmission systems seem to have been the stumbling block with other forms of power, together with the high torque at low speed directly available from steam reciprocating engines. It is not

clear whether hydraulic torque converters were included at that time in the assessment of the possibilities.

A saturated-steam, coal-fired boiler was suggested with particular attention to be paid to the position of the washout plugs and inspection doors to facilitate maintenance. Oil firing and superheating were considered but rejected, although the option to convert to oil firing was put forward. Water feed was to be by a combination of a small feed pump and non-lift-type injector. A simple hinged extension to the chimney and steam blower were recommended to provide draught to the fire. The

The only attempt in Britain at a crane designed for use under overhead lines, in advance of the introduction of hydraulic rams, was a diesel-electric 6½-ton tail-less crane with an extendable jib for permanent-way work, manufactured by Taylor Hubbard of Leicester in March 1960. A close-up of the front of No RDE 1764/6½ is seen at Hyndland on 4 September 1960. *Author*

quantities of coal and water on the superstructure were to be kept to a minimum, so as to maximise the potential counterbalance. Extra supplies of water to be carried elsewhere, such as on the match wagon, were advocated, while in those days, additional coal was deemed to be readily obtainable from attendant locomotives.

The controls were to be positioned high up, with a platform from where the driver could obtain a good view of his work. Amply-sized slewing clutches were called for to enable the slewing motion of the crane to be used to separate telescoped coaches. All-important hand and steam brakes were required, with the latter operating on all wheels of the crane with the steam cylinder on the superstructure, rather than routing a flexible hose to a cylinder on the carriage. It was assumed there would be insufficient room for vacuum brake cylinders on the crane carriage itself. The relieving bogies and match wagon, but not necessarily the crane, were to have automatic vacuum and handbrake with hand levers on both sides. Four vacuum brake-release valves on the crane carriage were called for, to enable the crane to be stopped precisely at the required position for work by an operative standing at track level beside the crane.

The advantage of vertically-pivoted outriggers, usual in mainland Europe and which might double as the connecting beams to the relieving bogies, was recognised, but considered unsuitable for use in United Kingdom due to loading-gauge restrictions and, if these were not square with the carriage, the loss of the crane's stability. In view of the high loads to be lifted over the side of the crane and to allow for the eventuality that not all girders could be extended, due to the possible presence of obstructions, four pairs of propping girders were advocated for the larger crane. Whilst three pairs might have been adequate, there were technical complications in fitting the middle pair in with the central king pin envisaged. Ratchet-operated screw jacks were to be provided at the girder ends to transmit the propping forces into the timber packing to be laid out on the ground. The extension and retraction of each propping girder was to be achieved by means of a ratchet-operated rack-and-pinion between the girder and its housing. When in the housings, the girders were to be positively locked in position to prevent them creeping while the crane was being hauled in train formation.

Super-elevation of the track on curves adversely affects the stability of a crane, and cant indicators were therefore called for.

In certain parts of the country, to increase the crane's stability for particularly heavy lifts, it was the practice to secure the crane to the adjacent track, upon which a locomotive would be stood, by means of warwicks. For this purpose, four evenly-spaced 'D'-shaped shackles along the side of the carriage were specified to which the warwicks could be attached.

As well as having the capacity to lift vertically, it is often useful to drag a load horizontally some distance, both to separate it from the wreckage and secondly to bring it within reach of the hook, thereby saving time in manoeuvring and re-setting-up the crane. For this purpose, it was proposed that a 300ft, 6-ton haulage rope was fitted to the new cranes, together with anchor points on each end of the crane to which sheaves could be attached to provide the facility to haul off-line from the superstructure of the crane.

The means of providing lighting on the crane was reviewed and an upward-facing jib-head light to detect overhead obstructions, as well as general downward lighting was recommended. The disadvantages of a steam turbo-generator were felt to be the quantity of water consumed and the high-pitched whining noise created. Petrol-driven generators, as used overseas, were discounted as too large to fit the British loading gauge. The preferred means of providing power for lighting was a small steam reciprocating engine driving a DC generator.

Buffers, if fitted to the crane carriage, should be mounted on hinges, so that they could be folded back at the site of operations and thereby increase the portée. It was recognised that the maximum speed at which the crane could be run in train formation was crucial and a maximum of 60mph was advocated. The benefit of roller bearings, as often used overseas, was noted, but it was stated that there was little to choose between plain and roller bearings in terms of reliability and, in the event of a failure, plain bearings were easier to repair. Articulated jibs were recommended, whereby the crane's superstructure was locked in line with the carriage for running in train formation and the jib, when resting on the match truck, was allowed to pivot laterally at the front of the superstructure – see drawing (Figure 12) on p.36 (LMS Craven 36T). The alternative of running the crane with the jib carried on the derricking ropes was discounted as impractical for the long-jib cranes envisaged.

The reserve stability available beyond the indicated safe load, used for design and to be given in the safe-load tables, was to continue to be the usual 25–30% and was to include being stable backwards under no load with the hook on the ground. The tail radius was to be limited to a maximum of 16ft 3in, 1ft more than then-current practice. Rail clips were also called for to hold the crane to the track.

On the smaller crane, two speeds to the main hoist were agreed by the Committee and a majority was in favour of an auxiliary hoist of 10-ton capacity on the larger crane, to afford a speedy means of handling smaller loads. This would obviate the need to use the large ram's-horn hook for small lifts and would gain a useful extra few feet in reach. In the event of there being insufficient room for an auxiliary hoist and a hauling rope, the latter was to be preferred.

The attainable speeds of the various motions were considered and the following agreed:

Motion	Speed
Slewing	One complete revolution per 1½ minutes
Derricking	From travelling position to minimum radius in 2 minutes
Lifting – main hoist with and without an auxiliary hoist:	
with full load	10/15ft/min
with light load	40/60ft/min
Lifting – Auxiliary hoist	60ft/min
Travelling:	
unloaded	4mph
with max 'free on rail' load	2mph

Emphasis was placed on the torque available when slewing rather than absolute speed of rotation. Due to the small purchase available when the jib was lowered and the large length of rope to be wound in, raising the jib from rest on the match wagon to its working position was one of the most onerous tasks required of the boiler's capacity. Higher lifting speeds were expected of the main hoist, if an auxiliary hoist was not provided. It was anticipated that at least two axles of the crane would be driven and that the clutch wheels to engage the gear should be positioned so that they could be operated from the track side.

In addition to the individual performance expected of each motion, the simultaneous movements of slewing the superstructure, or derricking the jib, while operating either the main or auxiliary hoist; derricking and slewing; and slewing, or derricking, while travelling, were called for, provided the last two were without detriment to other movements.

Although over the years it had become the practice to provide cover to the driver, protection was now sought for the machinery of the crane as well, by means of a long canopy attached to the derricking bridle. A ram's horn, having a single hole through the root for attaching

The Ad Hoc Committee may have reported, but its recommendations had yet to be implemented when the third-most-serious accident to occur on a British railway happened in dense fog on 4 December 1957. The late-running 4.56pm express passenger train from Cannon Street to Ramsgate, formed of eleven bogie coaches hauled by a Bulleid light Pacific, passed the Down Through colour-light inner home signal of St John's Signal Box at danger in foggy conditions. This led to it colliding with the rear of the 5.18pm ten-coach electric multiple unit train from Charing Cross to Hayes which was standing at the Park's Bridge Junction colour-light home signal. With the brakes of the electric train applied to hold it stationary on the rising gradient, the shock of the collision was severe, leading to the telescoping of the eighth coach into the ninth coach.

The momentum of the Ramsgate train forced the leading coach into the rear of the engine's tender, resulting in the displacement of the latter against a steel column supporting the heavy girders of a two-span bridge which carried the Nunhead to Lewisham line over the four main tracks. With their support removed, the two girders promptly subsided on to the train below, completing the destruction of the leading coach and crushing the second coach and the leading half of the third. About two minutes later, the 5.22pm eight-coach electric train from Holborn Viaduct to Dartford, which was moving slowly on to the bridge towards a signal at red, was fortunately stopped very promptly by the motorman when he saw the girders at an angle; this train was neither derailed nor damaged, but the leading coach was tilted. Ninety people lost their lives. *FJJ Prior collection*

Prior to the delivery of the new cranes, an ex-LMS Cowans Sheldon 50-ton from Crewe and Craven 50-ton crane from Rugby set about recovering Stanier 2-8-0 No 48616 on 21 July 1960 at Turvey, on the line from Bedford to Northampton. *K.C.H. Fairey, Colour-Rail*

a heavy-duty shackle, was specified to the main lifting block, which should be of the minimum depth practical to afford the maximum headroom clearance over the loads to be lifted.

To support the jib while in train formation, a match wagon was required. The Committee strongly recommended the well type to ease the task of accessing and stowing the heavy items of lifting tackle required in connection with the working of a crane. Trays containing sufficient packing for normal work were also advocated. Much consideration was given to lifting tackle. It was concluded that standard lifting tackle was not possible, because of the large variety of designs of locomotive in use on the regions. The need to attempt to standardise the lifting points on diesel and electric locomotives in future was recognised. A sandwich type of lifting beam was suggested, of capacity to match the maximum of the crane and with sufficient spread to reach outside the width of diesel and electric locomotives, and additional holes at closer centres suitable for use with steam engines. Lighter-duty lifting beams for coaches and wagons, together with a variety of wire-rope slings of 5-ton, 35ft long to 40-ton, 8ft 6in long; 6-ton to 36-ton or 65-ton bow shackles; engine lifters; cable protectors, etc. were also considered necessary.

The following chapter looks at how the Committee's findings were translated into the BTC crane orders placed with Cowans Sheldon but, like the issue of train control or train protection, the reaction was very much a case of shutting the stable door after the horse had bolted. As

always, it was a matter of too little and too late, for it would take the best part of a decade before the desperately needed new cranes were ready for service.

Some improvements were introduced piece-meal before then, but the debris of countless accidents had to be swept away during the remainder of the 1950s, including Britain's third-worst railway accident, which took place at St John's near Lewisham in 1957. This event undoubtedly gave new impetus to the issue of breakdown-train provision and served as another timely reminder to the powers that be, who five years after Harrow and Wealdstone were undoubtedly flagging. Fortunately for them, steps to authorise the ordering of such equipment had been taken just two and a half months earlier, although it took another two years before these orders were placed!

In a similar vein the cause of so many accidents, the lack of a train-protection or train-control system like that devised by the Great Western Railway in 1906, rumbled on as a matter of managerial debate rather than being implemented on the ground. The loss of life caused by the absence of such a safety feature now ran well into a four-figure total, and this was not to the credit of the national transport system nor any of the politicians who had been responsible for it since 1948.

On a positive note, the BTC crane orders did achieve what the Ad Hoc Committee intended, and it restored the morale of the men (and latterly men and women) who have worked with them.

The early deliveries of diesel locomotives were not immune to suffering accidents either, as this view of an English Electric Class 4 diesel-electric locomotive demonstrates. On 13 May 1966, a freight train of covered hopper wagons from Northwich to St Helens (Ravenhead) loaded with soda ash had divided on the southern approach to the bridge over the Manchester Ship Canal, between Norton Crossing and Acton Grange Junction. The rear portion ran back down the steep grade colliding with No D322 heading the 20.40 overnight sleeper train from Euston to Stranraer, killing the crew and writing off the locomotive. An ex-LMS 50-ton Craven crane attends, while the fire and ambulance services are still on the scene. *Colour-Rail*

Whilst working the 03:24 from Northfleet to Dunstable cement train on 11 October 1977, Class 33/0 No 33036, in multiple with sister No 33043, collided just outside of Mottingham station with an already derailed Merry-Go-Round coal train from Welbeck Colliery to Northfleet cement works, causing both locos and five bogie cement wagons to roll down the embankment. As can be seen, locomotive No 33036 almost reached the back garden of 413 Sidcup Road, Mottingham, and nearly seven weeks later is here about to be lifted out by a pair of ex-SR 45-ton Ransomes & Rapier steam cranes, Nos DS1560 and DS1561. *Author's collection*

8
The Modernisation Cranes

Supply of 30- and 75-ton Cranes

The Committee submitted its report in late 1955. No doubt this was reviewed and considered by the Board and a recommendation made that suitable funds should be applied for in the next available financial programme. In the event, 22 cranes were authorised on 19 September 1957 under the Motive Power Breakdown Crane and Equipment Long Term Replacement Programme, at an estimated cost of £1,010,000, following which tenders were invited.

In the intervening period, the recommendations of the Committee had been amended to two types of steam cranes, one capable of a maximum lift of 30 tons at 16ft radius and the other 75 tons at 18ft radius. In effect, both were a watering down of the Committee's recommendations.

Although apparently of greater maximum capacity, the larger crane could lift only 65 tons to a radius of 20ft, instead of the 25ft originally sought. Whilst regrettable, this was probably a sensible recognition that such a performance could not be achieved by the manufacturers with the technology available at the time, within the axle-load and loading-gauge limitations imposed. As will be seen, it took considerable technical advances over the next decade to achieve the Committee's ambition.

On the other hand, the reversion to the LMS policy of 30-ton cranes for secondary duties was, as events were to demonstrate clearly all too soon, particularly unfortunate. Whilst this may have been appropriate in the late 1930s, twenty years later needs were about to change dramatically, with the result that both the LMS and BR 30-ton cranes were being withdrawn concurrently, as small goods wagons were phased out. Also, no other grouping company had adopted this capacity and, in addition to the London Midland Region, only the Western and Southern regions could be persuaded to accept a pair each, the regions in the East of the country, including Scotland, declining them, receiving only the 75-ton version. It is a great pity, therefore, that the 35 tons at 18ft, as originally recommended, or as the future was to show even 50 tons, was not sanctioned instead. Interestingly, the

Specification for the larger cranes called for hinged outriggers rather than propping girders. Prices were sought, in the case of the 75-ton cranes for quantities from one to twelve, and these were submitted towards the end of that year.

Offers were received for both capacities from Joseph Booth & Bros of Rodley, Leeds, Cowans Sheldon & Co Ltd of Carlisle and Ransomes & Rapier Ltd of Ipswich, and solely for the 75-ton cranes from Steels Engineering Products Ltd (Coles Cranes) of Sunderland. In general terms, bids complying with the Specification were received from all three manufacturers for the 30-ton cranes, whereas only Booth and Cowans appear to have submitted compliant tenders for the 75-ton cranes.

Particular features and comments of the tender review for the 75-ton cranes were as follows:

Booth

Not a particularly advanced design, except that pivoted outriggers were fitted. Otherwise, it followed the general well-tried pattern of construction for a steam breakdown crane. The quotation followed the BR Specification very closely. Any deviations were said to be dictated by the restrictions imposed by the loading gauge. The firm sought the opportunity to re-quote for a diesel-driven design incorporating the latest developments in crane control operation.

Cowans Sheldon

This design also followed the well-known features of steam breakdown cranes and incorporated two sets of sliding propping girders and dolly jacks at each corner.

Pivoted outriggers were offered as an alternative for the 75-ton crane. In this version, the telescopic propping girders between the first and second, and third and fourth axle were replaced by hinged outriggers mounted on each corner of the carriage, with the dolly jacks repositioned to the position vacated by the propping girders. In train formation, the outriggers were swung beside the relieving bogies and served to transmit the redistributed load from the crane to the bogie. At the site of operations, the load would be released and the outriggers repositioned normal to the carriage to provide propping to the crane.

The outriggers would appear to have provided a propping base of approaching 20ft, compared with 17ft 6in. Even so, once swung parallel with the track and connected to a transverse beam projecting outside the frame of the bogie, the reach was only sufficient for a 5ft wheelbase to the bogie, with a larger projection at the buffer end to achieve the same overall length. The lateral translation of the bogies relative to the crane's carriage while negotiating a curve, would appear to have been accommodated by the ability of the outriggers to rotate at both ends. Presumably, the cross beam was also pinned at its point of support on the bogie to allow the latter to rotate relative to the carriage.

The firm also submitted proposals for the same designs of crane incorporating a diesel engine. On these, the boiler was to be replaced by a Rolls-Royce supercharged oil engine with 'Twin Disc' hydrostatic torque converter driving a reversing gearbox instead of the cylinders. The designs broadly followed the specification, and again any deviations were said to be dictated by the loading gauge.

Ransomes & Rapier

This was a standard steam breakdown crane, none of the innovations suggested in the BR Specification having been incorporated. The firm's specification was not very precise or detailed and in assessing the tender many assumptions had to be made. There were a number of deviations from the BR Specification, which the firm thought it advisable to make.

A preliminary general arrangement drawing shows a four fixed-axle carriage, producing an axle load of 17 tons, with a maximum of 15 tons on the two axles of the relieving bogies, and resulting in a total weight with match wagon of 149 tons. A relatively low-height carriage frame was to be achieved by side plates outside the springs, necessitating openings to access the spring shackles and blocking screws. To attain reasonably similar axle loads to the company's previous 45-ton cranes, the king pin was positioned just behind the second axle. The high propping forces on a 17ft-wide propping base necessitated double telescopic propping

girders, each consisting of a heavy welded 'I'-section within a rectangular welded box section. These were located in front of the first axle and between the third and fourth. A dolly jack was placed against the lower framing on each side, centrally between the second and third axle, the purpose of which seems obscure. An all-welded steel jib with numerous stiffeners was proposed, giving a radius of operation for lifting from 18–40ft. Although a chain-driven hauling drum was provided, no auxiliary hoist is apparent.

The low carriage allowed room for a 6ft 11in-high boiler, pressurised to 150psi, and a 14sq ft grate. This was designed to produce an evaporation rate of 1,200 to 1,600lb/hour. The steam drove a pair of horizontally-mounted 9½ x 14in cylinders, driving a crankshaft at 250rpm. These were intended to lift 75 tons at 10ft/min, or 25 tons at 30ft/min. Derricking from train formation to maximum radius (40ft) would take 2 minutes and another 2½ minutes to minimum radius (18ft). 1½ minutes was required to slew a full revolution, while the crane could travel with 15 tons at 250ft/min.

The foot of the jib was articulated, with large catches on the outside of the crab sides to retain it in position when lifting. The drive for the derricking gear was by external horizontal shaft to a worm gear and two-stage spur gearing. Water was carried in an 85-gallon tank beside the boiler with another 185 gallons beneath the driver's position. A further 1,000 gallons was available in a tank on the match wagon. Vacuum brake cylinders are apparent on both relieving bogies and the match wagon.

Steels

This was by far the most advanced design, incorporating all the novel features of the BR Specification (except the tubular jib) as well as many other up-to-date features, making full use of modern engineering practices and techniques. The crane incorporated a diesel-electric drive. Deviations from the BR Specification were mainly the result of the difference in the form of power offered.

All cranes

All cranes appear to have met the requirements relative to capacities and duties.

The quotations for the 75-ton cranes were as follows:

Manufacturer	Motive power	Means of propping	Max axle load (tons)	Price (£ per crane)			Delivery	
				1 No	6 No	12 No	1st crane (months)	Rate (weeks)
Booth	Steam	Outriggers	16	39,083	36,068	36,086	20	8
Cowans	Steam	Outriggers	17	43,480	39,312	38,895	16	6
	Steam	Girders		42,724	38,558	38,160		
	Diesel	Outriggers		44,995	40,492	39,840		
	Diesel	Girders		44,238	39,746	39,065		
Steels	Diesel	Outriggers	13¼	51,750	51,150	50,430	12	8
Rapier	Steam	Girders	17	65,107	51,360	49,615	18	10

In view of their price, the non-compliance of the Steels and Rapier quotations were to be of no further consequence. As subsequent events were to show, Cowans alternatives were clearly of interest in some quarters. However, apart from the longer delivery period, there must be further explanations to account for Booth's failure to secure the order. Perhaps the design offered was insufficiently developed to be relied upon for such a large and important investment for the main order, with time and funds unavailable to construct a prototype. Also, the requirement for both 75 and 30-ton cranes will have been born in mind as an overall package with consideration given to the benefits to be derived by obtaining all from one supplier. In the event, orders for a total of twenty-two cranes were placed with Cowans Sheldon on 11 November 1959, as follows:

Capacity (tons)	Motive power	Quantity	Fulfilled by Works Nos	Region allocated to:
30	Steam	8	C59-C65	London Midland (6 No.) and Western (2 No.)
30	Diesel	2	C66-C67	Southern (2 No.)
75	Steam	10	C78-C87	London Midland (3 No.), Eastern (2 No.), North Eastern (2 No), Scottish (1 No.) and Western (2 No.)
75	Diesel	2	C88-C89	Southern (2 No)

Despite the specification of outriggers for the larger cranes, all were provided with telescopic propping girders. The reason for this may have been that outriggers are disadvantaged when trackside obstacles, such as bridge girders or platforms, are encountered, preventing them being set at right angles. In addition, a relaxation seems to have been granted in respect of both types of crane for the requirement for a well-type match wagon, which in the event were conventional wagons with wells only for the hooks and blocks, together with lockers suspended from the underframe for the larger cranes. One wonders though whether the adoption of a well-type match wagon might have permitted a greater turnover to the top of the jib into the swan neck, thereby allowing a considerable shortening in overall length and consequential reduction in weight of this critical element.

Deliveries commenced in late 1960 with the steam 30-ton cranes at a cost of £25,646 each. The maximum axle load was a little less than 13 tons, as weighed. This was originally intended to be limited to 12 tons, for use on lightly-laid branch and colliery lines and within a loading gauge 12ft 11in high and 8ft 9in wide. Their route availability was RA5. These were of 0-6-4 wheel arrangement and showed some similarity with Cowans earlier 30-ton cranes for the LMS in 1941–4, with the king-pin offset from the centre towards the leading end of the carriage, thereby maximising the portée that end at the expense of the other. Telescopic propping girders were provided at the leading end and between the third

axle and the bogie. The superstructure was mounted on a 6ft 11in pathway with 28 tapered rollers.

The 45ft-long jib was of all-welded construction, with less angle to the swan neck and a longer upper section than usual on previous designs, making the length of the jib and the overall length of crane and match wagon greater than previously experienced. The box-section jib was fabricated from steel plate with solid sides and slotted top and bottom plates. Internally, it was stiffened, generally by ring stiffeners with occasional U stiffeners to accommodate the hoisting ropes.

The propping base was also less at 14ft, rather than the 17ft of the LMS cranes. A 6-ton hauling rope was provided at the front of the superstructure, together with points for the attachment of sheaves on the headstocks at both ends. The buffers at both ends were mounted on hinged plates, thereby enabling them to be swung back at the scene of operations, thus increasing the portée by the 1ft 9in length of the buffers.

The eight 30-ton steam cranes were inspected at the Works and tested between 29 November 1960 and 29 March 1961, whilst the larger steam cranes were similarly dealt with between 15 February and 13 November 1962, taking up duty during 1962.

These 75-ton cranes were a 50% increase on the previous maximum crane capacity and clearly intended for front-line work, but still within a loading gauge of 12ft 11in high x 8ft 9in wide. At a total weight for the crane and match wagon of 151 tons and with a 17-ton limiting axle load, a four-axle rigid carriage was assisted in train formation by an improved design of two-axle relieving bogie at each end. This resulted in a load and route availability of RA8. Relatively unusually for British practice, the superstructure was mounted centrally on the carriage by means of a 7ft-diameter pathway with 40 tapered rollers. The consequence of this was that, whilst equal portée distance was obtained at each end, due to the large counterweight on the tail of the crane, the axle loads on one relieving bogie were approaching the maximum permitted, whereas those on the other bogie were somewhat less. Pairs of telescopic propping girders were provided symmetrically about the king pin, between the first and second and third and fourth axles of the carriage, giving a propping base of 17ft 6in. In addition, screw dolly jacks were fitted at each corner of the carriage.

The final cost of the larger steam cranes was an average of £40,674 each. To achieve the specified lift of 75 tons, the tail radius was a record, for Britain at least, of 17ft. This meant that in the 'free on rail' condition their stability was critical and it was not long before one or two had toppled over. The jib was the same style as the smaller cranes but larger, and was also equipped with a 12-ton auxiliary hoist in lieu of the 6-ton hauling winch. In this case the top and bottom of the box section was made up from individual flange and transverse plates, rather than cut from a whole plate.

Coal-fired 6ft 6in-high Spencer Hopwood squat vertical boilers at a working pressure of 150psi were fitted to both sizes of the crane and each was equipped with one LMR standard injector and one feed pump. The diameter was 4ft 6in for the smaller and 4ft 9in for

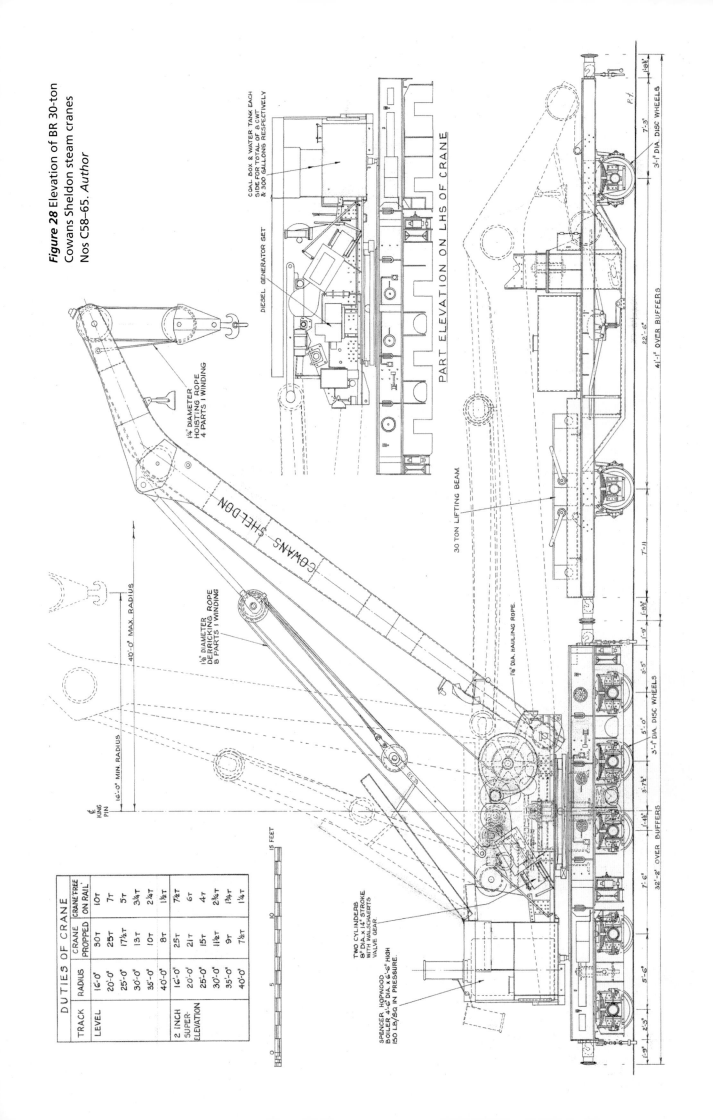

Figure 28 Elevation of BR 30-ton Cowans Sheldon steam cranes Nos C58–65. *Author*

COWANS SHELDON

PART ELEVATION ON LHS OF CRANE

COAL BOX & WATER TANK EACH SIDE FOR TOTAL OF 8 CWT & 300 GALLONS RESPECTIVELY

DIESEL GENERATOR SET

30 TON LIFTING BEAM

1¼" DIAMETER HOISTING ROPE 4 PARTS 1 WINDING

1⅛" DIAMETER DERRICKING ROPE 8 PARTS 1 WINDING

1⅛" DIA. HAULING ROPE.

40'-0" MAX. RADIUS

16'-0" MIN RADIUS

C̸ KING PIN

TWO CYLINDERS 8" DIA. x 14" STROKE WITH WALSCHAERTS VALVE GEAR

SPENCER HOPWOOD BOILER 4'-6" DIA. x 6'-6" HIGH 150 LB/SQ IN PRESSURE.

3'-1" DIA DISC WHEELS

7'-3"

22'-6"

41'-1" OVER BUFFERS

7'-11

1'-8½"

1'-9"

3'-5"

5'-1" DIA. DISC WHEELS

3'-1" DIA. DISC WHEELS

3'-7½"

1'-4½"

7'-6"

32'-2" OVER BUFFERS

5'-6"

2'-5"

1'-9"

DUTIES OF CRANE			
TRACK	RADIUS	CRANE PROPPED	CRANE FREE ON RAIL
LEVEL	16'-0"	30T	10T
	20'-0"	25T	7T
	25'-0"	17½T	5T
	30'-0"	13T	3¾T
	35'-0"	10T	2¼T
	40'-0"	8T	1½T
2 INCH SUPER-ELEVATION	16'-0"	25T	7½T
	20'-0"	21T	6T
	25'-0"	15T	4T
	30'-0"	11½T	2¾T
	35'-0"	9T	1¾T
	40'-0"	7½T	1¼T

0 5 10 15 FEET

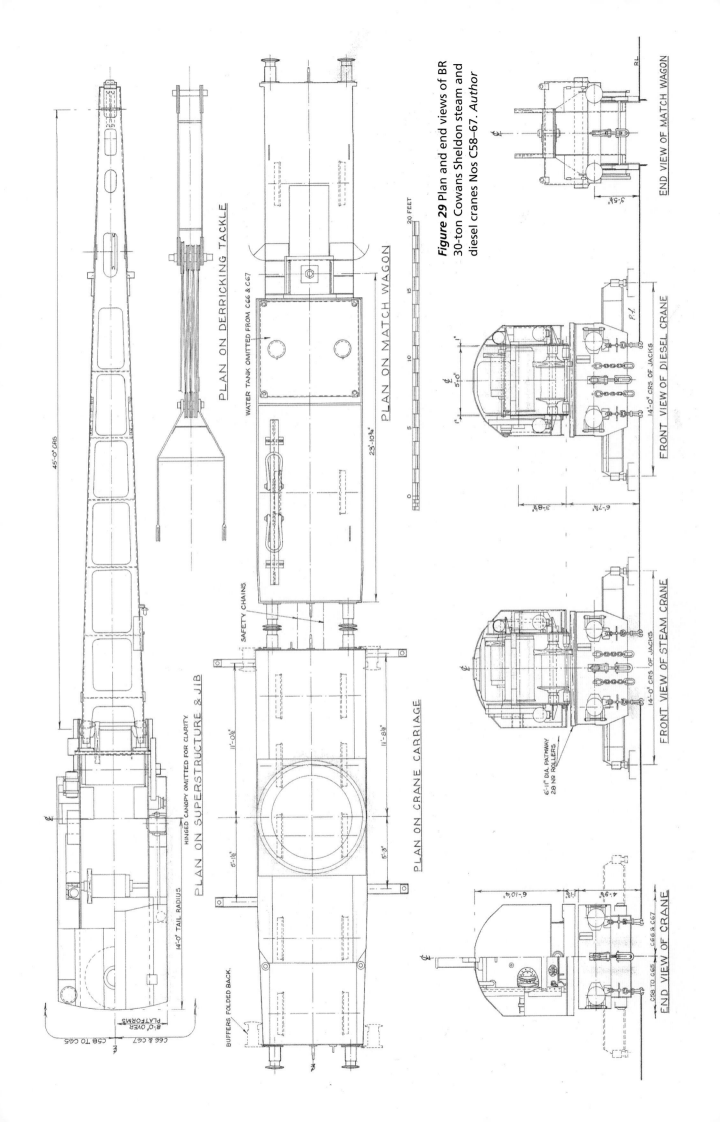

PLAN ON DERRICKING TACKLE

WATER TANK OMITTED FROM C66 & C67

PLAN ON MATCH WAGON

20 FEET

PLAN ON SUPERSTRUCTURE & JIB

HINGED CANOPY OMITTED FOR CLARITY

SAFETY CHAINS

PLAN ON CRANE CARRIAGE

BUFFERS FOLDED BACK.

8'-0" OVER PLATFORMS

C66 & C67
C58 TO C65

45'-0" CRS

14'-0" TAIL RADIUS

23'-10¾"

11'-8½"
11'-0½"
6'-1½"
5'-3"

END VIEW OF MATCH WAGON

R.L.

3'-5½"

FRONT VIEW OF DIESEL CRANE

P.L.

5'-0"
1"
1"
14'-0" CRS OF JACKS
3'-8⅜"
6'-7¾"

FRONT VIEW OF STEAM CRANE

6'-11" DIA. PATHWAY
28 N⁰ ROLLERS

14'-0" CRS OF JACKS

END VIEW OF CRANE

C58 TO C65
C66 & C67

6'-10¾"
1'-1"
4'-6¾"

Figure 29 Plan and end views of BR 30-ton Cowans Sheldon steam and diesel cranes Nos C58–67. *Author*

Figure 30 Elevation of BR 75-ton Cowans Sheldon steam cranes Nos C78–87. *Author*

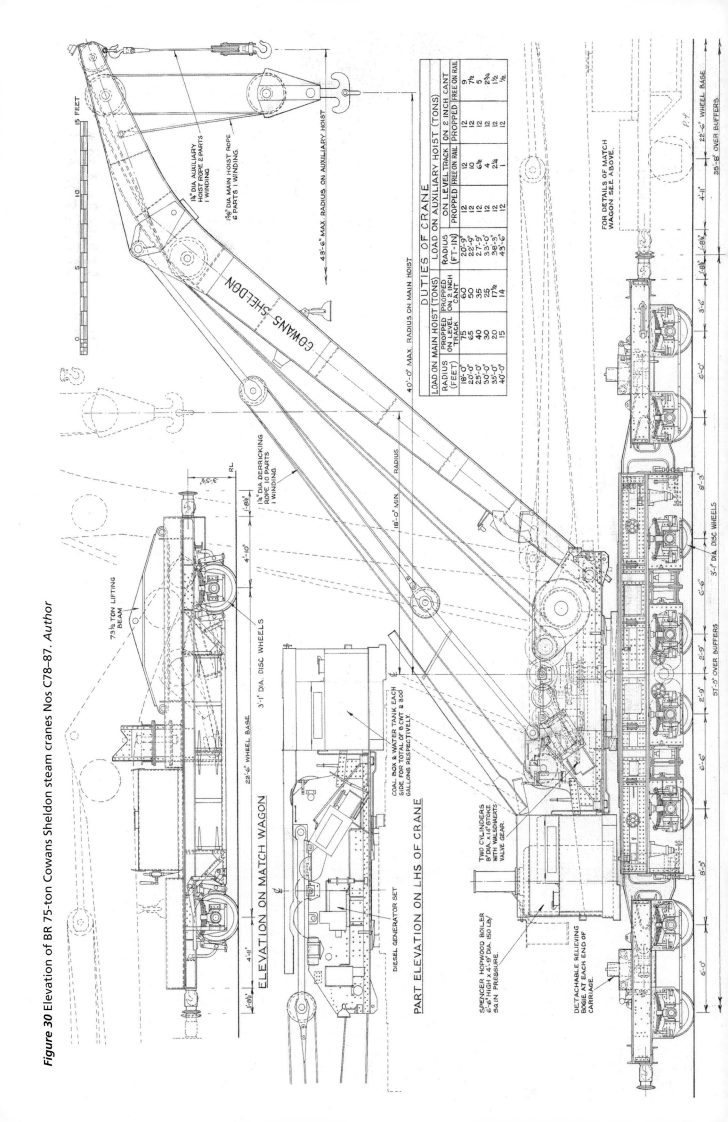

15 FEET

1¼" DIA AUXILIARY
HOIST ROPE 2 PARTS
I WINDING

1⅜" DIA MAIN HOIST ROPE
6 PARTS I WINDING

43'-6" MAX. RADIUS ON AUXILIARY HOIST

COWANS SHELDON

1¼" DIA DERRICKING
ROPE 10 PARTS
I WINDING

RL

18'-0" MIN. RADIUS

40'-0" MAX. RADIUS ON MAIN HOIST

DUTIES OF CRANE

LOAD ON MAIN HOIST (TONS)			LOAD ON AUXILIARY HOIST (TONS)			
RADIUS (FEET)	PROPPED ON LEVEL TRACK	PROPPED ON 2 INCH CANT	RADIUS (FT-IN)	ON LEVEL TRACK		ON 2 INCH CANT
				PROPPED	FREE ON RAIL	PROPPED	FREE ON RAIL
18'-0"	75	60	20'-9"	12	12	12	9
20'-0"	65	50	22'-9"	12	10	12	7½
25'-0"	40	35	27'-9"	12	6½	12	2¾
30'-0"	30	25	33'-0"	12	4	12	1½
35'-0"	20	17½	38'-3"	12	2¼	12	½
40'-0"	15	14	43'-6"	12	1	12	

FOR DETAILS OF MATCH
WAGON SEE ABOVE.

73½ TON LIFTING
BEAM

3'-1" DIA. DISC WHEELS

3'-5¾"

1'-8½"

4'-10"

22'-6" WHEEL BASE

4'-11"

1'-8½"

ELEVATION ON MATCH WAGON

DIESEL GENERATOR SET

COAL BOX & WATER TANK EACH
SIDE FOR TOTAL OF 8 CWT & 300
GALLONS RESPECTIVELY.

PART ELEVATION ON LHS OF CRANE

TWO CYLINDERS
8" DIA. x 14" STROKE
WITH WALSHAERTS
VALVE GEAR.

SPENCER HOPWOOD BOILER
6'-6" HIGH x 4'-9" DIA. 150 LB/
SQ.IN PRESSURE.

DETACHABLE RELIEVING
BOGIE AT EACH END OF
CARRIAGE.

3'-1" DIA. DISC WHEELS

35'-8" OVER BUFFERS

22'-6" WHEEL BASE

4'-11"

1'-8½"

P.4

3'-6"

6'-0"

8'-3"

6'-6"

2'-9"

2'-9"

6'-6"

6'-0"

6'-0"

8'-3"

57'-5" OVER BUFFERS

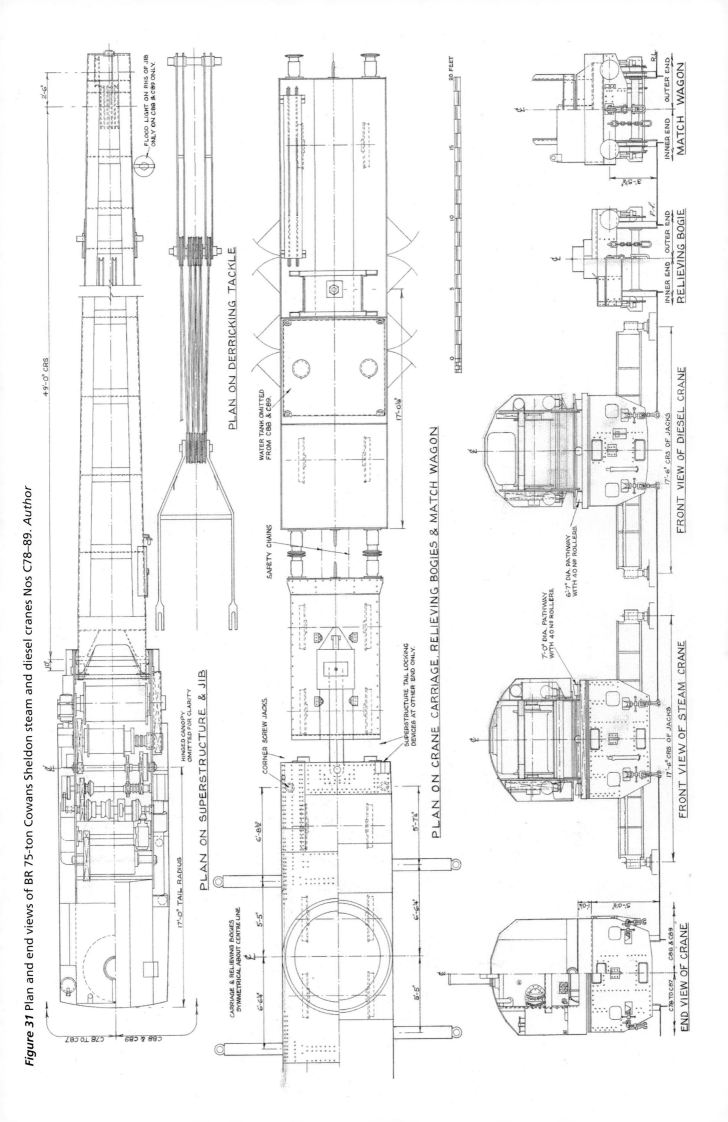

Figure 31 Plan and end views of BR 75-ton Cowans Sheldon steam and diesel cranes Nos C78–89. *Author*

Above Much bridge work is carried out during overnight possessions of the track, usually at weekends. Such a case is illustrated here one cold Saturday night, on 3 February 1968, as Wimbledon Park's 75-ton crane prepares to remove one of the main girders from a road over-bridge being renewed at the former Bramshot Halt between Farnborough and Fleet, on the ex-LSWR West of England mainline. Note the electric lights at the jib head and beside the crab. *Author*

Left A view of the rear end of 30-ton crane, No RS1086/30 at Bescot on 1 February 1969 shows the boiler and access to the man-holes and mud doors, so important for washing out and inspection, together with the firebox damper and hinged buffers. Note that the chimney extension has been removed and 'KEEP CLEAR' and overhead electrified line notices and zebra warning stripes have been applied as part of the repaint following overhaul. *Author*

the larger designs. These provided steam to a pair of 8in-diameter x 14in inclined cylinders mounted on the crab sides and actuated by Walschaert's valve gear. On the smaller crane, 30 tons at 25ft/min and 15 tons at 50ft/min lift speeds could be achieved, whilst the larger crane managed 75 tons at 10ft/min, increasing to 20ft/min with 37½ tons on the main hoist, and 12 tons at 45ft/min increasing to 90ft/min with 6 tons on the auxiliary hoist. An extended canopy was provided for the machinery within the crab sides and other external moving parts were encased. Additionally, a small canopy was fitted over the driver's position.

A total of 8cwt of coal and 300 gallons of water were carried on both types of crane in small bunkers and tanks on each side of the boiler, plus 1,000 gallons on the match wagon. During protracted clearing-up operations and pre-planned long weekend working, steam cranes can exhaust their supply of feed water. Somewhere in the breakdown train there is therefore likely to be a tank of reserve water for just such an eventuality. Alternatively, most civil engineering sites will have a temporary supply for its own activities and arrangements could easily be made with the contractor for a water hose from the supply to be run out to feed the crane's tanks.

A Stones 1kW steam turbo-generator for lighting had originally been proposed, but instead Lister hand-starting diesel 2kW generating sets were mounted on the left-hand side, providing power to the electric floodlights at the jib head and sides of the superstructure and carriage, plus a bulkhead light on the jib pointing upwards to illuminate any overhead obstruction, and another light for the load/radius indicator fitted on the right-hand side towards the bottom of the jib. The lanterns on the carriage were capable of being dismantled and stowed in lockers mounted on the match wagon. Whilst these afforded excellent lighting for the work, the noise created by the engine was usually enough to ensure that adequate lighting from another, quieter, source was laid on, especially if mains electricity could be accessed.

The match wagons were four-wheeled, with trussed underframes and supported the jib on a swivelling crutch designed to draw the jib forward by 10in as it was lowered on to it, thereby providing the clearance at the foot end of the jib to permit articulation as the crane traversed curves in train formation. A 73½-ton or 30-ton lifting beam, as appropriate, was mounted on the wagon. The match wagons for steam cranes carried detachable 1,000-gallon water tanks to supplement the crane's feed water.

Both the carriages and match wagons of the 30-ton cranes were fitted with automatic vacuum brake (AVB) gear, whereas the 75-ton cranes were equipped with air brakes activated by a proportional valve and only the match wagon had AVB. A handbrake lever was provided on the match wagon from the outset, whereas these were sometimes subsequently added to the relieving bogies. 3ft 1in-diameter plain-disc rail wheels were mounted on SKF roller bearings of 150mm diameter on the crane and relieving bogies, and 4in diameter on the match wagon. These permitted the cranes to be hauled by a locomotive in train formation at speeds of up to 60mph.

BR 30-TON COWANS SHELDON STEAM CRANES						
No	Year built	Works No	Match wagon No	Remarks and Allocation	Date Withdrawn	Disposal
139	1959	C58	DB 998526	Newport Ebbw Jct 12/59, Worcester 4/72	c1976	To Birmingham Railway Museum, Tyseley by 3/77
140. TDM1099	1959	C59	DB 998527	Banbury 12/59, to LMR 1963, No RS1099/30, Chester 29/10/66	2/82	Scrapped at Chester by TW Ward 1982
RS 1087/30	1961	C60	DB 998520	Hellifield 2/61, Skipton 6/63, Carnforth 3/4/67, Spring's Branch 4/11/68, Bletchley 4/73	12/76?	To KWVR c 1976, SVR Bridgnorth 26/7/82
RS 1086/30	1961	C61	DB 998519	Stoke 2/61, Bescot 29/4/68, Spare to Crewe 9/69, Longsight to 14/4/73	c 1973	To CIE 6/73 Inchicore* 5/79, No 641A
RS 1088/30	1961	C62	DB 998521	Barrow 2/61, Bletchley 4/67–1975	1976	Accident, cut up Bletchley 1976
RS 1089/30	1961	C63	DB 998522	Nottingham 2/61, Toton 1964, Newton Heath 3/68, Carlisle (Spare) 1973	Withdrawn	To CIE 6/73 Inchicore* 7/79–3/01, No 645A
RS 1090/30	1961	C64	DB 998523	Newton Heath 4/61, Longsight 17/6/65–5/6/73, Willesden (spare) 9/73, Bescot 1975–76	c 1976	Cut up 1976
RS1091/30 ADM1091	1961	C65	DB 998524	Saltley 30/4/61, Edge Hill 1969, Allerton 5/2/69, Chester	1977	24/6/77 at Bridgnorth, scrapped 2010/11

Notes:
1. Dates shown in *italics* are spot dates upon which the crane is known to have been at the depot concerned
2. * = Converted to 5ft 3in gauge at Inchicore circa 1973

A rear three-quarter view of Cowans Sheldon 30-ton steam crane No C58, allocated by the Western Region to Newport and seen there on 8 October 1961, not long after delivery. The Western Region numbered it 139. As was their wont, Swindon have added the cast-iron notices with extensive instructions to the water tank sides. Perhaps these afforded increased stability to the crane! *N.E.W. Skinner*

An elevated view of No RS1087/30 at Hellifield on 25 May 1962, where it had been allocated in February 1961. This clearly shows the lined livery style. It moved to Skipton a little over a year later and transferred to Carnforth on 3 April 1967. It then went to Spring's Branch on 4 November 1968 and was at Bletchley from April 1973. Upon withdrawal about two years later, it was preserved on the KWVR and moved to Bridgnorth on the Severn Valley Railway on 26 July 1982. *W.D. Cooper*

Above Now in preservation, but in rather faded red, No ADB139 was at Tyseley on 7 July 1981 when this photograph was taken. *P. Bartlett*

Left Newton Heath's 30-ton steam crane, No RS1090/30 is seen at work within the platforms of the Macclesfield branch at Cheadle Hulme station, carrying out the installation of steel box girders and deck as part of the reconstruction of an under-bridge for a road-widening scheme in 1964. The old bridge superstructure has been removed and a pair of new girders is in place awaiting the lifting in of the deck units. Another crane, this time a 45-ton Ransomes & Rapier, can be seen in the background, together with various bridge and permanent-way materials stacked about, including temporarily dismantled pre-cast-concrete platform units. Earlier during the work, temporary bridging waybeams had been in use to enable the abutments to be reconstructed, requiring a temporary speed restriction of 10mph. Unfortunately, on 28 May 1964, an excursion train from Gnosall to York was derailed due to excessive speed on the curve, resulting in three fatalities. *Author's collection*

Above As part of the rebuilding of Cheadle Hulme station under the Modernisation Plan, 30-tonner No RS1090/30, by then at Longsight, dismantles the old footbridge early in 1966. Note the difficulty caused by the overhead wires, despite them being temporarily tied back, obstructing the operation of the jib. Cranes were not well-suited to work under overhead catenary and the route mileage of the London Midland electric lines was in the process of growing considerably. Unfortunately, this region had been the recipient of the largest number of 30-ton cranes. *M.S. Welch*

Right No RS1090/30 again, on 5 June 1973, in Ashwood Dale on the Midland Railway's Buxton branch, this time re-railing a 16-ton steel end-door mineral wagon after a derailment due to excessive speed on suspect track. *M.S. Welch*

The right hand side of No ADM1091/30 at Arley on the Severn Valley Railway on 7 July 1977. *P. Bartlett*

The jib support to the same crane on its match wagon, No DB998524. *P. Bartlett*

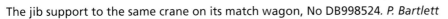

Cowans Sheldon's advertisement in the *Railway Gazette* for 23 February 1962 depicting a 30-ton steam crane. *Author's collection*

75-ton steam breakdown crane No RS1092/75, having arrived from Willesden behind Derby Type 2 diesel No D5029, is seen lifting into position a pre-cast pre-stressed concrete beam on 12 April 1963 as part of the deck renewal of an over-bridge at Norcott Hall, between Berkhamsted and Tring. This will have been required in connection with overhead electrification of the West Coast mainline. Note the use of the lifting beam so that the concrete beam is lifted from the ends. *Colour Rail*

The red of York MPD's 75-ton steam crane No DB 967159's livery glistens in the sunlight in June 1965, showing off the black and straw lining and the details picked out in black, white and yellow. *Keith R. Pirt, Colour-Rail*

Closer view of No RS1092/75 north of Northampton on 20 May 1962 during bridge works. *M.S. Welch*

BR 75-TON COWANS SHELDON STEAM CRANES						
Nos		**Year built**	**Works No**	**Match wagon No**	**Remarks and Allocation**	**Date converted**
1st	**2nd**					
DB966111	ADB966111	1961	C78	DB998517	Stratford *4/64–10/84*	1977
DB966112	ADB966112	1962	C79	DB998518	King's Cross *3/64*, Finsbury Park *11/67 to 4/72*,	1978/9
RS1092/75	ADM 1092	1962	C80	DB998534	Willesden 1962, Derby 5/65, Toton 1968	c 1977
RS1093/75	TDM 1093	1962	C81	DB998535	Wellingborough 26/4/62, Cricklewood 9/65 to *4/72*, Willesden 9/6/76–4/79	1977
RS1094/75	ADB365	1962	C82	DB998536	Kingmoor 1962 *to 1977*	1977
RS1075/75	-	1962	C83	DB998537	Polmadie 1962	1977
(ADB)142	RS1095/75	1962	C84	DB998539	Canton 1962 *to 6/3/76*	c 1977
141	ADB141	1962	C85	DB998538	Swindon Rail Yard 11/62, Bristol *31/12/71–19/4/75*	c 1977
DB967159	ADB967159	1962	C86	DB998540	York *1964 to 11/67*, Doncaster *14/1/69 to 4/88*	1978
DB967160	ADB967160	1962	C87	DB998541	Gateshead *1964 to 4/88*	1977/8
Note: 1. Dates shown in *italics* are spot dates upon which the crane is known to have been at the depot concerned.						

One of the Western Region's 75-ton cranes again, in this case No 141, receiving the final touches of a repaint on 23 August 1971, following an overhaul at Swindon Works. The lining has been omitted and the ends of the crane and inner ends of the relieving bogies and match wagon have been painted black. Note the lifting beam on the match wagon. *Author*

One of the Western Region's 75-ton cranes utilises its lifting beam to re-rail a Class 47, No D1736, on 30 July 1964. Note the auxiliary hoist at the outer end of the jib and the propping girders extended with the jacks screwed down on timber packing. Brake levers and ladders have been fitted to the relieving bogie. *BR, WR, author's collection*

A brand-new 75-ton steam crane standing outside Cowans Sheldon's St Nicholas Works in Carlisle. Although painted and lined, the crane and match-wagon numbers have yet to be applied. *BR, LMR, author's collection*

A close up view of Gateshead's 75-ton steam crane No DB 967160 on 1 May 1971, showing the heavy riveted-steel sections to side members of the carriage. Note that the extended canopy over the machinery has been removed, the chimney extension has been shortened and the spreader plates for the propping-girder jacks to bear on are kept in pockets on the side of the carriage ready for use. *J. Chris Dean*

Looking down on the superstructure of 75-ton steam crane No RS1092/75 in action at South Hampstead on 1 November 1964. The blurred motion indicates that the cylinders are rotating the crankshaft. The driver can engage various clutches to bring into use gears to operate the motions of lifting on either the main or the auxiliary hoist, derricking the jib, slewing the superstructure and travelling the crane slowly along the track. *M.S. Welch*

Diesel-mechanical Cranes

As noted previously, during the tender process several bidders had submitted alternative proposals for utilising diesel instead of steam power. In view of further developments since the original submission (for authority to purchase the twelve 75-ton and ten 30-ton steam cranes) was made, it was felt that it would be beneficial if some experience was gained with diesel cranes. The change to electric and diesel power was already more advanced on the Southern Region and worthwhile experience would, therefore, be gained in the shortest possible time on this Region under conditions similar to those which were to apply to all regions in fifteen years' time. It was therefore proposed that the two 75-ton and two 30-ton cranes required by the Southern Region should be diesel, rather than steam cranes.

As the tender prices for the twenty-two steam cranes had been lower than anticipated, it was expected that the additional cost of the diesel cranes could still be accommodated within the original authorised figure of £1,010,000, whilst it was hoped that economies in operating the diesel cranes would be achieved.

The steam cranes were therefore followed later by similar, but diesel-powered cranes for the Southern Region, capable of being worked down the restricted Tonbridge to Hastings via Battle line. It is understandable

that the Southern Region would wish to have breakdown cranes capable of operating on this line, but its existing more recently acquired 36- and 45-ton cranes with relieving bogies were already cleared to pass along the line, so it is debatable whether both the 30- and 75-ton types needed be capable of this as well. The Schools class 4-4-0 locomotives, specially designed for the line, had been displaced by diesel-electric multiple units in 1960. Eventually, the problem was removed as part of the electrification in 1983 by singling the line at the points of constriction.

On the two 30-ton cranes, steam power was replaced by a Rolls-Royce C4NFL four-cylinder vertical in-line diesel engine rated at 119bhp gross at 1,800rpm, driving through a 'Twin Disc' three-stage hydrokinetic torque converter. These two cranes cost £24,958 each.

On the two 75-ton cranes, a Rolls-Royce C4SFL four-cylinder vertical in-line supercharged diesel engine with a Type F10,000 three-stage torque converter was used. This drove the motions of the crane by the same mechanical arrangement of gears as the steam crane, the driveshaft from the engine compartment to the drive box passing up the right-hand side of the driver's position. The drive mechanism permitted a continually varying increase of lifting speed with decrease in load in each gear. This pair of cranes cost £46,479 each.

Instead of an open cab, the crane operator was now located in a closed cabin with small lever controls and access on the left-hand side only. It is reported that complaints were received to the effect that the driver's position was so noisy and with such poor visibility that he could not receive the supervisor's instructions. Initially, a man was positioned at the lower end of the jib to relay instructions, and later two-way radios were introduced. Apart from the more-modern form of prime mover, the design of the machinery of the cranes was similar to the steam cranes and the opportunity to improve the driver's view of operations by moving his position forward on the crane was not taken. The water tank was omitted from the match wagons.

Although the 30-ton diesel cranes were delivered approximately 12 months after their steam equivalents, much of the design appears to have been developed in parallel and many of the details are similar. Achieving this within the Tonbridge to Hastings loading gauge must have caused considerable difficulties, and as a consequence the rear end of the 30-ton crane carriage and crane end of the match wagon were tapered in plan. It is noted on the Crane in Train Formation drawing that, due to 'growth during manufacture', crane No C66 encroached the gauge at one top corner of the operator's cab by $^3/_8$-inch when standing on a 5-chain curve.

BR (SR) 30-TON DIESEL-MECHANICAL CRANES							
Nos		Year built	Works No	Match wagon No	Remarks and Allocation	Date Withdrawn	Disposal
1st	2nd						
(A)DB 965183	ADRC 96100	1962	C66	DB 998530	Feltham 6/62, Clapham Jct 1/9/70, Horsham *9/80–4/01*, Doncaster Electrification Construction Depot *04/03–07/05*.	1996	To Power Traction, Donc. Carnforth *12/11*
(A)DB 965184	ADRC 96101	1962	C67	DB 998531	Bournemouth 9/62, Eastleigh *18/10–11/69*, Horsham *9/80 to 08/04*.	1996	To Forest of Dean Railway c5/05
Notes: Dates shown in *italics* are spot dates upon which the crane is known to have been at the depot concerned.							

Should this have been the form of propulsion adopted for all the cranes supplied in the early 1960s? Diesel-powered 30-ton crane at Cowans Sheldon's works prior to delivery to the Southern Region. The driveshaft on the right-hand side of the crab can be seen running from the engine housing to the reduction gear and brake box in place of the crank disc. The water tank on the match wagon has been omitted and the full-height side rails extended up to the swivelling crutch for the articulated jib. *BR, LMR, author's collection*

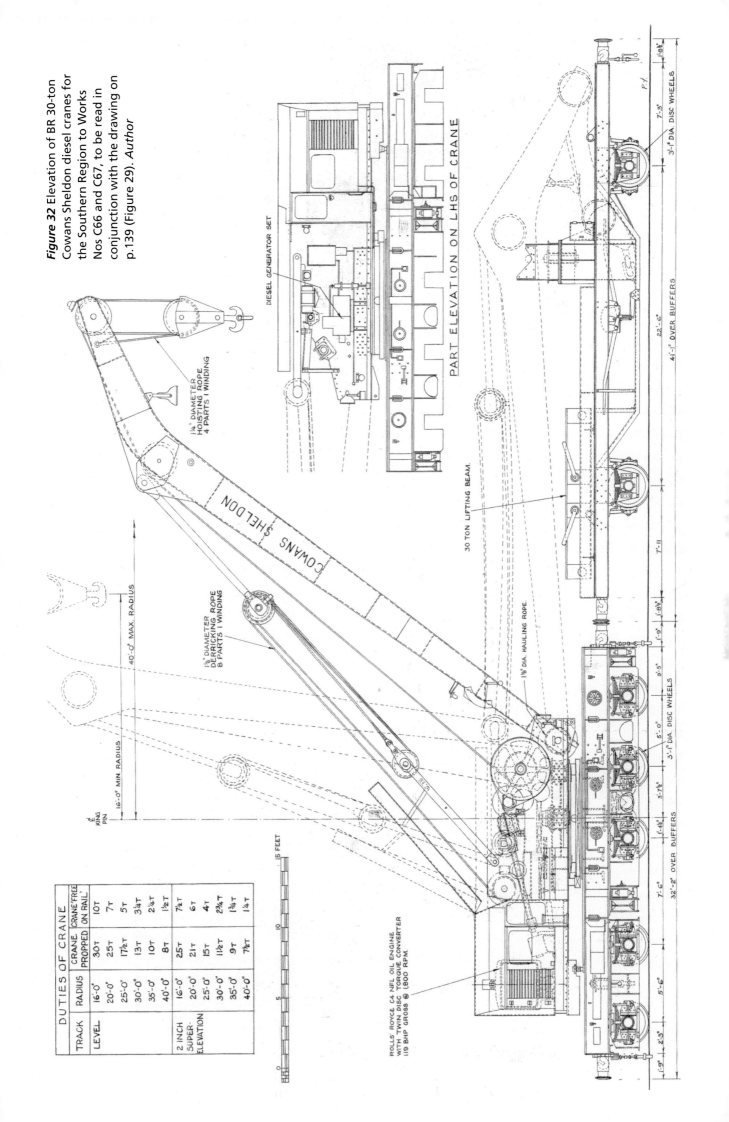

Figure 32 Elevation of BR 30-ton Cowans Sheldon diesel cranes for the Southern Region to Works Nos C66 and C67, to be read in conjunction with the drawing on p.139 (Figure 29). *Author*

DIESEL GENERATOR SET

PART ELEVATION ON LHS OF CRANE

1¼" DIAMETER HOISTING ROPE 4 PARTS I WINDING

COWANS SHELDON

1⅛" DIAMETER DERRICKING ROPE 8 PARTS I WINDING

30 TON LIFTING BEAM.

1⅛" DIA. HAULING ROPE.

40'-0" MAX. RADIUS

16'-0" MIN RADIUS

₵ KING PIN

ROLLS/ ROYCE C4 NFL OIL ENGINE WITH TWIN DISC TORQUE CONVERTER 119 BHP GROSS @ 1,800 RPM.

3'-1" DIA. DISC WHEELS
7'-3"
1'-8¼"

22'-6"
41'-1" OVER BUFFERS

7'-11"
1'-8¼"
1'-9"
3'-5"
5'-0"
3'-1" DIA. DISC WHEELS
3'-7½"
1'-4½"
32'-2" OVER BUFFERS
7'-6"
5'-6"
2'-5"
1'-9"

5 FEET
10
15
0
5

DUTIES OF CRANE			
TRACK	RADIUS	CRANE PROPPED	CRANE'FREE' ON RAIL'
LEVEL	16'-0"	30T	10T
	20'-0"	25T	7T
	25'-0"	17½T	5T
	30'-0"	13T	3¾T
	35'-0"	10T	2¼T
	40'-0"	8T	1½T
2 INCH SUPER- ELEVATION	16'-0"	25T	7¼T
	20'-0"	21T	6T
	25'-0"	15T	4T
	30'-0"	11½T	2¾T
	35'-0"	9T	1¾T
	40'-0"	7½T	1¼T

Not long after, on 20 April 1962, No C66, together with its mate C67, had been delivered to the recently-created diesel roads at Stewarts Lane Motive Power Depot at Battersea, London, but not yet numbered or allocated to a depot. *Author*

A side view of the 30-ton diesel crane No DB965183 at Eastleigh on 18 October 1969 to compare with p.143 (30T CS) showing the steam version. The cover to the generator has been discarded. *Author*

These two photographs show the driver's view forward and up the jib of a 30-ton diesel crane during a bridge-deck renewal at Vauxhall station on 27 March 1971. As can be seen, the view is very restricted and the driver is almost totally dependent on his supervisor's instructions for the operation of the crane. The extended canopy, load/radius indicator and partial enclosure of the machinery can be seen. *Author*

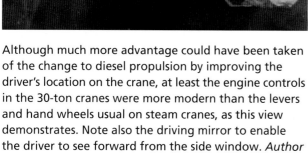

Although much more advantage could have been taken of the change to diesel propulsion by improving the driver's location on the crane, at least the engine controls in the 30-ton cranes were more modern than the levers and hand wheels usual on steam cranes, as this view demonstrates. Note also the driving mirror to enable the driver to see forward from the side window. *Author*

No ADRC96101 on the load pad at Ashford (Kent), where it will have been tested following an overhaul in 1993. Notice that its carriage has now been painted black. By this time, the crane was in the custody of the Electrification Department and stationed at Horsham. *M. House*

BR (SR) 75-TON DIESEL-MECHANICAL CRANES								
Nos			Year built	Works No	Match wagon No	Remarks and Allocation	Date Withdrawn	Disposal
1st	2nd	3rd						
DB 965185	ADB 965185	ADRC 96200	1964	C88	DB 998532	Hither Green 5/64, Eastleigh 4/65 to *4/75*, Ashford *30/9/80–3/93*.	by 10/96	Sold to Phillips & cut up 8/98
DB 965186	ADB 965186	ADRC 96201	1964	C89	DB 998533	Nine Elms *c6/64*, Wimbledon Park *7/67–9/80*, Eastleigh *8/86*, Ashford Repair Crane Depot *4/88*, Stewart's Lane *c1988 to 3/93*, Ashford Plant Depot OOU *30/9/94*.	by 10/96	Sold to Phillips & cut up 9/97

Notes:
1. OOU = Out of use
2. Dates shown in *italics* are spot dates upon which the crane is known to have been at the depot concerned.

In the case of the 75-ton cranes, the requirement of achieving the Tonbridge to St Leonard's via Battle loading gauge seems to have resulted in the need for a total redesign of the structure to the carriage, with shallower main longitudinal members to lower the overall height. Whereas on the steam cranes these members were fabricated in the traditional manner from heavily-riveted steel plates and angles, the diesel cranes utilised a very heavy steel structural-column core, or bearing pile section with plates welded top and bottom, whilst both ends of the carriage to the 75-ton cranes were also tapered in plan. More-modern welded construction was also used for the telescopic propping girders and girder boxes. The roller path on which the superstructure rotated was also reduced to 6ft 7in, but still with 40 rollers. Difficulties were experienced when it came to placing an order for the Rolls-Royce engines and for a time Cummins engines were considered as an alternative. Each crane cost £41,787 and, despite being a fixed-price contract, a claim for extra costs was submitted by Cowans to BR.

A close-up of the Nine Elms' crane again, this time on a cold day during the renewal of the Bridge No 9 over a filled-in canal on the Windsor line between Wandsworth Town and Putney on 23 January 1966. The sockets within which the relieving-bogie cantilever beams fit can be seen in the end of the carriage. Note that, when raised for use, the fork at the foot of the jib, in shadow, bears down on the heavy circular crossmember between the crab sides. The lighter member further forward supports the rubbing strips on the underside of the jib when this is lowered prior to travelling in train formation. This permits longitudinal movement, and allows the jib to articulate in relation to the superstructure, which is locked with respect to the carriage, as the assembled crane moves round a curve. *Author*

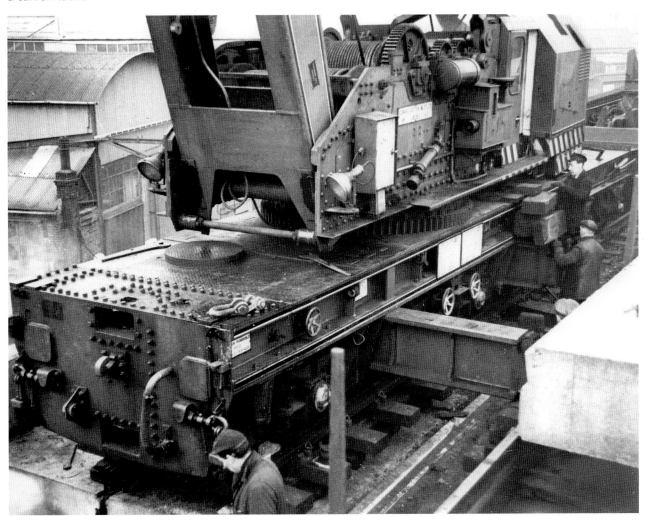

A detailed view of Nine Elms' crane No DB 965186 on 6 June 1964, showing the crane superstructure mounted on the carriage via the live ring of tapered rollers. The end of the driveshaft enclosed gearing to the main cross-shaft, warwicking shackles and clutch wheels can also be seen. Compare the shallow, smooth-steel section of the main carriage beam with the deeper heavily-riveted girder used on the steam cranes, shown on p.152 (CS75T). *M.S. Welch*

Right, Figure 33 Elevation of BR 75-ton Cowans Sheldon diesel-powered cranes for the Southern Region to Works Nos C88 and C89, to be read in conjunction with the drawing on p.141 (Figure 31). *Author*

Left One of the Southern Region's diesel 75-ton cranes, No DB 965186 allocated to Wimbledon Park, being drawn out of the sidings at Chertsey on 3 March 1970 by a Birmingham RCW Type 3 diesel locomotive. *Author*

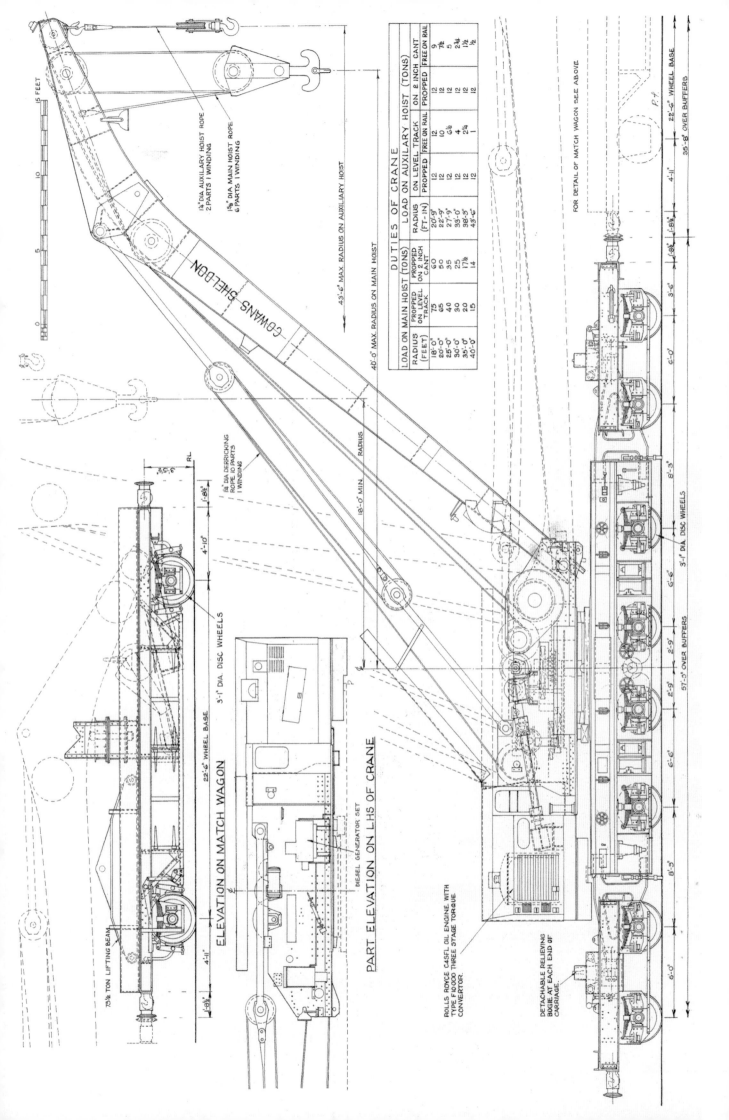

DUTIES OF CRANE

LOAD ON MAIN HOIST (TONS)			LOAD ON AUXILARY HOIST (TONS)				
RADIUS (FEET)	PROPPED ON LEVEL TRACK	PROPPED ON 2 INCH CANT	RADIUS (FT-IN)	ON LEVEL TRACK		ON 2 INCH CANT	
				PROPPED	FREE ON RAIL	PROPPED	FREE ON RAIL
18'-0"	75	60	20'-9"	12	12	12	9
20'-0"	65	50	22'-9"	12	10	12	7½
25'-0"	40	35	27'-9"	12	6¾	12	5
30'-0"	30	25	33'-0"	12	4	12	2¾
35'-0"	20	17½	38'-3"	12	2¼	12	1½
40'-0"	15	14	43'-6"	12	1	12	½

1¼" DIA AUXILIARY HOIST ROPE
2 PARTS 1 WINDING

1⅝" DIA MAIN HOIST ROPE
6 PARTS 1 WINDING

COWANS SHELDON

1¼" DIA DERRICKING ROPE 10 PARTS 1 WINDING

43'-6" MAX RADIUS ON AUXILIARY HOIST

40'-0" MAX. RADIUS ON MAIN HOIST

18'-0" MIN. RADIUS

15 FEET

10

5

0

FOR DETAIL OF MATCH WAGON SEE ABOVE.

3-5½"

RL

1-8½"

4'-10"

3'-1" DIA. DISC WHEELS

22'-6" WHEEL BASE

75½ TON LIFTING BEAM

1-8½"

4'-11"

DIESEL GENERATOR SET

ELEVATION ON MATCH WAGON

PART ELEVATION ON LHS OF CRANE

ROLLS ROYCE C4SFL OIL ENGINE WITH TYPE F10000 THREE STAGE TORQUE CONVERTOR.

DETACHABLE RELIEVING BOGIE AT EACH END OF CARRIAGE.

22'-6" WHEEL BASE

35'-8" OVER BUFFERS

4'-11"

1-8½"

1-8½"

3'-6"

6'-0"

8'-3"

3'-1" DIA. DISC WHEELS

6'-6"

2'-9"

57'-3" OVER BUFFERS

6'-6"

8'-3"

6'-0"

Liveries

All the new cranes were painted in accordance with *General Instructions 10 – Covering the repainting and treatment of .... breakdown cranes and other service stock*, issued in July 1959. For cranes, this consisted of a bright red livery, including the bridle gear and sheaves, jib and blocks and hooks, with black and straw lining to the coal box, water tank, (or cab/engine enclosure, including the rear of the diesel cranes, together with cab roof and canopies), carriage and relieving-bogie sides. The match wagon was also red, including the solebars, tool boxes, water tank, jib crutch and lifting beam. The sides and tool boxes were lined. Lettering was in lining yellow (straw).

Right Wimbledon Park's crane at Raynes Park, again showing the end of a 75-ton crane as the jib is being raised. The lower part of the deep headstock to the match wagon supports the well within which the hook and block of the auxiliary hoist fits when the jib is lowered. *Author*

Below Southern Region's diesel 75-ton crane, No DB 965186 from Wimbledon Park, on bridgeworks at the London end of Raynes Park station on 15 October 1967. Note that the propping girders are partially extended, but the jacks are not yet screwed down on packing and the right-hand relieving bogie has been removed and set to one side to enable the crane to approach closer to the work area. The lattice jib of a road-mobile crane can also be seen in the background. *Author*

The Scottish Region's No RS1075/75, initially allocated to Polmadie, seen at that depot in September 1964. This shows off her original scheme of lining particularly well in the sunlight. It should be noted that this crane's number partially duplicated the ex-LMS 30-ton Cowans Sheldon crane No RS1075/30. *W.O. Potter, author's collection*

Notice plates attached to the crane were white, with lettering and borders picked out in black, except for the additional plates the Western Region insisted on adding to its cranes, which had white lettering and borders on a black background. Springs, spring hangers and axle boxes were black. The roller-bearing covers were yellow with a 1½in-wide horizontal red stripe. Black was also applied to the side shackles, wheel centres, tops of the relieving bogies and match trucks, boiler, tank tops, buffers, draw gear, cab roof and canopies (of steam cranes), steps and grab handles. White was used on the end of the jib (although the lining was carried through), handbrake wheels (edged in black), and wheel tyres. The travelling clutch wheels were orange/yellow. The ends of the pipes to fully-automatic-brake-equipped vehicles were painted freight stock red (bauxite), or white to piped vehicles. The two Southern Region 75-ton diesel cranes had yellow and black diagonal zebra safety markings on the lower portion of the tail and lifting blocks from the outset.

The numbers and allocations were applied by the regions and therefore tended to vary. The London Midland and Scottish regions added the number, in the former LMS list, i.e. RS10xx/75 or 30 as appropriate, to the jib sides and sometimes to the crane tank sides as well, but in other cases the depot name in shaded lettering was positioned above and below the 'lion rampant' totem. The Eastern, North Eastern and Southern regions used the BR departmental list of numbers in the series DB96xxxx, the Southern applying the number to the side of the engine housing. In 1974, the Civil Engineers Plant System (CEPS) of numbering was set up.

This included an allocation of numbers for M&EE steam and diesel cranes in the 95xxx and 96xxx series respectively.

As the existing stock of cranes went through the works for an overhaul, they were also generally repainted in the new red livery, although the styles tended to vary depending on the individual Works carrying out repair and the date. At subsequent repaints, the ends of the crane and inner ends of the relieving bogies and match wagons, together with the jib cradle, trussing and W irons of the jib cradle often became black, whilst the steps and grab handles were painted white. Incidentally, additional steps and grab handles were fitted to the cranes and match wagons as time passed. The tendency over the years was for an increasing awareness of the need for hazard-warning stripes and notices, including the overhead-electrification flashes. From small beginnings, the extent of zebra markings grew on the tail of the crane and lifting blocks, until eventually yellow replaced the red body colour and black lettering was applied.

From the mid-1970s, in the yellow livery style, all under-framing and running gear below the main member of the crane carriage and relieving bogies and the solebar of the match wagon was painted black, with the roller-bearing covers, propping girders and girder and dolly jacks picked out in yellow. The roof, canopy and tops of the bogies and floor match wagon were also black. The bridle gear, clutch wheels and buffer beams generally continued to be painted red, occasionally alongside the lifting points on the bogies and match wagon. Sometimes, however, black and yellow zebra stripes were applied to the buffer beams and crane-carriage-ends of the relieving bogies and match wagon, with just the buffer housings red. The letters of 'COWANS SHELDON' attached to the jib side were also picked out in red. The brake wheels, grab irons, ladders, vacuum-pipe standards and notice plates, with black lettering, continued to be white, and on the converted cranes the air reservoirs on the crab sides were also white. The depot to which the crane was allocated and the safe working load (SWL) was emblazoned in large letters along the length of the jib, first in white during the later red era and subsequently in black with the yellow livery, when imperial tons gave way to metric tonnes, typically: 'To lift 75 tons or S.W.L. 50 tonnes'.

Allocation

The allocation of the new 75- and 30-ton cranes was a reflection of the changes taking place with BR as a whole and particularly in the motive-power field at the time. Initially, the larger cranes were sent to the strategic depots, allowing the cascading of the existing cranes to some less-important depots. Subsequent changes were then usually dictated by possible closure of steam sheds and a move to the new diesel depot. There was little point in allocating a crane to a depot solely handling multiple units, whether diesel or electric powered, when a diesel locomotive would inevitably be required to haul the breakdown train to the scene of an incident.

The 75-ton cranes tended not to be displaced from the more important sheds until the arrival of the telescopic-jib cranes a decade and a half later. The 30-ton cranes on the other hand were intended to replace worn-out existing ancient and smaller cranes, typically of 15- or 20-ton capacity dating from before or around the end of the 19th century. Inevitably, it was these secondary depots that tended within a few years to face closure plans with the implementation of modernisation schemes. Eventually, the reduction in number of depots, the decline of the train of loose-coupled wagons, together with a reduction in the pool of suitable manpower from which to recruit into the breakdown gangs, left few locations to which to allocate a breakdown crane, and the presence of a second crane at one site, sometimes acting as regional spare, was not uncommon.

The London Midland Region received by far the largest allocation of 30-ton cranes and sent these to their less-important motive-power divisions. For instance, initial allocations were to depots at Hellifield, Stoke, Barrow, Nottingham, Newton Heath and Saltley, thereby permitting three old 15-ton cranes to be withdrawn and releasing further cranes for cascading to other depots, which in turn released more old cranes for scrapping in due course. All of these 30-ton cranes tended to move on as their depots changed status and divisions amalgamated with adjacent ones and/or sheds being closed. Additional locations therefore included Skipton, Carnforth, Spring's Branch, Bletchley, Bescot, Longsight, Toton and Allerton. Even then the cranes usually ended up as spare within ten years.

The Western Region sent its two 30-ton cranes first to Newport Ebbw Jct and Banbury. Subsequently, the Banbury crane fell into the hands of the LMR to add to its existing collection and was transferred to Chester, while the Newport crane was moved to Worcester. The Southern Region's two diesel 30-ton cranes, having been delivered to Stewart's Lane in April 1963, were sent to replace a pair of 1907-vintage ex-LSWR Stothert and Pitt 20-ton cranes at Feltham and Bournemouth. On closure of these sheds, the Fetham crane moved to Clapham Jct carriage depot and the Bournemouth crane to Eastleigh. Later they were both transferred to the Electrical Engineer's Power Supply Section for use handling mainly transformers for traction feed, and were kept at Horsham, No ADRC 96100 later moving on to the Doncaster Electrification Construction Depot.

The Eastern Region received its two 75-ton cranes at the end of 1961 and allocated them to Stratford and King's Cross, the latter crane moving out to Finsbury Park on the closure of Top Shed. The LMR's three cranes were initially sent to Willesden, Wellingborough and Kingmoor. Perhaps due to the electrification of the West Coast mainline and the consequent risk of obstruction to crane working, the Willesden and Wellingborough cranes were soon on the move to Derby and later Toton, and Cricklewood respectively. The Scottish Region's crane went initially to Polmadie. The Western Region's pair was allocated to Cardiff Canton and Swindon Works, the latter's crane subsequently being transferred to Bristol. York and Gateshead were the recipients of the North Eastern Region's two cranes and, following amalgamation with the Eastern, the York crane went to Doncaster.

The Southern Region had to wait until 1964 for its two diesel versions of the 75-ton crane and when they arrived they were sent initially to Hither Green and Nine Elms. However, both soon ended up on the Western Division when the Hither Green crane was transferred to Eastleigh, although later this was moved on to Chart Leacon (Ashford, Kent). In all cases, the initial allocation of the 75-ton cranes to the important depots mentioned previously led to the cascading of their existing cranes, usually reasonably modern and of significant size, to other depots, which in turn would relinquish their older cranes for either further cascading or withdrawal.

9

The 75-tonne Telescopic-jib Cranes

The Working Party

Ten years after the order for the 30- and 75-ton steam and diesel cranes had been placed, as discussed in the previous chapter, a further review of breakdown arrangements was undertaken by a specially constituted Working Party, similar to the Ad Hoc Committee of 1953, under the chairmanship of Kenneth RM Cameron. This committee reported in April 1970.

As before, a major consideration was the need to meet the changing requirements of British Railways. Since the previous review, steam traction had been completely eliminated. Coal was no longer a regular fuel on the railways and the number of staff familiar with steam was rapidly diminishing. There was, therefore, an urgent need to do away with steam as a means of propulsion for breakdown cranes. In addition, improvements in maintenance regimes and the rationalisation of railway operations had led to a vast reduction in the number of motive-power maintenance depots to meet the needs of the reduced fleet. The work now undertaken at the depots tended to be carefully planned, with little flexibility to permit the temporary withdrawal of staff to take out the breakdown train in an emergency, as such a practice would throw maintenance schedules into disarray and risk delay to the return of units to traffic.

Previously, members of the breakdown gang learned their trade by personal observation on the job. Supervisors in particular usually started off at an outlying depot and built up experience as their careers progressed. In current times however, special training is expected, which tends to lead to the need for a team dedicated to breakdown work alone. Further, in the past the breakdown train might have been the first to arrive on site with specialist equipment with which to carry out rescue operations, while by the 1970s the emergency services would have often got there first by road, leaving the breakdown gang to carry out the recovery and clearing-up operations.

Modern locomotives and rolling stock tend to be more sophisticated and therefore prone to damage from mishandling, and re-railing of these locomotives by dragging over ramps is no longer likely to be appropriate. Very often, the locomotives are heavier than their steam counterparts

would have been, and the overall load cannot be reduced by splitting off the tender to be dealt with separately. Today's locomotives also require lifting only at specific points allowed for in their design and these points are intended for lifting in maintenance shops rather than out on the line, perhaps with the locomotive lying in a far from a vertical position. The means of attaching lifting equipment almost inevitably requires the use of specialist lifting brackets, frequently unique to the class of vehicle concerned, together with a lifting beam. The point of lift is almost invariably at a greater reach than was common in the days of the steam railway, when a pair of 'J' hooks would have merely been passed under the buffer beam or headstock.

Appendix 5 details a report on the problems encountered during the recovery of a pair of Type 3 English Electric diesel locomotives in 1964. It was written to detail any problem areas arising when using the new lifting equipment in a double crane lift, and is believed to be the first time that the Western Region's two 75-ton Cowan Sheldon cranes were used together when recovering a mainline diesel locomotive on a running line.

As the railways developed towards the present era, the traditional strut-jib breakdown crane became less able to cope. An increasing mileage of track featuring overhead electrification equipment hindered the use of fixed-length strut-jib cranes, resulting in greater use of alternative means of re-railing vehicles, such as specialist jacking equipment, and also provided scope for use of the telescopic jibs by then usual for road-mobile cranes. The higher overall operating speeds for a railway increasingly devoted to passenger carrying rather than conveying freight, was leading to a requirement for service stock, such as breakdown trains, to approach these speeds, with consequential effects on the design of the vehicle suspension and the necessity to adopt air braking. The use of heavily super-elevated track of up to 150 mm (6in) associated with the upgrading of line speeds was becoming much more widespread. The resulting inclination of a crane on the rails is detrimental to its load-lifting performance and, whilst hydraulically-powered cranes can often be levelled when propping up, such a tilt still would have an adverse effect on stability when 'free on rail'. There was also a need to pay greater attention to operator

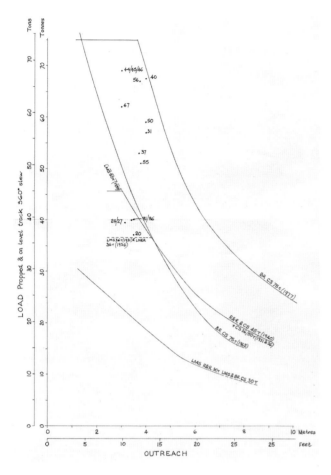

Figure 34 Graphs of load against outreach required to lift one end of diesel and electric locomotives, for cranes built from 1936 to 1977. The outreach required to undertake a lift of a locomotive is considered to be the distance from its front to the point at which a lift may be applied to the locomotive, and the outreach available is the lifting radius of the crane minus the distance from the kingpin to the front, or the crane's portée. *Author*

does depend on arriving at the site the right way round in relation to the recovery to be carried out. Nonetheless, this type of crane was still very useful in handling multiple units and other items of rolling stock. On the other hand, in the absence of smaller locomotives and the traditional four-wheel wagons, there was simply no further use for the 30-ton cranes in breakdown and recovery work.

Until this point, the usual practice was to quote the maximum load that a crane could safely lift with the jib orientated anywhere in its 360° slewing circle. The lifting of modern locomotives mentioned previously might be with the jib generally in line with the carriage, when the stability of the crane was likely to be greater than with the jib over the side. For instance, the propping base of the 75-ton cranes in-line, provided by the dolly jacks at the side of the carriage, was 24ft 3in, compared with 17ft 6in across the jacks at the ends of the propping girders. In these circumstances, it was worth recalculating the performance of the crane to improve the safe lifting capacity with the jib in-line and thereby permit the crane to lift to the greater reach required for so many of the larger diesel locomotives.

Following the ministrations of the Committee, further rationalisation was recommended to meet the then-current perceived requirements with the change over from steam to diesel or electric traction and the decline of individual wagon freight movements. Under these plans, all cranes of less than 36-ton capacity were earmarked for prompt withdrawal. These were to be replaced by new thoroughly up-to-date diesel-powered cranes and all existing 75-ton and some 45-ton steam cranes were to be upgraded by conversion to diesel propulsion, following which a reduced fleet of 25 cranes, all diesel propelled, was envisaged by the early 1980s.

The features recommended by the Working Party for the new cranes were as follows:

a) High-capacity 152.4 tonne (150 ton) crane capable of lifting 71.1 tonnes (70 tons) at 9.14m (30ft) radius, or more importantly 4.27m (14ft) portée or outreach from the front of the carriage

b) Medium capacity 76.2 tonne (75 ton) crane able to lift 45.7 tonne (45 tons) at 6.09m (20ft) radius

As will be realised, the high-capacity type was way beyond the specification then available and inevitably would require new cranes to be constructed. The medium-capacity crane on the other hand might be achieved by modernisation of the existing 75- and 45-ton cranes. The committee made various stipulations for the proposed new cranes, with a view to obtaining extremely reliable, robust and modern high-capacity cranes with maximum outreach performance, flexibility in operation, easy to set up for work and suitable for the arduous working conditions to be found on the

comfort and health-and-safety aspects of work on the railway, including noise control.

The elimination of alternative routes, quadruple lengths of track and refuge sidings, together with the singling of some double-track lines, rendered it more difficult to divert trains held up by any incident to enable them to proceed on their way and allow the breakdown train through to reach the site. The reduction in crane numbers led to increased distances being covered by individual cranes.

One of the most onerous duties for any breakdown crane is the requirement to lift one end of a larger diesel or electric locomotive whose point of lift is some distance in from the end. In these circumstances the available portée, or reach in front of the crane, is more significant than the mere radius at which the specified load can be lifted. This is illustrated by the graph above (Figure 34) showing the load anywhere on the 360° slewing circle plotted against the outreach in front of the carriage provided by the existing and the future types of cranes proposed, and that required to be able to lift various classes of locomotive. From this, it can be seen that the original 75-ton cranes could lift their maximum load only at rather small outreaches and that therefore, strictly speaking, many classes of locomotive were beyond their capability. The need for cranes with greater capacity was thereby clearly demonstrated.

It is interesting to note that in the lower load ranges, the outreach of the old 45-ton cranes was remarkably good. The reason for this was that, unlike the 75-ton cranes, which had a symmetrical layout, the kingpin of the 45-ton ones was offset to one end of the carriage. The advantage of this was that it enabled the crane to approach closer the object to be lifted and evened out the maximum axle loads when in train formation, but this railway. Matters covered included: strut jib, diesel-electric transmission system on the grounds of reliability, the preferred speed of carrying out the crane's motions, limiting tail radius, facilities within the driver's cab, braking systems, ancillary equipment, powered outriggers, stability factors, lighting and the provision of a safe-load indicator for both propped and free-on-rail conditions.

The 75-tonne Telescopic-jib Cranes

During the intervening period between the respective 1955 and 1970 studies, great strides had been made in the design and manufacture of road-mobile and other forms of cranes, particularly in welding techniques for high-strength steels, hydraulic systems and rams to provide the crane's motions, and with the adoption of telescopic jibs, all leading to a vast increase in maximum possible load capacity. Most of these elements could be applied to rail-mounted cranes.

Between the time of the Working Party's review in 1969 and another census in 1973, a further reduction in the number of derailments was recorded, the consequence of which was that financial authority was obtained from the Investment Committee on 14 August 1973 to place orders for only six machines of the larger size and for converting the existing ten 75-ton steam cranes to diesel as part of a package for breakdown and re-railing equipment at a cost of £2,355,000. Nonetheless, a little over a year later the Executive Director Systems & Operations was seeking an additional £1,110,000, the estimated cost for the new cranes increasing from £960,000 to £1,596,000, and the conversions from £200,000 to £344,000!

Tenders for the supply of new 75-tonne cranes were invited from a range of European rail-crane suppliers against a comprehensive specification drawn up by the Chief Mechanical and Electrical Engineer's Department which, however, called for a telescopic, rather than a strut jib. The result was that the order was fulfilled by Northern Engineering Industries, Clarke Chapman Cranes Ltd's Cowans Sheldon branch from their St Nicholas Works, Carlisle in 1977. These cranes were of an innovative new design, at least as far as high-capacity cranes in United Kingdom were concerned, and were the first telescopic-jib cranes supplied by the company. In times of considerable inflation, the tender price was £386,673 and the final cost ended up at an average of £432,535 each.

A newly-constructed 75-tonne telescopic-jib crane stands outside Cowans Sheldon's St Nicholas Works in 1977. In the yellow livery and BR emblem, but as yet with no number, lettering or notice plates, other than the company's name and BR's double-ended arrow. Note also that the buffer housings have been painted red. The hydraulic rams to swing the outriggers have yet to be fitted. *Cowans Sheldon, S.M. Baker & R. Taylor collections*

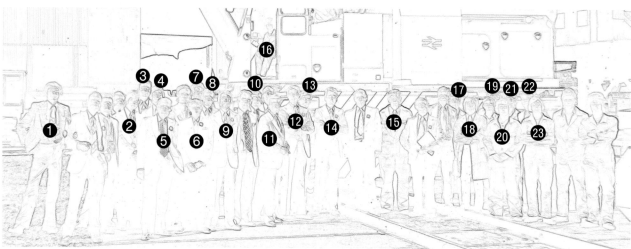

A number of Cowans Sheldon's personnel and BR officials stand proudly in front of the crane. Those identified include:

1. Tom Smith – Hydraulic Engineer
2. David Edgington – Series Crane Manager
3. Gerald Burton – BRB
4. John Steele – Commercial Manager
5. Tom Barlow – Works Superintendent
6. John Walker – Buyer
7. Ken Moseley – BRB Doncaster
8. Harold Sowden – Company Secretary
9. Raymond McCreadie – Works Manager
10. Alan Bisby (with glasses) – BRB Doncaster
11. Jack Haswell – Chief Engineer
12. Peter Robinson – BRB Doncaster

13. Roger Baker – Managing Director NEI Cranes
14. Simon Baker – General Manager
15. Tom Mark – Electrical Foreman
16. Raymond Cartner – Fitter
17. Jimmy Carswell – Charge-hand Fitter
18. John Hind – Project Manager
19. Joe Carswell – Charge-hand Fitter
20. Jimmy Cartwright – Fitter
21. Bobby Carswell – Fitter
22. Fred McMurray – Fitting Shop Foreman
23. Steven Cowen - Fitter

Cowans Sheldon, M. Buttkereit collection

Crewe Diesel Depot's 75-tonne telescopic-jib crane No ADRC 96713 is shown at Crewe Diesel Depot on 24 July 1987 in the yellow livery. *M.S. Welch*

Cowans Sheldon 75-tonne diesel crane No ADRC 96715 awaits the call of duty at Upperby, Carlisle, on 12 August 1991 with hook drawn up against the underside of the telescopic jib. *P. Fidczuk*

Another view of ADRC 96715 at Upperby. Note the counterweight in travelling position near to the driver's cab and the lifting beam carried on the relieving bogie. The propping-jack spreader plates and extension pieces are also slung on the underside of the bogie. *P. Bartlett*

The most obvious feature of the new cranes was the adoption of the telescopic jib. Not only would this afford improved access under obstructions such as overhead line equipment, but it enabled the match wagon to be dispensed with, thereby substantially shortening the length of the crane in train formation, together with the elimination of the need for any articulation of the jib. The reduction in the width of the jib foot also made the accommodation of the driver's cab more readily achievable. The jib was of rectangular cross section of welded steel plate, in two lengths, and was capable of having a fly jib temporarily fitted for the purpose of lifting light loads at large radius. Instead of mechanical operation of the motions by means of gears, shafts, wire ropes and tackle, these functions could now be performed by hydraulic motors and cylinders.

The other major change over previous practice in the United Kingdom was the adoption of hinged outriggers. These were swung out from the side of the crane carriage to provide the props when making all larger lifts, whilst in train formation they provided the means by which some of the dead load of the crane was dispersed into the relieving bogies at each end of the carriage.

As previously mentioned, to achieve the constraints of the specification inevitably led to some design compromises. The narrow width of the track gauge severely restricted the crane's stability when free on rail, while the amount of counterbalance that could be incorporated was limited by the risk of overturning. Any increase in total dead load in the carriage was constrained by the maximum permitted axle load and practical limits to the number of axles, their minimum spacing and the effect on the crane's outreach of over-lengthy carriages. For many decades, all larger cranes in the United Kingdom had adopted four-axle carriages with relieving bogies at each end and the king pin just forward of the second axle, as exemplified by the 45-tonners discussed previously. On the other hand, the 75-tonners with a symmetrical carriage had uneven axle loads, with the rear relieving bogie carrying a greater load than the forward one.

In adopting diesel propulsion from the outset for the new cranes, it was possible to devise a counterweight which could be moved along the rear portion of the superstructure. While travelling and working free on the rail, with the option to slew through the full 360°, the 20.1-tonne counterweight would be stowed in a forward position towards the centre of the crane. This could, however, be moved to the rear of the superstructure to improve stability when working in a propped condition, or free on rail within ±10° of the crane's longitudinal centreline. It was only by the adoption of such a feature that the axle loads, within the prescribed limits, could be optimised throughout, and the required load and reach performance could be achieved.

The main powerplant was a Rolls-Royce C6TFL diesel engine capable of developing 280bhp at 2,000rpm, which drove hydraulic pumps supplying the hydraulic system operating the various motions. Electrical transmission was costly and impractical in the space available within the superstructure and a hydraulic

No ADRC96710 from Bristol, with the assistance of strut-jib 76-tonne No RDH1092 from Toton, demonstrate the lifting of Type 2 diesel locomotive No 24066 at Doncaster during a large-plant demonstration on 5 July 1978. Note the counterweight at the rear position for lifting when propped. Also, the uninterrupted wasp stripes on the right-hand outrigger suggest that the power unit has yet to be fitted. *M.S. Welch*

system was the only possible solution once the choice of telescopic jib had been made. The main pumps were close-coupled to the engine. Of these, variable-displacement pumps supplied the rotating functions of the main hoist or travel motion and auxiliary hoist or slew motion, while a fixed-displacement pump drove the ram functions of the telescopic and derricking motions of the jib. A triple-belt-driven auxiliary pump powered the travelling counterweight and outriggers; the servo systems, travel counterweight locks and travel clutch cylinders; and the make-up oil for closed-loop systems and hoist and slew-brake release. The whole power pack was mounted longitudinally on a 'Joloda' track, which enabled it to be withdrawn from the rear for overhaul. Facilities for routine maintenance were catered for by the provision of full-length platforms each side of the sound-proofed engine housing.

The hydraulic system was capable of fine-precision, slow-speed independently variable control of the motions by means of proportional pilot-operated control valves, together with throttle control of the engine. This was particularly important for hoisting, slewing and travelling, especially while positioning a load precisely; but could also provide faster movement for lower loads.

Two hydraulic rams provided the telescoping function of the jib and another pair the action of derricking the jib at the maximum rated load of 75 tonnes. These rams were protected by positive-lock valves to lock the rams and thereby prevent slip in the unlikely event of a hose or pipe fracture.

The main hoist drum was situated on the superstructure behind the jib, the barrel incorporating an epicylic reduction unit driven by a fixed-displacement piston motor. A 6-tonne auxiliary winch was positioned at the front right-hand side of the superstructure, opposite the cab. Its rope could also be rigged over a sheave at the jib head to enable it to be used as an auxiliary hoist of either 6 tonnes, if single part, or 12 tonnes when reeved with a block in two parts.

The power pack provided sufficient power to enable three motions, such as hoisting, derricking and telescoping, to be carried out simultaneously. In the event of a total breakdown of the power pack, facilities existed for individual motions to be connected to a hand pump, or the Maschinenfabrik Deutschland (MFD) power pack carried on breakdown trains. By this means, the motions could be actuated and restored, albeit slowly in the case of the hand pump, to their stowed position. One depot is understood to have adapted their Bruff road/rail breakdown unit to fulfil the role.

A close view of the carriage and superstructure of No ARDC96710 at Eastleigh on 25 May 2009 during the Eastleigh 100 Open Weekend. *Author*

A side view on the same occasion with the counterweight in the travelling position. Note that the top of the outrigger hinge and more obviously the ends of the roller bearings on the left-hand side are painted white, while those on the right are blue. This was to assist in informing all involved in which direction to describe a crane's movement. *Author*

A rear view of the crane and relieving bogie. Note the lifting beam carried on the bogie. *Author*

Clarke Chapman Patent Relieving Bogie

Up until this point, all British breakdown cranes had used telescopic propping girders, and those adopting four-wheeled relieving bogies employed a pivoted cantilever girder coupled to each end of the crane carriage to share some of the dead-weight with the adjacent bogie while in train formation. In this configuration, the length of the cantilever could be the optimum to enable it to apply the load at the bogie centre and hence achieve equal load on each axle. Also, the ability of the girder to rotate in plan at each end meant that the crane and the bogie were free to move laterally and turn as the ensemble traversed a curve. The length of the outriggers, however, was dictated by other parameters, such as the stability requirements of the crane and practical limitations in use. If now the outriggers were to double up as the means of transmitting load to the bogies as well, they were not long enough to reach the bogie centre and furthermore, once the pair at each end was connected, were inflexible.

To accommodate these issues, Manfred Buttkereit of Clarke Chapman, by then Cowans Sheldon's parent company, invented a sophisticated modified version of the relieving bogie, for which a patent application was filed in the United Kingdom and was granted on 6 August 1975 as No GB 1 498 859. The British patent, however, expired on 10 February 1982 due to non-payment of the renewal fee. There were two aspects to this patent, firstly to couple rigidly to the outriggers to enable the load to be placed at the bogie centre, and secondly in doing so to maintain the ability of the bogie to move laterally relative to the crane when negotiating curves.

The first was achieved by engaging the ends of the outriggers (132 – see drawing on the next page (Figure 35)) in an extension (102) to a coupler (90), so that the top was initially connected by bearing surfaces (108) and (114), which were brought into firm contact by operation of the outrigger jacks. In plan, these bore down on a bearing plate (32) at the end of a lever (22) inside the bogie frame. The coupler (90) was carried on a spherical bearing (92) at the centre of the bogie supported on the lever (22), akin to a steelyard along the longitudinal centreline of the bogie. The bifurcated ends (28) of the lever at the crane end were supported on the bogie frame relatively close to the transverse centreline (34), whilst the remote end extended to behind the headstock (24) where it was latched to the frame (50–64). Whilst this maintained equal distribution of load onto each axle, the pivoted end carried a high proportion of the load, and the latched end the remaining smaller amount, thereby simplifying the release mechanism (66–84) included to assist in coupling and uncoupling.

Above this mechanism was a locking catch to secure the paired outriggers to the bogie. The safety catch (118) was pivoted on the horizontal transverse pin (120), so that as the outriggers entered the bogie, the catch rode up on the chamfered top of the outrigger and dropped over the lug cast into the outrigger top, locking the outrigger into the bogie.

The second matter of negotiating a curve was accomplished by a vertical pivot (100) between the

coupler (90) and the extension (102) to the spherical bearing (92), thereby permitting lateral displacement and rotation of the crane relative to the bogie. On either side of the top trunnion were units that supported the main weight-transfer beam when uncoupled.

Connecting the crane and bogie

When preparing to resume train formation, the outriggers (132) at the end of the crane (12) were swung towards each other into the travelling position and locked together along the line of the track by means of the coupling pin (136). At the side of the bogie at the outer end was hand lever (76). Operating this in either direction changed the direction of the pulling force of the tension spring (84) causing the shaft (66) to rotate the hook lever (60).

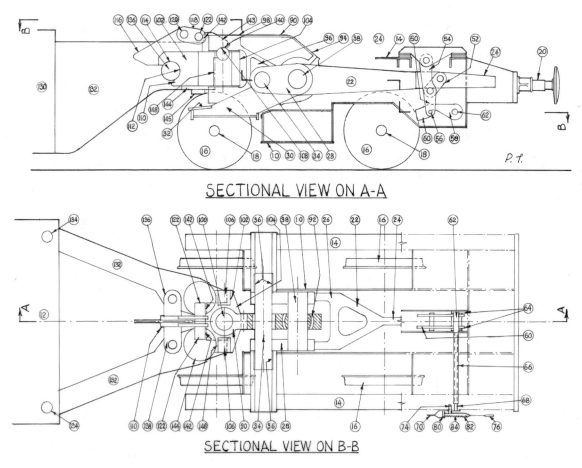

SECTIONAL VIEW ON A-A

SECTIONAL VIEW ON B-B

Figure 35 Longitudinal and plan sectional views of Clarke Chapman's patented relieving bogies. *Author*

Turning the hand lever in the clockwise direction put the hook lever under tension and ready to snap into the locked position as soon as lever (22) was lifted by the force of the outrigger jacks.

The crane was then moved towards the stationary bogie, which had its brakes on, to effect preliminary coupling between them due to pin (122) having been raised up over the sloping faces on the top tip of the outriggers (143) and dropped behind the projecting catches (142). Also as the bogie and crane came together, the inclined face (116) of the vertical plate extension (110) of the coupler passed between the two outriggers until its crutch (112) rested against the bearing surface (138) of coupler (136) between the outriggers. In bringing the crane and bogie together, as (116) rose over (136), this caused longitudinal lever (22) to rotate slightly downwards and lift (32) to its raised position. At this point the two vehicles were connected together and could, if necessary, be drawn in a train, but the bogie was not yet performing its intended function of taking some weight from the crane.

Engagement of the crane with the coupling casting on the relieving bogie was achieved by operating the jacks (145) at the extremity of the outriggers (132) which now bore down on plate (32) of the longitudinal load lever (22). This automatically caused the bearing interfaces to come firmly into contact (108/140 & 114/138). By this means the coupling casting became attached rigidly to the joined outriggers, while continued movement of the jack tended to rotate the coupler (90) because it was prevented from moving downwards by the spherical bearing (92).

The longitudinal load lever (22) having been set in a raised position by the trigger mechanism (50) with lower surface (60) resting on pin (56), was now raised by load applied at the opposite end, causing connecting lift-link (52) to pull the drop-link (54) towards the headstock, in turn causing the pin at its bottom end (56) to engage with the hook element of a lever (58). Further load on the lever (22) through the spherical bearing (92) was now equally shared by the two wheel axles. The jacks (145) of the outriggers were now gently retracted to cause slight reverse movement in lever (22) and positively engage pin (56) in the hook of lever (58).

The outer (i.e. bogie) end of the coupling casting was joined to the main load-transfer beam by means of a substantial trunnion with a vertical axis, allowing articulation in a horizontal plane only. Thus when the crane negotiated a curve, the coupling casting trunnion was displaced from the centreline towards the outside of the curve, but this was accommodated by means of the pivot in the coupler and spherical bearing on the load lever.

The extension (24) to the longitudinal load lever (22) afforded the opportunity in the event of failure of the outrigger jacks, in an emergency, very gently to raise this using the crane's hook, or to be raised by a jack placed within the extension of the bogie structure behind the headstock.

Disconnecting the bogie from the crane

To reset the longitudinal lever (22) in its upper position, the relieving pre-select hand lever (76) was operated against the spring (84) to its raised position, which

	COMPONENTS OF THE CLARKE CHAPMAN PATENT RELIEVING BOGIE			
Component	Description		Component	Description
10	Relieving bogie		90	Load-transfer coupler pivoted on 92
12	Carriage of crane		92	Spherical bearing on 38
14	Frame of relieving bogie		94	Vertical element of 90 forked at crane end
16	Wheels of relieving bogie		96	Aperture in 94 through which 34 freely passes
18	Axle between wheels 16		98	Limb of 94 embracing 104
20	Buffers at outer end of relieving bogie		100	Vertical pin connecting 94 & 102
22	Longitudinal lever transferring load to 10		102	Part of load-transfer coupler member of relieving bogie
24	Extension of 22 towards buffers		104	Concave part of coupler member of 102
26	Forked portion of 22		106	Limbs of 102/104 carrying hardened steel pin
28	Limbs of 26 extending towards crane		108	Upper bearing surface of 106
30	Lower level extensions of 28		110	Vertical link of 104
32	Transverse connecting plate between 30		112	Recess in 110
34	Transverse intermediate fulcrum pin supporting 28 and on 14 journaled to 36		114	Bearing surface of 112 to transmit draw bar forces
36	Transverse journal in 14 for pin 34		116	Vertical plate extension of 110
38	Transverse pin between bogie & 22 centred between axles		118	Safety device pivoted at 120 to extension of 116
			120	Pivot between 116 & 118
50	Holding mechanism for lever 22		122	Horizontal pin welded to 118
52	Lift-link between 22 & 50			
54	Drop-link pinned at top to frame 14		130	Headstock of crane
56	Pin on 54 which engages with hook 60		132	Hinged outriggers cantilever beams to crane
58	Longitudinal member pivoted to 14 by pin 62		134	Vertical axes of outrigger pivots
60	Hook on 58 which engages with pin 56		136	Coupling pin between outriggers 132
62	Transverse pin to support one end of 58		138	Bearing surface on 136 corresponding with 114
64	Journals to 62		140	Downward-facing bearing surface corresponding with 108
66	Hollow transverse shaft attached to 62		142	Vertical bearing surface (catch) corresponding with 122
68	Transverse shaft extension of 66 journaled to 14		143	Sloping edge on top corner of 132
70	Lever with elongated slot		144	Cylinder of hydraulic jack on outrigger 132
74	Short transverse shaft through 70 & on the end of which is 76		145	Piston of hydraulic jack on outrigger 132
76	Relieving pre-select hand lever on 74 with lower side limb		148	Outer surface of jack cylinder 144
80	Pin on 70			
82	Pin on side limb			
84	Tension spring connecting 80 & 82			

turned shaft (62). Lever (58) only disengaged from the hook on pin (56) however, once the jacks (145) were actuated causing lever (22) to rotate about the fulcrum (34) and releasing the hook from pin (56). With retraction of the jacks, lever (22) was able to rotate about the fulcrum again, which allowed the coupler (90) to come out of contact with the outriggers (132) of the crane and also caused holding mechanism (50) to revert to its normal position. The safety device (118) was then lifted clear of the catches on the top of the outriggers by means of a lever on the side of the bogie at the crane end. With withdrawal of the crane, the extent to which

the load-transfer coupler could fall was limited by a rubbing pad, thereby presenting the components at an appropriate height for reconnection.

In the past, with traditional relieving bogies, there had often been difficulty in coupling up the bogies on anything other than straight and level track. On the new bogies, a fully articulated bearer permitted the coupling-up under any track condition and catered for the subsequent movement of the crane and bogie as the assembly travelled along the line. Although the point of connection could be off-centre from the bogie, the patented load transfer system provided longitudinal

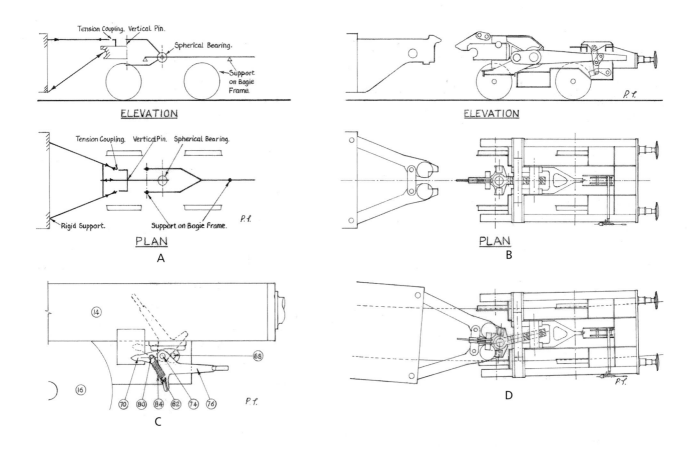

Figure 36 A) Schematic and force diagram for Clarke Chapman relieving bogie; B) View of relieving bogie separated from crane; C) Scrap view on relieving pre-select lever; D) Crane and relieving bogie in plan on 80m radius curve. *All Author*

Main sequence of connecting the bogie to the crane and the transfer of load.

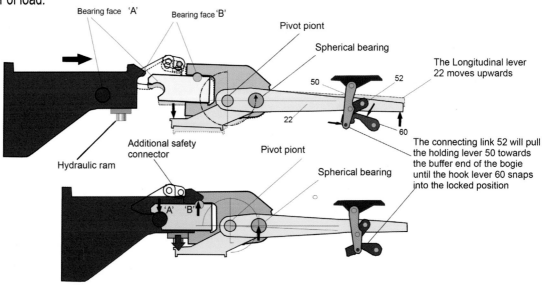

1. Connect both outriggers 132 with coupling pin 136

2. Drive outriggers slowly into the bogie till the coupler is in contact with bearing face 'A' and 'B'. The guide plate 116 will align the coupler 102 into the right position.

3. Activate the hydraulic ram and apply pressure on to the connecting plate of the lever extension 32.
As the hydraulic pressure is increased the coupler will be locked under tension with the outrigger arrangement.
As the hydraulic pressure is increased further some of the weight of the crane is transferred on to the bogie.
When the end of the lever 22 reaches the preset position the locking device is activated and will retain the lever in a predetermined position.

4. The hydraulic pressure of the ram can now be released.
The predetermined load of the crane is now transferred over the spherical bearing on to the bogie.

Figure 37 The sequence of connecting the bogie to the crane and the transfer of load. *Manfred Buttkereit*

The inner end of the Clarke Chapman relieving bogie designed to receive the ends of a pair of outriggers from the crane and showing the brake hoses. Beyond the horizontal grey areas are the bearing plates onto which the jacks press. *W. Lee*

rigidity in the vertical plain between the crane and bogie when in travelling mode, thereby affording equal load distribution into the two axles.

Using the outriggers to bear on the relieving bogies meant that the jacks had to be positioned some distance above rail level, whereas when propping the crane the ground support was likely to be at rail level or lower. To make up this difference in height and reduce the amount of packing required, aluminium sections with interlocking spigots were provided and, when out of use, carried in purpose-made racks on the relieving bogies.

To enable the crane to move about the site of operations under its own power, it was first necessary to swing in the outriggers. These could not sensibly take up their travelling position, because more often than not they would then obstruct the work. Provision had therefore been made for them to be folded back against the side of the crane. In this position, they would not totally satisfy load-gauge requirements for normal travel, but it was considered adequate for moving about on site at slow speed and in particular clearing platform edges.

Telescopic 75-tonne No ADRC96713 and strut-jib 76-tonne No ADRC96709 cranes set about restoring No 45074 to the rails at Chinley North Jct on 16 January 1982. The Type 4, following a misunderstanding between the driver and signalman, had gone through the trap points the day before. Note the stack of three aluminium sections on top of piles of timber packing to take the reaction loads imposed by the outriggers. *M.S. Welch*

75-tonne crane No ADRC96712 from Old Oak Common makes its way behind Type 4 diesel locomotive No 47341 through Oxford one evening in August 1990. *G. Spink, courtesy 53A Models*

In train formation, the crane was designed to travel at speeds of up to 75mph (120kph). It was not easy to accommodate this requirement and yet also provide satisfactory ride characteristics for slow speeds when propelling itself 'free on rail'. Whereas all previous cranes had used blocking screws to render the wheel springs inoperable when the crane was travelling under its own power with the jib raised from the match wagon, this was no longer considered acceptable to the permanent-way engineer. Coil springs and hydraulic dampers were therefore employed to provide the vertical suspension, and guide posts to restrain the wheel sets in the horizontal directions. Most wheel axles were mounted on twin spherical bearings, but the centre pair in the crane carriage had roller bearings to permit a lateral displacement of up to 40mm when negotiating curves down to 80m radius (4 chains). Under test, the prototype crane satisfactorily reached speeds of 85mph (135kph).

The outer axles of the carriage were fitted with gearboxes driven by two-speed hydraulic motors through a single-spur reduction to provide the crane's self-propulsion at speeds of up to 5mph (8kph). Engaging and disengaging the travel gears was achieved by means of a sliding pinion inside each gearbox being moved in and out of mesh by a hydraulic ram. The crane and relieving bogies were fully equipped with an automatic two-pipe air-brake system acting on disc brakes, and a through-vacuum brake pipe for use when in train formation, while the direct air brake could be operated by the driver from the cab when self-propelling. The telescopic 75-tonne cranes could shunt a 100-tonne load on a 1 in 35 gradient.

The superstructure was mounted on a slewing ring of tapered rollers, with the slewing motion achieved by means of a pair of epicyclic slewing units driven by fixed displacement motors positioned diametrically opposite each other outside the main-jib-foot support frame.

Structurally, a telescopic jib in supporting the load acts largely in bending, rather than principally as a strut member in compression as was the case for the previous types. Greater strength was also required to cater for dynamic-loading effects while travelling and laterally to prevent collapse of the cross-section of the jib. The result was a much heavier jib, which worked against the crane's overall stability. To limit the weight as far as practical, therefore, a high-tensile, low-alloy steel was used which brought with it challenges in welding techniques for such material to avoid cracking and consequential risk of fatigue failure. Particular attention was given to the sliding surfaces of the telescopic sections, with wear-resistance pads at the critical points. The length of the telescopic jib was infinitely variable between a minimum of 10.89m (35ft 9in) and a maximum of 15.93m (52ft 3in) by the operation of twin double-acting hydraulic cylinders by means of twin double-acting hydraulic derricking rams between the underside of the jib and the top plate of the revolving structure. The jib could be inclined at any angle between 55° and -6° to the horizontal. With the jib fully retracted, the minimum radius of operation was 4m. When propped and operating with the jib at an angle of less than 15° to the horizontal, due to the high hydraulic pressures induced in the derricking rams, the lifting capacity was severely restricted.

The lift capabilities on the main hoist for the various conditions of the crane and when level and on super-elevated track, or cant, of up to 50mm (2in) are given in Table 1 and shown graphically in the drawing below (Figure 38). Within an angle of ±10° from the longitudinal centreline, the crane could lift greater loads when free on rail than through the full 360° slew. It could operate on cant of up to 150mm (6in) and this had the effect of reducing the permissible load by between 1 and 3 tonnes when propped, and ½ tonne when free on rail through 360° slew, but by as much as 5 tonnes when working over the end. Propped, the auxiliary hoist when rigged with two falls could take 12 tonnes out to 12m radius, reducing to 8.5 tonnes at 14.75m, but when 'free on rail', the permissible load started to fall below 12 tonnes from a radius of 7.5m and could not operate at more than a 12m radius.

With the upper section of the jib retracted, there was no longer a large overthrow on rounding curves and therefore articulation was unnecessary. With its relatively short jib, on a superstructure centrally placed on the carriage, the crane could travel in train formation with the jib either way round.

With the elimination of the match truck by virtue of the telescopic jib, another place had to be found to stow the ram's-horn hook. Due to the relative lateral movement while rounding curves, it was not considered expedient to rest the hook on the relieving bogie. Instead, a procedure was adopted whereby, while the jib was in the fully-depressed position and completely retracted, a pair of special short stowage ropes was attached between the lower section of the jib and the ram's-horn. Once the ropes were fitted, the jib was gently extended sufficiently to draw the hook against the underside of the upper jib section, where it was secured in place by a pin and the jib finally withdrawn to its fully-retracted position.

A 74-tonne lifting beam could be stowed on either of the relieving bogies, whichever was at the opposite end from the jib.

The crane operator's cab was situated on the front left-hand side of the superstructure, from where he had an excellent view of the work area – an unimaginable improvement on the situation on all previous cranes. From this fully-enclosed, environmentally-controlled position, the operator had access to all controls. The operator's supervisor on the ground would be in communication by means of two-way radio, for which purpose individual call signs were allotted to each of these and other surviving cranes, so, by 1985: 'RAIL CRANE 01 to 23'. The operator's response was, however, transmitted by a public address system mounted on the crane, so that all in the vicinity were aware of the intended movements.

To enable the driver to monitor the stability of the crane, a simple readout of load and radius was initially provided on the first four cranes which could be compared against a chart of the crane's performance duties. With such a wide range of conditions under which loads were to be measured, it was not at first found feasible to devise an automatic over-load system of sufficient accuracy. This was especially a problem at low loads, when the hysteresis effect of the sheaves and the safe load was less than the weight of the jib itself. The last two cranes, however, were equipped from new, and the earlier cranes retro-fitted, with a multi-input alarm system, which monitored the condition under which the crane was working and illuminated the display of the actual load and cant against that permitted. It also recorded the maximum cant over which the crane had passed since starting work and used this as the limiting condition when 'free on rail'. This data was processed by an on-board multi-duty computer and

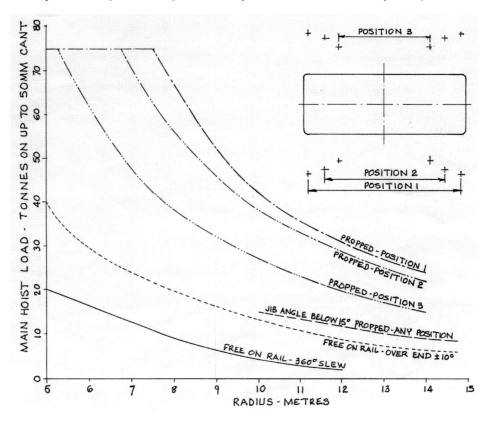

Figure 38 Load/radius performance curves for Cowans Sheldon 75-tonne telescopic-jib crane. *Author*

continually compared with the permissible duties of the crane to assess the safety of a lift. An audible warning was given of any 'out of duty' condition. A mechanical load/radius indicator and wandering lead, which could be used to sound a warning to the driver should the rear wheels start to lift off the rail during a heavy lift, were provided as a back-up.

Safety features were designed and built into various features of the crane, where possible, in an effort to ensure that it could only be operated in a safe, reliable way and to improve the life expectancy of the components. These features comprised a planned procedure for setting up and packing away the cranes, including the engaging and disengaging the travelling gear; the adoption of transit collars for the derricking rams; the removal and insertion of various pins in the relieving bogies to ensure the taking up of the appropriate load while in train formation; counterweight position locks; brake-isolating levers; and a battery-isolating switch. Striker bars at the jib head activated limit switches to prevent over-hoisting, or over-lowering the block. A slew lock was provided so that the superstructure was positively locked against rotation and its rear supported off the carriage while in train formation. Warning hooters were attached around the crane, to be sounded prior to commencing a movement. A dead-man's button had to be depressed during the operation of the travel and slewing motions. A log book was provided and kept with the crane at all times.

The arrival of such sophisticated items of equipment emphasised the need for a thorough training programme for the breakdown staff that would be called upon to use the cranes, and this was undertaken at Kingmoor over the winter of 1980/1. In due course, a video was produced to assist in this process.

Originally, it was necessary to pull the outriggers round to position by hand, but it was soon found that these were so heavy that manpower was insufficient to move them into position, especially on super-elevated track. A design modification had to be implemented to provide hydraulic rams to power this function and, because the angle moved through exceeded 180° and everything had to be folded back within the loading gauge for travelling, the rams operated through a rack.

The outriggers were also part of coupling the crane to the relieving bogies, but it was not unknown when passing over a hump in the track for the train to separate at this point. To alleviate the problem, additional top blocks were made and fitted to prevent uncoupling while in motion. The slew lock pin, which kept the superstructure in line when travelling, was also modified by the provision of an interlock to prevent the travel gear being left in, or re-engaged, until the slew lock was released. In 1979, re-engagement of the travel gear with the slew lock engaged on one of the cranes ruined the travel motors, valves and pipe-work, resulting in a repair cost of £26,000.

To afford greater route availability, Glasgow's crane No ADRC96711, was from the outset provided with less ballast weight. It could, however, still lift a maximum of 75 tonnes, albeit at a lesser radius than the remainder of the fleet. Later, its maximum capacity was reduced to 60 tonnes. Perhaps as a consequence, when rebuilding of the whole class was undertaken, as described later, this crane was the candidate for withdrawal and the source of spare parts for the remainder.

BR 75-TONNE COWANS SHELDON TELESCOPIC JIB CRANES					
Nos		Year built	Works No	Remarks and Allocation	Overhaul/ Current status
1st	2nd				
ADB 966094	ADRC 96715	1977	31145	Kingmoor 1980–4/4/88, Upperby 2/91–3/93, Stratford 30/9/94–1997, Old Oak Common 3/97–2/98, Thornaby 11/02, Hither Green 2004, MoD Ludgershall 07/05, Oak Common 6/06–5/08, Toton 5/08–31/3/09, Bescot 2010–4/12.	1999–2002/ Extant
ADB 966089	ADRC 96710	1977	31146	Bristol 1977–9/80, Upperby 10/85, Cardiff 4/88–3/90, Crewe 2/91–4/98, (national spare 3/93), Old Oak Common 06/8/00–2006, Old Oak Common OOU 2006–5/09, Knottingly 4/12.	1999–2000/ Extant
ADB 966091	ADRC 96712	1977	31147	Old Oak Common 1977–6/00, Old Oak Common (National spare) 6/8/00–6/01, Derby Etches Park OOU 2002–07/05, Holgate Wagon Works 05/06–27/5/08.	1998–2000/ Withdrawn post-2006 & scrapped R Hull, Rotherham 5/08
ADB 966092	ADRC 96713	1977	31148	Wigan 1977–10/85, Crewe 7/87–2007, Wigan 5/08–4/12.	8/97– 11/98/ Extant
ADB 966093	ADRC 96714	1977/8	31149	Holbeck 1978, Healey Mills 4/81, Cardiff Canton 10/85–2005, Newport/Margam to 2005–6/08, (national spare) 4/12.	4 to 6/97/ Extant
ADB 966090	ADRC 96711	1978	31150	Eastfield 1978–10/85, Haymarket 3/4/88–2/91, Motherwell 3/93–3/95, down-rated, Thornaby 3/97.	Withdrawn 12/97, Stripped for spares and scrapped at Gateshead 1999

Notes:
1. OOU = Out of use
2. Dates shown in *italics* are spot dates upon which the crane is known to have been at the depot concerned.

No ADRC96712 at Old Oak Common during a display of recovery equipment on 19 September 1985. *P. Bartlett*

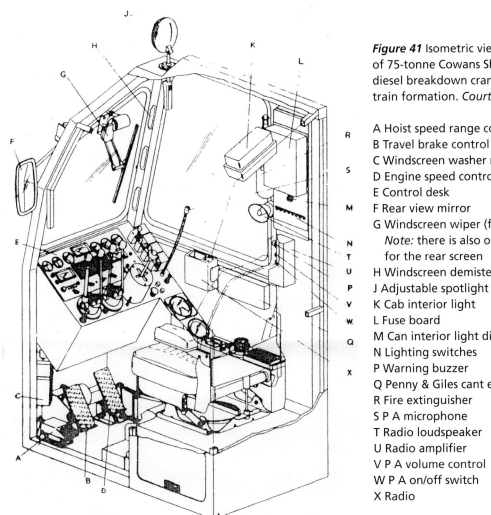

Figure 41 Isometric view of the operator's cab of 75-tonne Cowans Sheldon telescopic-jib diesel breakdown cranes Nos 31145–31150 in train formation. *Courtesy of I Mech Engineers*

A Hoist speed range control pedal
B Travel brake control pedal
C Windscreen washer reservoir
D Engine speed control pedal
E Control desk
F Rear view mirror
G Windscreen wiper (front screen).
　Note: there is also one fitted but not shown for the rear screen
H Windscreen demister outlets
J Adjustable spotlight
K Cab interior light
L Fuse board
M Can interior light dimmer
N Lighting switches
P Warning buzzer
Q Penny & Giles cant equipment
R Fire extinguisher
S P A microphone
T Radio loudspeaker
U Radio amplifier
V P A volume control
W P A on/off switch
X Radio

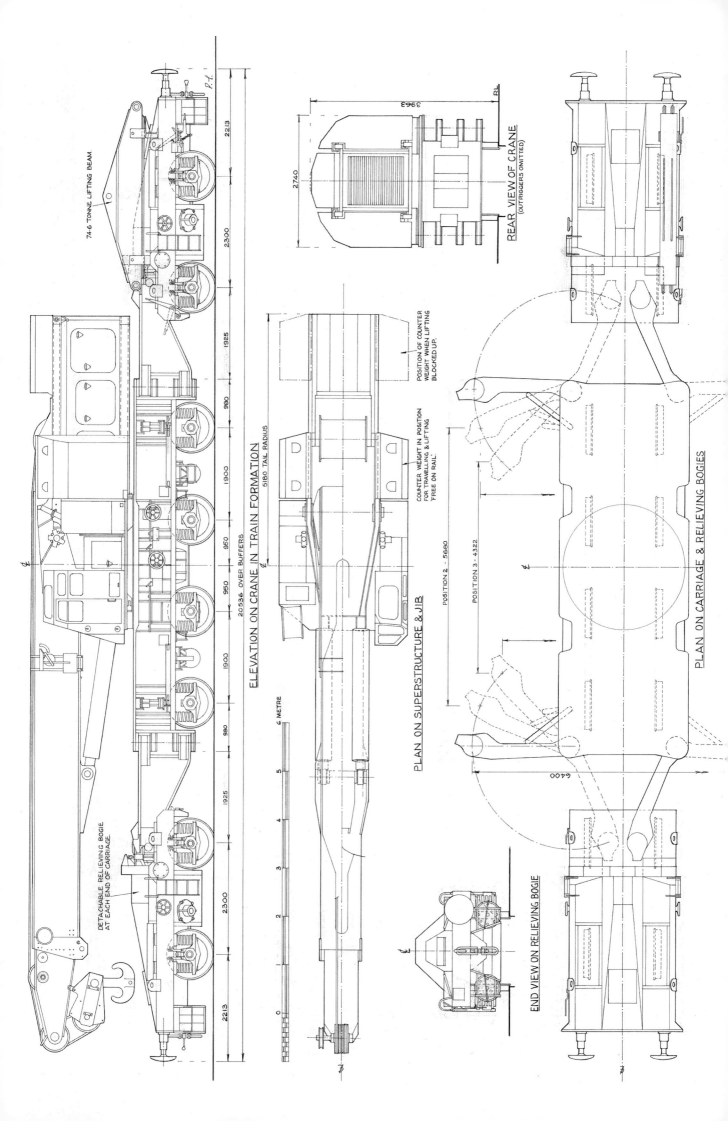

74·6 TONNE LIFTING BEAM.

DETACHABLE RELIEVING BOGIE
AT EACH END OF CARRIAGE.

22¦3   2300   1925   980   1900   950   950   1900   980   1925   2300   22¦3

20536 OVER BUFFERS

ELEVATION ON CRANE IN TRAIN FORMATION

3963

2740

REAR VIEW OF CRANE
(OUTRIGGERS OMITTED)

5180 TAIL RADIUS

POSITION OF COUNTER
WEIGHT WHEN LIFTING
BLOCKED UP.

COUNTER WEIGHT IN POSITION
FOR TRAVELLING & LIFTING
'FREE ON RAIL.

PLAN ON SUPERSTRUCTURE & JIB

0 1 2 3 4 5 6 METRE

END VIEW ON RELIEVING BOGIE

POSITION 2 - 5680

POSITION 3 - 4322

6400

PLAN ON CARRIAGE & RELIEVING BOGIES

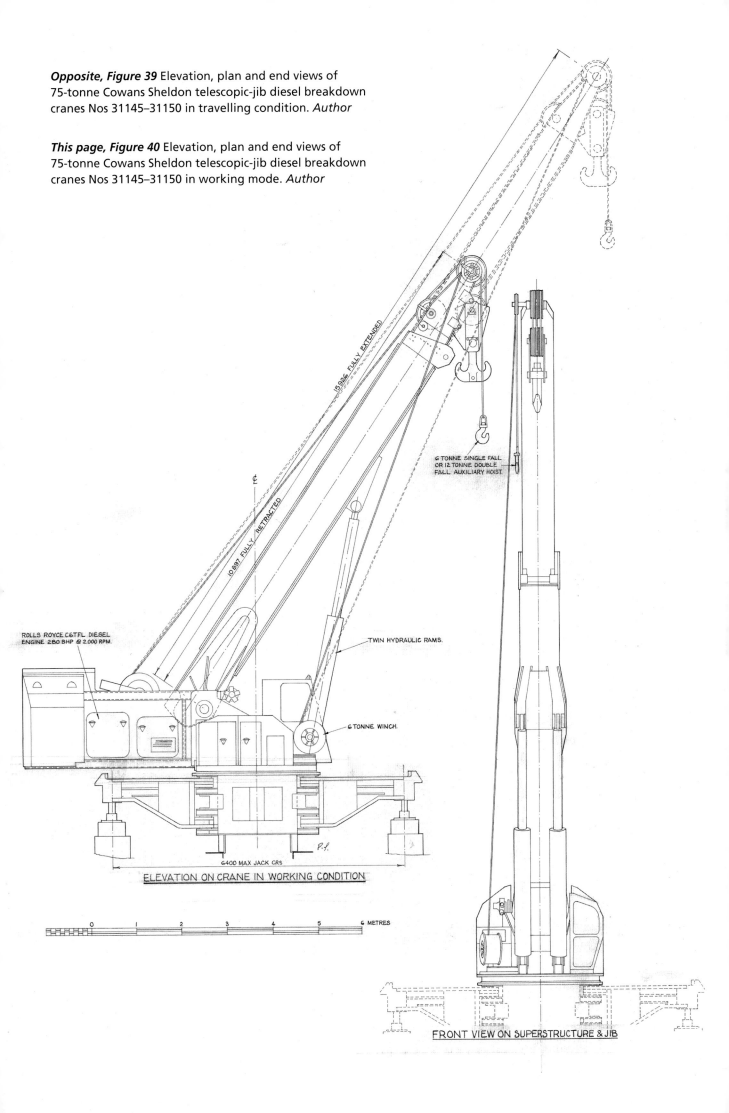

Opposite, Figure 39 Elevation, plan and end views of 75-tonne Cowans Sheldon telescopic-jib diesel breakdown cranes Nos 31145–31150 in travelling condition. *Author*

This page, Figure 40 Elevation, plan and end views of 75-tonne Cowans Sheldon telescopic-jib diesel breakdown cranes Nos 31145–31150 in working mode. *Author*

15926 FULLY EXTENDED

10897 FULLY RETRACTED

6 TONNE SINGLE FALL OR 12 TONNE DOUBLE FALL AUXILIARY HOIST.

ROLLS ROYCE C6TFL DIESEL ENGINE 280 BHP @ 2,000 RPM.

TWIN HYDRAULIC RAMS.

6 TONNE WINCH.

6400 MAX JACK CRS

ELEVATION ON CRANE IN WORKING CONDITION

0   1   2   3   4   5   6 METRES

FRONT VIEW ON SUPERSTRUCTURE & JIB

No ADRC96713 at work at Chinley N. Jct on 11 October 1983. *M.S. Welch*

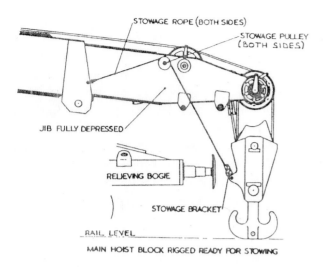

STOWAGE ROPE (BOTH SIDES)
STOWAGE PULLEY (BOTH SIDES)
JIB FULLY DEPRESSED
RELIEVING BOGIE
STOWAGE BRACKET
RAIL LEVEL
MAIN HOIST BLOCK RIGGED READY FOR STOWING

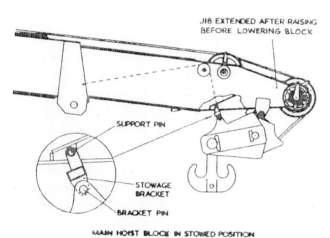

JIB EXTENDED AFTER RAISING BEFORE LOWERING BLOCK
SUPPORT PIN
STOWAGE BRACKET
BRACKET PIN
MAIN HOIST BLOCK IN STOWED POSITION

Figure 42 Stowage arrangements for the block of 75-tonne Cowans Sheldon telescopic-jib diesel breakdown cranes Nos 31145–31150 in train formation. *Courtesy of I Mech Engineers*

A view looking backwards from the jib foot of a 75-tonne crane while undergoing overhaul in the works of Clarke Chapman at Gateshead. *D. Carter collection*

Allocation

Nos 31145 to 31150 were delivered in 1977 and 1978. Initially, they were allocated by British Rail Nos ADB 966089 to ADB 966094, but not in the same order as the works numbers, and it appears unlikely that such numbers were actually applied before being superseded by their new ADRC series of numbers.

Upon delivery, these cranes were allocated to Carlisle (Kingmoor), Bristol, Old Oak Common, Wigan (Spring's Branch), Healey Mills and Glasgow (Eastfield). The Kingmoor crane then moved to Stratford via Upperby, while both the Bristol crane and the Wigan crane found their way to Crewe, one as national spare. The Healey Mills crane went to Cardiff, and Eastfield's went first to Haymarket and then to Motherwell.

Towards the end of the millennium, five of these cranes were in turn thoroughly overhauled by Clarke Chapman at Gateshead. The updates included an improved safe-load indicator, a new Cummins diesel engine, an enhanced hydraulic system, six additional brake disks, improved slew-ring bolts to overcome fatigue failures, better lighting of the work area and a new operator's cab on anti-vibration mountings with a rear-facing video monitor and radio and public address systems. No ADRC96711, the sixth crane,

was withdrawn in December 1997 and during the following year some of its parts were recovered for use in repairing the remainder of the fleet.

In 2006, No ADRC96710 struck an over-bridge and suffered damage, following which it was stored out of use at Old Oak Common until eventually overhauled at Eastleigh. On 31 March 2009, No ADRC96715 struck a 132kV overhead electricity power cable while preparing to undertake a lift at Fairwater Yard, Taunton, causing serious damage to the crane's electrical systems. It was repaired at NEI Sunderland. At the time of writing, there are just four of these cranes left, three allocated to main depots, with one spare to cover as necessary. It would seem that the electronic equipment within these cranes is so sensitive to the ingress of moisture during inclement weather that they have to be kept under cover when not in use.

Liveries

Livery for the new telescopic cranes was all-over yellow from the outset, with black and yellow diagonal zebra hazard markings on the ends of the tail, outer ends of the counterweight, ends of the carriage, buffer beams of the

The headstock of the carriage. On the left-hand outrigger, the power drive to its positioning mechanism can be seen between the two hinge pins. Towards the outer end, folded into a recess is the short arm used to connect the pair of outriggers before being coupled up to the relieving bogie. *D. Carter collection*

The winding drum to the winch or auxiliary hoist. *D. Carter collection*

relieving bogies and on the sides of the outriggers. Red was applied to the block and ram's-horn hook, and the shanks of the buffers, while the wheel centres, springs, axle-horn guides and buffer heads were black. The maker's name was applied in black letters and 'SWL 75 TONNES' in red to the jib side, together with BR's double-ended arrow logo in red on the side of the counterweight. The handbrake wheels, wheel tyres, grab irons, steps and ladders were painted white. In service these cranes were numbered ADRC96710 to ADRC96715.

TABLE 1: COWANS SHELDON 75-TONNE TELESCOPIC JIB BREAKDOWN CRANE – DUTY TABLE																					
Radius (m)	MAIN HOIST (All Loads in Tonnes)																	AUXILIARY HOIST, 1 or 2 Falls			
	BLOCKED Full 360° Slew												FREE ON RAIL					BK'D	FREE ON RAIL		
Outrigger/base (m)	Position 1/6.40				Position 2/5.68				Position 3/4.32				Full 360° Slew			Over-end		1, 2, 3	Over-end	Full 360° Slew	
Jib Angle	Above 15°		Below 15°		Above 15°		Below 15°		Above 15°		Below 15°		Above & Below 15°					Above & Below 15°			
Counter Weight Position	R1	R1	R1	R1	R1	R1	R1	R1	R1	R1	R1	R1	F	F	F	R1	R1	R1	R1	F	F
Cant (mm)	50	150	50	150	50	150	50	150	50	150	50	150	50	100	150	50	150	150	150	50	150
5	75	75			75	75			75	75			20	19.5	18.5	40	35	6/12	6/12	6/12	6/12
5.25	75	75			75	75			75	71			19.5	18.5	17.5	36	32	6/12	6/12	6/12	6/12
6.75	75	75			75	73			51	48			13.5	13	12	25	21	6/12	6/12	6/12	6/12
7.5	75	72			62	60			42	40			11	10.5	10	21	17	6/12	6/12	6/11	6/10
8	67	65			56	63			38	37			9	8.5	8	20	16	6/12	6/12	6/9	6/8
9	52	50			46	43			32	30			6	5.5	5	16	13	6/12	6/12	6/6	5/5
10	42	41	15	15	38	36	15	15	27	26	15	15	4.5	4	3.5	13	10	6/12	6/10	4.5/4.5	3.5/3.5
12	31	30	12	12	29	27	12	12	20	19	12	12	2	1.5	1	9	7	6/12	6/7	2/2	1/1
14	24	23	9	9	22	21	9	9	15	14	9	9	0.5	0	0	7	5	6/9	5/5	-	-
14.75			8.5	8.5			8.5	8.5			8.5	8.5	0	0	0	6	4.5	6/8.5	4.5/4.5	-	-

Notes:
R1 = Counter weight in rear position for lifting when propped and free-on-rail over-end condition.
F = Counter weight in forward position for travelling and when lifting free-on-rail through 360° slew condition.
   = No duty available.

From tentative beginnings, over a period of thirteen years the Southern Region's diesel-powered 75-ton crane has developed into the 75-tonne telescopic version described above. No. DB965186 from Wimbledon Park is being drawn out of the sidings at Chertsey on 3rd March 1970 by a Birmingham RCW type 3 diesel locomotive. *Author*

10
Conversion of Steam Cranes

Conversion of 75-ton Steam Cranes

Within a decade of the introduction of the British Transport Commission (BTC) cranes during the early 1960s, steam motive power had been eliminated from British Railways and the continued use of this form of propulsion on breakdown cranes was becoming more and more of an anachronism. Whilst initially there remained plenty of men brought up and trained in the use and maintenance of steam power, with the passing of time gradually these men retired to be replaced by younger staff familiar only with diesel or electric propulsion. Moreover, with the decline of freight traffic, and in particular the elimination of the smaller wagons in unfitted goods trains and shunting at wayside station yards, the need for the smaller 30-ton variety of crane had virtually disappeared. Also, the hindrance caused to crane operations by the presence of the increasing mileage of overhead-electrification equipment rendered strut-jib cranes less useful.

The 30-ton steam cranes were therefore withdrawn in the early 1970s, after not much more than ten or a dozen years' service, examples being preserved at Birmingham Railway Museum and a pair on the Severn Valley Railway (of which one was scrapped due to its poor condition). Two others were acquired by the Irish Railways, CIE, shipped from Barrow-in-Furness to Dublin North Wall on 11 June 1973 and in due course re-gauged at Inchicore for further use on the Irish system, where they remained until laid aside in 2002. Two years later, as in the interim no preservation society had shown interest, they were cut up.

The Southern Region's diesel-powered cranes having proved satisfactory, the British Railways Board Working Party, in its report of 1970, proposed an examination of the feasibility of the conversion of the remaining 75-ton steam cranes. The provision of kits of parts to railways overseas, consisting of diesel engines and hydraulic power packs enabling them to convert their existing steam-propelled breakdown cranes to more up-to-date means of propulsion, had become almost routine to Cowans Sheldon by this period.

Following the enactment of the Transport Act in 1968, the British Rail Workshops were permitted to undertake work for organisations outside BR. As a consequence of the rationalisation, the remaining expertise in the design and construction of rail-mounted cranes and associated lifting equipment was brought together from the five separate regions as a unit of the Plant & Machinery HQ, part of the Director of Mechanical & Electrical Engineer's Department at Doncaster. When Derby Locomotive Works was tendering for the conversion of five of the Ministry of Defence's 45-ton cranes of both Cowans Sheldon and Ransomes & Rapier build, they approached this unit to undertake the work. On winning the contract, this specialised unit undertook the detailed design, while the work was carried out at Derby, the first conversion being completed in 1974. Although the conversion work was basic, replacing the steam propulsion by diesel power, the task nonetheless gave those involved valuable experience for the future, particularly regarding the diesel-hydraulic drive element.

In due course, following the delivery of BR's six new telescopic-jib 75-tonne cranes in 1977, the opportunity was taken to give a new lease of life to BR's 75-ton steam cranes by providing them with diesel-hydraulic propulsion and uprating their lifting capacities. All the work was undertaken by British Rail Engineering Ltd to designs prepared by the Headquarters Plant and Services Section of the Chief Mechanical and Electrical Engineer, British Railways Board. Between 1977 and 1979, all ten cranes were taken into Derby Locomotive Works, where their boilers, water tanks, coal boxes and cylinders, small diesel generators, etc were removed and replaced by a General Motors Detroit 6V-71N diesel engine which developed 238bhp at 2,100rpm. This drove a Sundstrand Series 25 variable-displacement hydraulic pump which provided a flow of oil to two Sundstrand Series 22 fixed-displacement hydraulic motor/brake and speed-reduction units located on each crab side. These drove the main crane driveshaft through two shaft-hung Holroyd Croft reduction units. All valves required for the closed-loop circuit were contained within the hydraulic pump and motors. Cooling was achieved by a heat exchanger mounted in front of the diesel-engine water radiator. The transmission system was developed to avoid any alteration to the existing gear mechanisms on the crane, and as far as possible to retain the original operating techniques. The work involved the fitting of a new derricking drum, gear wheel and associated shafts, to accommodate a new derricking rope of the same diameter as the original, but of enhanced performance.

Each hydraulic motor was fitted with a flexible drive coupling and fail-safe brake assembly, which in the event of the circuit pressure being lost through a leak or hose failure would prevent the load falling before the normal service brakes were applied. Normal service brakes were retained with the exception of the steam travelling brakes, which were replaced by a crane air-brake when the crane was travelling under its own power, with the standard two-pipe automatic train brake for use while being locomotive hauled. The air supply for the crane air-brake was provided by a compressor mounted on and driven by the diesel engine. Through-vacuum brake piping was retained on the crane.

Electrical power for the crane was provided by an alternator driven by the diesel engine. Two sets of 24-volt batteries were fitted, one for normal engine starting purposes and the other for auxiliary circuits. In the event of the starting batteries being flat, the auxiliary set could be brought into circuit in parallel to provide an alternative starting facility. A mains-supply battery charger was located permanently on the crane.

The original cab on the crane was replaced by a combined engine housing and driver's cab, separated by a soundproof bulkhead which also contained the power-pack instruments and gauges, together with an access door to the engine compartment for routine maintenance. The layout of the cab was modernised by the addition of a front bulkhead and control panel, drop-down side windows and sliding doors, cab heater and improved lighting. Hinged side and rear panels were provided to the engine housing for access for maintenance purposes.

In addition, considerable efforts were made to minimise noise levels in the cab, primarily from the diesel engine and power pack, to 85dBA. For instance, the internal walls of the housing were fully lined with sound-insulation material, and acoustically-designed engine air inlet and outlet ducts were fitted to reduce sound levels from the transmission system.

The minimum radius of the jib was reduced from 5.48m (18ft) to 4m (13ft) to give greater room for manoeuvre with maximum load, although it must be debatable how much use this was at such a short radius where the presence of the end of the crane and propping girders will have been a hindrance. At the same time, the extra water tanks on the match truck, if not already discarded, were removed and dual-pipe air-brake gear added, whilst retaining the vacuum brake. Parts of the cranes were strengthened. 7.45 tonnes (7.33 tons) of additional weights were added to the superstructure, at the top of the crane carriage each side of the slewing ring and in the position previously occupied by the ash pan at the tail of the superstructure. This was to replace the greater weight of the steam equipment and to slightly improve the load/radius capability.

As well as listing the reduced loads to be lifted on superelevation of up to 150mm (6in) when propped and 100mm (4in) when free on the rail, the new duty tables also included separate consideration of the crane working over the end when both propped and free on rail on up to 50 mm of cant. This produced a significant improvement in performance compared with that for full slew through 360°, which were only marginally improved over the crane's original capability.

A distinction was also made between normal ratings when carrying out pre-planned duties, such as bridgeworks, and enhanced ultimate ratings only authorised for use under extenuating circumstances and under special conditions, but which will inevitably be encountered during breakdown work. This was really formalising and providing some control over the previous practice, where the experienced supervisor would be aware of the additional stability of his crane over and above the tabulated lifting capacity and would utilise this when necessary. The revised normal and ultimate lifting duties, when propped, following conversion are given in Tables 2 and 3. Note that the formal capacity appears to have been metricated at the same time as the conversions, from 75-ton to 76-tonne.

To help guard against loss of stability and possible structural overloading, two safety features were provided in the cab. An Ekco electronic load/radius indicator was fitted in the cab to give the crane operator a direct readout of the load on the hook and the true radius when working. Whilst this was not accurate enough to act as an automatic safe-load indicator, it was the first time the operator knew with any reasonable degree of accuracy the load he was lifting. A cant indicator, supplied by Penny and Giles, was also fitted to give the operator an indication of the actual super-elevation of the track on which the crane was standing and to record the highest cant over which the crane had travelled during the current phase of the work. The operator was also given a warning as he slewed the jib from the high to the low side of cant. Secondly, a wander lead and push-button linked to an alarm in the cab was available to an operator positioned at the rear of the crane to watch for the first tendency for a wheel to lift, indicating the approach to the limit of stability.

The effect of the conversion was to increase the total weight from 151.9 tons to 161.04 tonnes. Nonetheless, in this revised condition the route availability of the cranes was quoted as RA7 at 60mph, or RA6 when restricted to 15mph, which suggests a relaxation of the criteria for setting route availability. They could also negotiate a curve of 5 chains at a speed of 15mph.

If not already painted yellow, the cranes were certainly out-shopped in this colour following conversion. New numbers were soon issued for the converted cranes in the series ADRC 96700 to 96709. The depots to receive the converted cranes in the first instance included Stratford, March, Crewe, Motherwell, Bescot, Eastleigh, Doncaster and Thornaby, together later with Brighton (its crane was never used in anger), Toton, Wimbledon Park, Tinsley and Tyseley.

On withdrawal from Eastleigh, No ADRC96707 was sold and is now with Riley & Son's works adjacent to the East Lancashire Railway, whilst No ADRC96704 is in the hands of the Midland Railway Trust at Butterley and

No ADRC96706 was taken by the Churnet Valley Railway, but has since been scrapped. No ADRC96708 was acquired by Fragonset Railways for internal use at Tyseley, but has subsequently moved to the Battlefield Line, and No ADRC96701 was retrieved from the scrap merchant MRJ Phillips by Harry Needle, sent to Kineton for storage and cannibalising as a source of spare parts, and has since been scrapped.

BR 76-TONNE COWANS SHELDON CRANES CONVERTED TO DIESEL							
Nos		Year converted	Works No	Match wagon No	Remarks and allocation	Date Withdrawn	Disposal
Previous	New						
ADB 966111	ADRC 96701	1977	C78	DB 998517	Stratford 11/4/85–1994, Brighton 5/94– 3/95, Selhurst OOU 5/97– 9/98.	by 3/97	To H Needle 1998, Kineton 10/6/00, scrapped by R Hull 5/02
ADB 966112	ADRC 96702	1978/9	C79	DB 998518	Toton 2/91– 09/04, Old Oak Common OOU 22/5/08.	2007	Scrapped 5/08
ADM 1092	ADRC 96706	c1977	C80	DB 998534	Chart Leacon 4/88?– 2/91, Stewart's Lane 3/93, Toton OOU 9/94– 4/98.	by 4/98	Sold to Churnet Valley Rly 1998, scrapped
TDM 1093	ADRC 96703		C81	DB 998535	Crewe 6/6/81, Wimbledon 16/12/87– 3/95, Eastleigh OOU 3/97.	1996	Scrapped at Eastleigh late 1997
ADB 365	ADRC 96704	c1977	C82	DB 998536	Tinsley 4/88– 10/3/91, Doncaster 3/93, Toton (national spare) 30/9/94.	10/96	Sold to Midland Rly Trust late 1997
-	ADRC 96705	1977	C83	DB 998537	Doncaster 2/91, Thornaby 3/93–1994, Accident at Ryhope 5/12/92.	2/94	Scrapped by Thomson, Stockton
RS 1095/75	ADRC 96708	c1977	C84	DB 998539	Tyseley 4/88–30/9/94.	10/96	To Fragonset Railways, Tyseley early 1998, to Battlefield L 12/09
ADB 141	ADRC 96707	c1977	C85	DB 998538	Eastleigh 30/4/78–30/9/94.	3/97	Sold to MRJ Phillips, onto E Lancs Railway 3/98 & Riley Engrg at Bury 2003
ADB 967159	ADRC 96709	1978	C86	DB 998540	Doncaster 3/93, Thornaby 30/9/94– 11/01, Tees Shops (C&W), 02/04– 5/08.	2009	Accident at Denthead 4/9/98, to Great Central Railway 2/09
ADB 967160	ADRC 96700	1977/	C87	DB 998541	Thornaby 3/93.	11/93	Scrapped by Thomson, Stockton

Notes:
1. OOU = Out of use
2. t = metric tonne
3. Dates shown in *italics* are spot dates upon which the crane is known to have been at the depot concerned.

Figure 43 Elevation and end view of 76-tonne Cowans Sheldon steam breakdown cranes Nos C78–87 converted to diesel power. *Author*

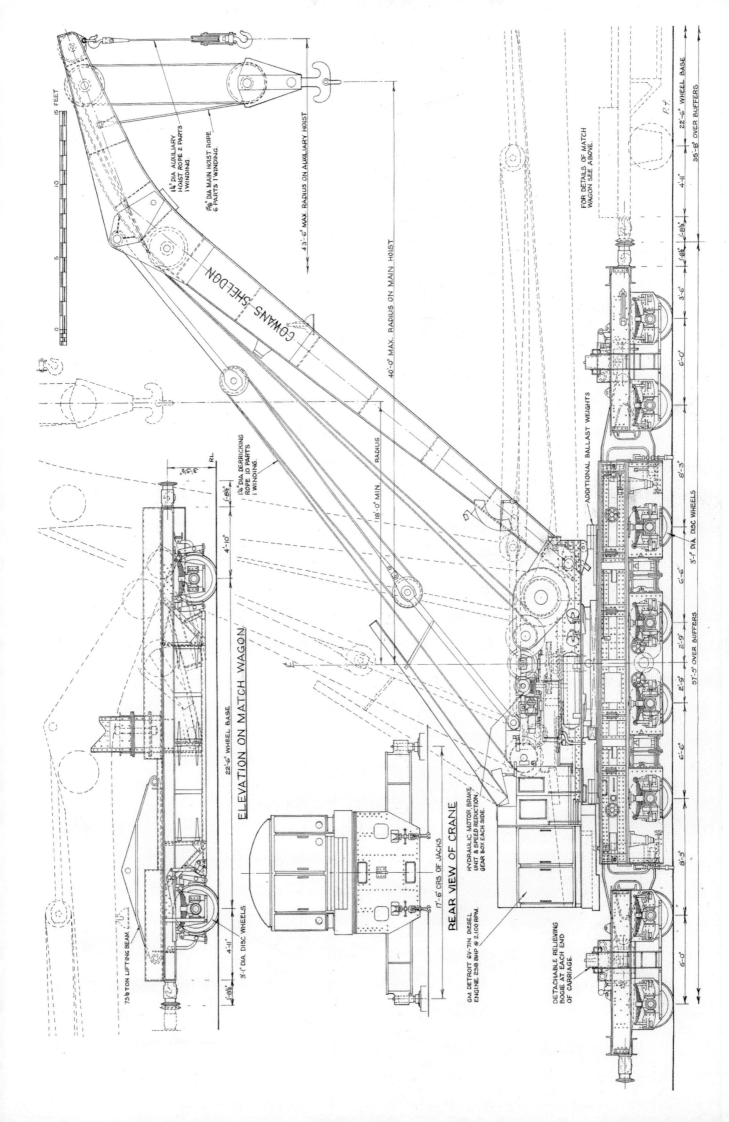

15 FEET

1⅛" DIA AUXILIARY HOIST ROPE 2 PARTS I WINDING.

1⅝" DIA MAIN HOIST ROPE 6 PARTS I WINDING.

43'-6" MAX. RADIUS ON AUXILIARY HOIST

40'-0" MAX. RADIUS ON MAIN HOIST

GOWANS SHELDON

18'-0" MIN. RADIUS

1¼" DIA DERRICKING ROPE 10 PARTS I WINDING.

RL

3'-5⅜"

1-8½"

4'-10"

22'-6" WHEEL BASE

ELEVATION ON MATCH WAGON

7⅜ TON LIFTING BEAM

3'-1" DIA DISC WHEELS

4'-1"

1-9½"

REAR VIEW OF CRANE

17'-6 CRS OF JACKS

GM DETROIT 6V-71N DIESEL ENGINE 238 BHP @ 2,100 RPM.

HYDRAULIC MOTOR, BRAKE, UNIT & SPEED REDUCTION, GEAR BOX EACH SIDE.

DETACHABLE RELIEVING BOGIE AT EACH END OF CARRIAGE.

ADDITIONAL BALLAST WEIGHTS

FOR DETAILS OF MATCH WAGON SEE ABOVE.

22'-6" WHEEL BASE

35'-8" OVER BUFFERS

4'-11"

1-8½"

1-8½"

3'-6"

6'-0"

8'-3"

3'-1" DIA DISC WHEELS

6'-6"

2'-9"

2'-9"

6'-6"

8'-3"

6'-0"

57'-5" OVER BUFFERS

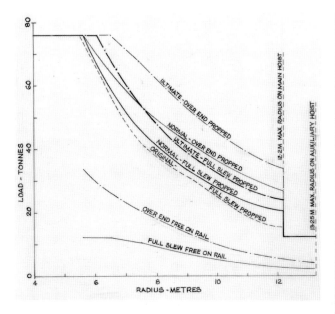

Above, Figure 44 Load/radius performance curves for Cowans Sheldon 76-tonne strut-jib crane following conversion. *Author*

Right Cowan Sheldon 76-tonne crane No ADRC 96701 in May 1994 at Hove soon after its transfer to Brighton being tried out by the gang. In fact, it is understood that it was never used in anger before being transferred away to Selhurst out of use and eventually scrapped. *M House*

Below Close up of converted crane No ADRC96708 of Tyseley at Washwood Heath on 19 February 1990. Additional ballast weights have been placed in the engine compartment to replace the weight of the boiler and on top of the carriage to improve the lifting performance. *P. Fidczuk*

Above Following conversion to diesel propulsion, No ADB141 at Stewarts Lane in the late 1970s. Note that the boiler and cylinders have been replaced by a new diesel engine, within an enclosure, and hydraulic drive units, while the water tank on the match wagon has been removed and the lifting beam transferred to its place. Twin-pipe air brakes have been fitted. *Caley Photographic*

Right A dramatic view of No ADM1092 from Toton engaged on bridgeworks at Luton in 1979, soon after conversion to diesel propulsion. *Caley Photographic*

No TDM1092 from Toton, and Willesden's No TDM1093 at Chinley on 10 September 1978 in the protracted process of re-railing diesel locomotive No 40044. Having run away with a heavy freight train, this had ploughed into a spillage of limestone from a previous accident. Lifting 133 tons in total weight, plus the effect of being buried in the limestone, set the overload bells furiously ringing, each time resulting in the necessity to reposition the cranes a little closer, with much retightening of the propping-girder jacks. *M.S. Welch*

	MAX. S.W.L. (TONNES)										
	BLOCKED						**FREE ON RAIL**				
RADIUS (m)	OVER-END	FULL SLEW					OVER-END	AUXILIARY HOIST ONLY			
								FULL SLEW			
	LEVEL 0 & 50	0	50	100	150		LEVEL 0 & 50	0	50	100	150
4*	76	76	76	76	65	MAX S.W.L. AUXILIARY HOIST 12.2 TONNES	-	-	-	-	-
5.6	76	76	72	67	62		33.6	12.2	12.2	9.9	8.5
6.5	64.5	59	53.5	50.75	47.75		26	12.2	10.6	9.4	8.1
7.5	53.5	46	43	41	37.5		20.5	10.4	8.1	7.3	6.9
9	42.25	33.5	31.5	30	26.5		13.5	7	5.5	5	4.7
10.5	33.75	25.5	24	23	19.75		8.2	4.75	4.3	3.2	3
12.2φ	26.75	20.5	18.5	17.5	14.75		5.4	2.8	2.2	1.9	1.6
13.25Θ	12.2	12.2	12.2	12.2	12.2		4	2	1.7	1.3	1

TABLE 2: COWANS SHELDON 76-TONNE DIESEL BREAKDOWN CRANE – DUTY TABLES, NORMAL RATINGS

* Indicates allowable minimum working radius of crane main hoist when working on the high side of 150mm super-elevated track.
φ Indicates maximum allowable working radius of main hoist.
Θ Indicates maximum allowable working radius of auxiliary hoist.
Over-end duties are applicable ONLY when crane is working on 0 and 50mm super-elevated track, they DO NOT apply for 100 and 150mm super-elevations.
Levels of track super-elevations are shown in mm.
Boxes marked thus [-] indicate no duty available.
Notes above also apply to the ultimate S.W.L. duty table.

No ADRC96700 from Gateshead deals with a smashed-up 20-ton goods brake van in Teesyard on 28 April 1988.
R. Watson

RADIUS (m)	ULTIMATE S.W.L. (TONNES)					
	BLOCKED					
	MAIN HOIST					
	OVER END	FULL SLEW				
		0	50	100	150	
4	76	76	76	76	75.5	
5.6	76	76	76	76	72.5	
6.5	76	68	62	59	55.5	
7.5	67	53.5	48.75	47	43.5	
9	52.75	39	36.5	34.75	30.75	
10.5	42	29.75	27.75	26.25	23	
12.2	33.75	23.75	21.5	20.25	17.25	
13.25	-	-	-	-	-	

TABLE 3: COWANS SHELDON 76-TONNE DIESEL BREAKDOWN CRANE – DUTY TABLES, ULTIMATE RATINGS

ATTENTION

Normal ratings must not be exceeded for pre-planned work (eg bridge operations).

Normal ratings may only be exceeded for those duties which have Ultimate ratings and at the discretion of the Supervisor in situations where he considers that the lifting operation has to be proceeded with and there is no alternative way of carrying out the operation, such as with other equipment or by repositioning the crane.

If the normal rating has to be exceeded, the appointed supervisor is to decide on the course of action after consultation with the crane driver.

If the Ultimate Safe Load rating is reached, further loading is not permitted.

Where the decision has been taken to exceed the normal ratings the crane must be operated with extra caution, only one motion operated at any one time, except where the manufacturer's instructions allow simultaneous operation of motions.

All lifts above the normal rating must be recorded in the log book and details must be sent to: Chief Mechanical & Electrical Engineer, Board HQ, Doncaster.

Conversion of 45-ton Steam Cranes

Soon after the return to service of the converted 76-tonne cranes, most of the earlier steam cranes were withdrawn, the last being ex-SR No DS1561 from Stewarts Lane, which went into retirement in April 1988. An exception, however, was the five (four LNER and one ex-WD) 45-ton Cowans Sheldon steam cranes by then at Thornaby, March, Stratford, Eastfield and Bescot. Between 1985 and 1987, these five were also converted to diesel propulsion in a similar manner to the 75-tonners. The original proposal was for seven 45-ton cranes to be converted, which means that two Ransomes & Rapier cranes must also have been considered. In addition, it was proposed to modernise the two diesel 75-ton cranes supplied to the Southern Region in 1964, but this appears not to have been put in hand.

As before, the work was carried out in the Crane Shop at Derby Locomotive Works. Once again, this involved removing the boilers, water tanks, coal boxes and cylinders and fitting a diesel engine in their place to power hydraulic motors driving the original driveshaft.

In addition, roller axle bearings were fitted, together with additional ballast weights, thereby enhancing the crane's lifting capacity to 50 tonnes at a radius of 6m (19.7ft) when propped and on level track. The lives of the cranes were not, however, markedly extended and withdrawals began within seven years.

The duties of the converted 50-tonne cranes are given in Table 4 on page 202 and illustrated in the drawing on p.197 (Figure 47). It will be noted that the minimum radius quoted is 5.2m (17ft), and whereas the original drawings clearly state that the minimum radius was 18ft, the jib is drawn at a scale minimum radius of 17ft. So perhaps it had been capable of this all along. To reflect the change in prime mover, these cranes were renumbered between ADRC96716 and 96720 and repainted yellow.

The newly-converted 50-tonne cranes were sent to Motherwell, Brighton, Chart Leacon (Ashford), Laira and Stewart's Lane. Since withdrawal, No ADRC96718 has passed into preservation at Llangollen in 1997 and No ADRC96719, after standing at Preston Park, Brighton, waiting to be cut up for years, was rescued and in April 2001 despatched to the Crewe Heritage Centre.

COWANS SHELDON 50-TONNE CRANES CONVERTED TO DIESEL							
Nos		Year built	Works No	Match wagon No	Remarks and allocation since conversion	Date of conversion & withdrawal	Disposal
Previous	New						
ADRC 95220	ADRC 96717	1939	6870	DE971589	Derby LW 10/84–10/85, Motherwell 2/4/88–3/91, Electrification Dept.	10/85–12/93	Scrapped at Ashford by Coopers Metals
ADRC 95218	ADRC 96719	1940	6871	DE941776	Derby LW 10/84–10/85, Brighton 4/88–3/93, Brighton (national spare) 30/9/94, Brighton OOU to 3/01. Replacement all-welded articulated jib following accident c1968.	8/86–1996/97	Sold to MRJ Phillips 4/97 for scrapping, Crewe Heritage Centre 4/01
ADRC 95217	ADRC 96716	1940	6872	DE901720	Derby LW 10/84–10/85, Ashford Crane Repair Depot 4/88–2/91. Match wagon retained and converted into tunnel ventilation fan.	10/85–12/93	Scrapped at Ashford by Coopers Metals
ADRC 95219	ADRC 96720	1940	6873	DM39600 DE961665?	Derby LW 10/84–10/85, Chart Leacon 4/88, Stewart's Lane (SR relief crane) 2/91, No. LDRC 96720 by 12/91 Electrification Dept Paddock Wood.	1/87–7/94	Scrapped at Paddock Wood by Coopers Metals
ADRC 95221	ADRC 96718	1943	8053	DB998523	Derby LW 10/84–11/86, Laira 4/88–3/95.	5/86–c1997	To Llangollen Rly 30/3/97

Notes:
1. OOU = Out of use
2. Dates shown in *italics* are spot dates upon which the crane is known to have been at the depot concerned.

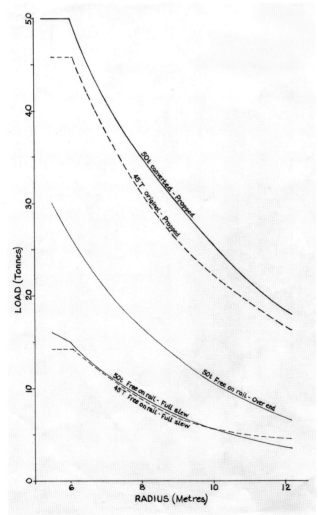

LOAD (Tonnes)

RADIUS (Metres)

Above 50-tonne No ADRC96716, converted from a Cowans Sheldon 45-ton steam crane supplied to the LNER in 1940, inside the train maintenance depot at Brighton on No 2 road in 1991. *M. House*

Left, Figure 47 Load/radius performance curves for Cowans Sheldon 50-tonne strut-jib crane following conversion. *Author*

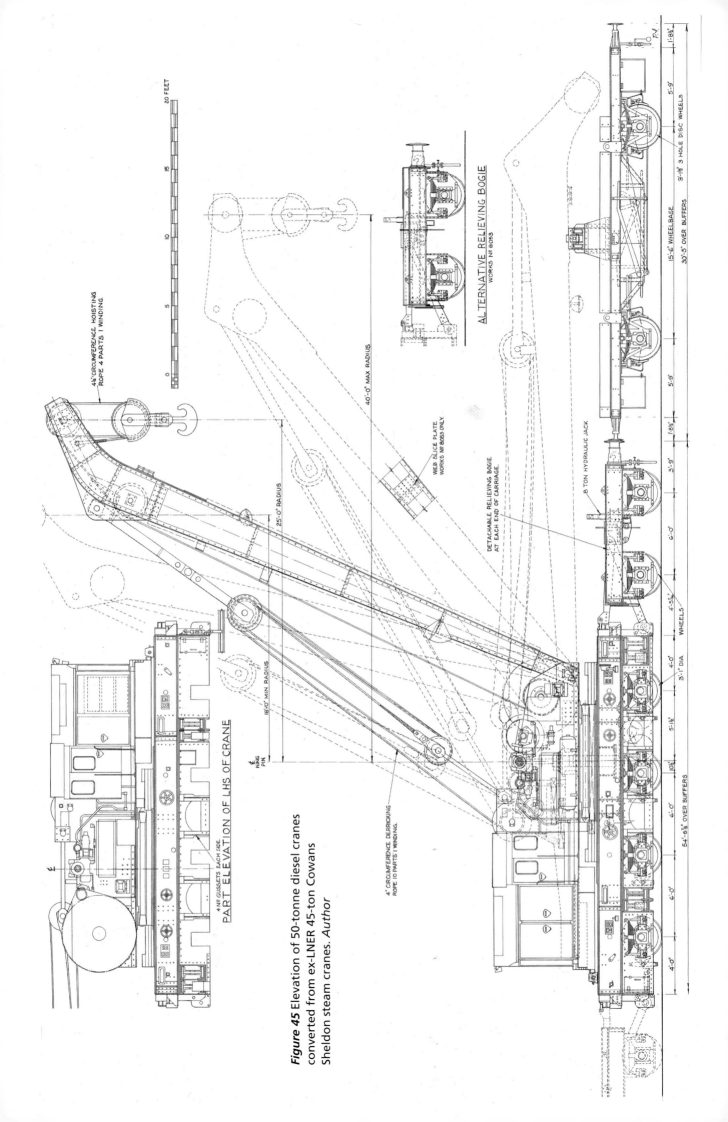

4½"CIRCUMFERENCE HOISTING
ROPE 4 PARTS 1 WINDING.

15
10
5
0

ALTERNATIVE RELIEVING BOGIE
WORKS № 8053

WEB SLICE PLATE
WORKS № 8053 ONLY.

40'-0" MAX RADIUS

DETACHABLE RELIEVING BOGIE
AT EACH END OF CARRIAGE.

P.J.

1'-8½"

5'-9"

3 HOLE DISC WHEELS

3'-1½"

15'-6" WHEELBASE

30'-5" OVER BUFFERS

25'-0" RADIUS

5'-9"

1'-8½"

8 TON HYDRAULIC JACK

3'-9"

6'-0"

4'-5½"

WHEELS

4'-0"

3'-1" DIA

18'-0" MIN RADIUS

₵
KING
PIN

5'-1½"

10½"

6'-0"

54'-6½" OVER BUFFERS

4'-0"

4 N° GUSSETS EACH SIDE.

PART ELEVATION OF LHS OF CRANE

4" CIRCUMFERENCE DERRICKING
ROPE 10 PARTS 1 WINDING.

Figure 45 Elevation of 50-tonne diesel cranes
converted from ex-LNER 45-ton Cowans
Sheldon steam cranes. *Author*

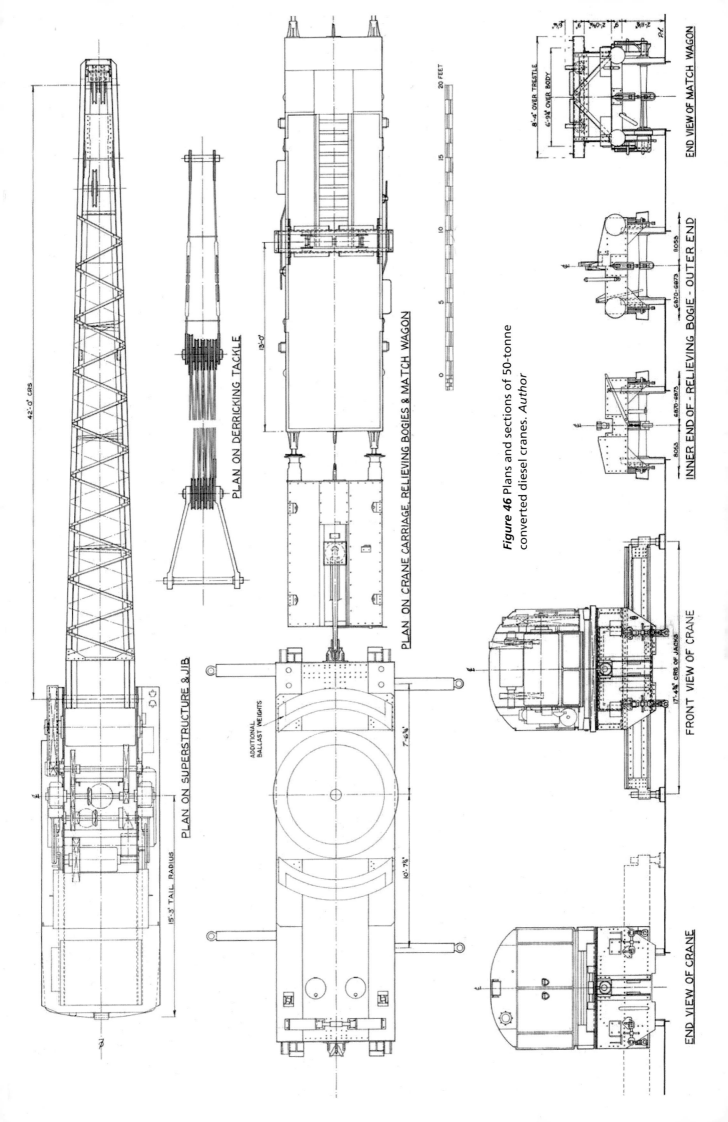

PLAN ON DERRICKING TACKLE

PLAN ON SUPERSTRUCTURE & JIB

42'-0" CRS

15'-3" TAIL RADIUS

PLAN ON CRANE CARRIAGE, RELIEVING BOGIES & MATCH WAGON

13'-0"

20 FEET

ADDITIONAL BALLAST WEIGHTS

7'-6¾"

10'-7½"

END VIEW OF MATCH WAGON

8'-4" OVER TRESTLE

6'-9¾" OVER BODY

INNER END OF - RELIEVING BOGIE - OUTER END

8053   6870-6873   6870-6873   8055

FRONT VIEW OF CRANE

17'-4½" CRS OF JACKS

END VIEW OF CRANE

Figure 46 Plans and sections of 50-tonne converted diesel cranes. *Author*

No ADRC96716 stands beside the works at Ashford (Kent). *M. House*

No ADRC96719, another of the former LNER cranes, handling an item of construction plant in connection with work to secure the chalk-cutting face at Brighton depot on 28 January 1991. Following an accident in 1968, this crane had received an all-welded replacement jib with an articulated foot similar to those fitted to the BR 30- and 75-ton cranes. *M. House*

No ADRC96719 stands outside the former Pullman Car Company's works at Preston Park, Brighton, in 1997 having been withdrawn and awaiting disposal. In the event it was acquired privately and sent to the Crewe Railway Heritage Centre. *Author*

A close-up of the carriage and superstructure of No ADRC96719 having its rear-axle wheels re-railed following derailment in Three Bridges yard in June 1991. Note the blue-coloured jacking bracket on the end of the crane. This was the colour code adopted to assist the supervisor in describing to the driver in which direction to travel. The other end was coloured white. *M. House*

A close-up of No ADRC96719 showing the hydraulic motor, piping and ancillary equipment, driver's cab and enclosure for the diesel engine fitted in place of the steam cylinders and boiler of the original crane. *Author*

TABLE 4: COWANS SHELDON 50-TONNE DIESEL BREAKDOWN CRANE – DUTY TABLE									
	BLOCKED				FREE ON RAIL				
	FULL SLEW				OVER-END			FULL SLEW		
CANT	0	50	100	150	0	50	100	0	50	100
MINIMUM RADIUS LIMITS (?)	5.2	5	4.6	4.2	5.5	6	7.5	5.5	6	7.5
RADIUS (m)	MAX. S.W.L. TONNES									
5.2	50	46	40	36	-	-	-	-	-	-
5.5	50	46	40	36	30	-	-	16	-	-
6.0	50	43	37.5	33.5	26.5	22	-	15	14	-
7.0	41	37	32.5	29	20.75	17.75	-	11.5	10.75	-
7.5	38	34.5	30.25	27	18.5	16	14	10.25	9.25	8.5
8.0	35	32	28.25	25	16.5	14.5	12.5	9	8.25	7.5
9.0	30	27.5	24.5	21.25	13.25	11.75	10.25	7	6.25	5.5
10.0	25.5	23.5	21	18	10.5	9.5	8.5	5.5	5	4.25
11.0	21.5	20	17.75	15	8.5	7.75	6.75	4.5	4	3.25
12.2	18	16.5	14.5	12.5	6.5	6	5	3.5	3	2.5

The maximum working radius of this crane on any cant is 12.2m
Boxes marked thus [-] indicate no duty available

11
Review of Breakdown Working and Trains

Alternatives to Cranes

As well as making recommendations for the next generation of cranes, in 1955 the Ad Hoc Committee had reviewed and considered alternative methods of recovery, which were about to become more necessary as an increasing mileage of track was fitted with overhead-line equipment in connection with electrification schemes implemented under the Modernisation Plan. Conventional jacks and re-railing ramps had long been part of the breakdown gangs' stock in trade, but the availability of lightweight, high-pressure hydraulic systems, including mobile motor-driven pumps, bridging rails and traversing jacks, offered realistic alternatives to cranes even when faced with moving heavy items. Later, in the right circumstances heavy-duty inflatable air bags were found to be useful in righting overturned vehicles.

The presence of overhead traction catenaries, unless of course they were brought down by the accident, considerably hindered the use of cranes, as exemplified here at Hadfield on 9 April 1981. The overhead-line equipment has been pulled back to one side to allow steam cranes Ransomes & Rapier 45-ton No ADRR95214 and Cowans Sheldon 50-ton No RS1005/50 to re-rail a bogie anhydrous-ammonia tank. The tank was turned upside down to drain it before lifting. *M.S. Welch*

With advances in motor transport and an improving highway network, earlier arrival at the scene of an incident could be achieved by road lorries kitted out with smaller and lighter breakdown plant and accompanied by a small number team of operators. Sometimes, these were even able to deal with events without the need for the breakdown train, which in certain cases might have taken some time to arrive. Further advantages were obtained by using combined road/rail vehicles that could travel close to the site by road and then transfer to the rails for the last leg of the journey.

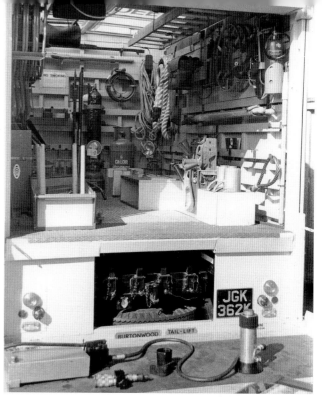

An open day at Eastleigh on 26 March 1972 provided the opportunity to see the rear of a first-generation breakdown lorry raised to expose the items of kit neatly arranged around the sides, on the floor and even hung from an otherwise-translucent roof. Note also the tail-lift to enable heavy articles to be lowered to, and later raised from, the ground. *Author*

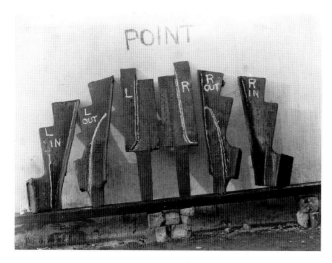

A selection of cast-steel re-railing ramps designed to suit a variety of situations. *Author's collection*

Subsequent to goods brake van, No ZTR DS 56153 hitting the stops at Three Bridges yard rather hard, a lightweight aluminium-alloy bridging beam was laid across the rails, on top of which was placed a small 20-ton Lukas LM Telescopic two-stage jack and traverser placed under the headstock. Note the hydraulic pipes leading off towards a portable control panel and pump. *M. House*

Travelling cranes were not past becoming derailed themselves, as this view of Regional Civil Engineer's 12-ton tailless Plasser & Theurer diesel-hydraulic No DRP 81517 at Three Bridges in June 1991 demonstrates. The breakdown gang set about using a pair of 60-tonne Lukas jacks on a lightweight aluminium-alloy bridging beam to restore the crane to the rails. *M. House*

The road/rail recovery vehicles, such as the Bruff, became popular with recovery teams due to their ability, unlike plain road vehicles, to approach close to the scene of the incident. These four-wheel road lorries featured a scissors-lift turntable, mounted under the chassis between the axles, together with small retractable rail wheels in front and behind the road wheels. Upon arrival at the railway line, the lorry would be driven part way across the track, the scissors-lift lowered and the lorry rotated so as to be in line with the rails and lowered down on them. The rail wheels were then lowered and the vehicle could run on the track.

These vehicles were provided with mobile power packs for hydraulic jacks and for air bags, together with good lighting. As well as accommodation for the driver and a small team, they were fitted out to carry a reasonable number of tools and packing, and were able to transport the staff in relative comfort with adequate facilities. They were preferred by railway management, because they could be despatched quickly without having to wait for a locomotive, driver and guard. They could go straight to the scene by road, bypassing the congestion likely on the rail system, following the incident.

Mercedes Unimog breakdown lorry fitted with retractable Ries rail undercarriage standing on the outlet road of the branch to the Shell oil refinery at Teesport on 12 January 1983, where several 100-ton oil-tank wagons had derailed. While on the track the rail-engaging undercarriage guides the vehicle, but traction is still by means of the road wheels. *R. Willis*

A Bedford four-wheel truck equipped by Bruff to run on the track, fitted out for breakdown work at the Toton Breakdown Train Centre. Note the accommodation for a small number of personnel behind the driver, the rail wheels lowered onto the track and the stem light mounted on the cab roof. *R. Willis*

The front end of the Bedford truck, showing the outlets for the hydraulic pipes. *R. Willis*

Right An unsuccessful attempt using air bags to right a Class 47 diesel locomotive, which overturned near Shrewsbury. On this occasion, the air bags only achieved an angle of about 45°, and in the end cranes had to be brought in to complete the job. *W. Lee*

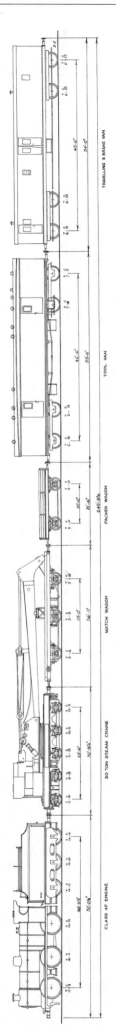

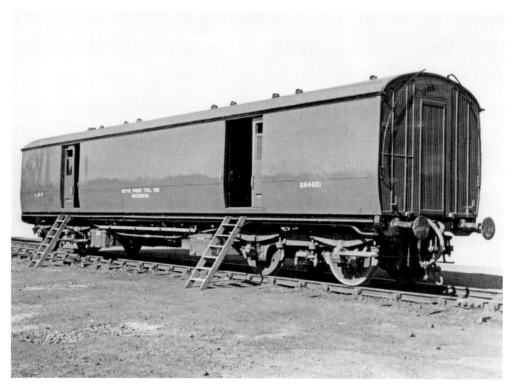

Above Tool vans were created by plating over the sides of surplus bogie coaches, providing two sets of wide sliding doors through which to pass items of heavy equipment stored inside. LMS No 284651 was an ex-Caledonian 57ft coach labelled for Inverness, although it is thought not to have ended up there. This photograph displays a short length of rail hung on hooks below the solebar, and the steps provided to enable access from the lineside. *BR, LMR, author's collection*

Left, Figure 48 The ideal arrangement of a breakdown crane, including a 30-ton Cowans Sheldon steam crane, as conceived by the LMS. *Author*

Mess and Tool Vans

Whereas breakdown cranes are necessarily purpose built and acquired new at some expense, the attendant vans and wagons of the breakdown train, as described in Volume 1, were frequently converted from redundant discarded revenue-earning vehicles. Whilst the former were not usually overworked and hence had a long life span, the vans had already had their lives extended and therefore tended not to last more than say fifteen to twenty years before they needed replacement.

As part of this process, the LMS had in the late 1930s reviewed its breakdown arrangements and tool- and riding-van requirements. Each of the depots allocated the new 30-ton cranes introduced in the early 1940s, mentioned previously, were also provided with new standard vans converted for breakdown work from a number of redundant bogie coaches. In addition, the LMS subsequently built sixteen further standard vans to replace existing vans that had reached the end of their economic life, although, due to the difficulties with the supply of materials during the war, some of the existing tools and equipment had to be temporarily transferred from the redundant to the new vans. Other companies or regions early during the BR period followed similar practices.

The Ad Hoc Committee defined the various types of vehicles as follows:

Packing wagons/vans

These were considered by some to be necessary to carry the chains and gear used with the breakdown cranes, as well as other equipment. Usually, an old four-wheeled, non-bogie vehicle of robust construction was adequate, provided such vans were normally fitted with vacuum brakes and a side-lever handbrake.

Tool vans

These were often four-wheeled bogie, automatic-vacuum-braked, ex-coaching-stock vehicles with a steel

Above Inside the van, a wide variety of tools, other equipment and materials were arranged in an orderly fashion on shelves and hooks, etc, even a ladder strapped to the roof, together with an oil lamp for illumination. *BR, LMR, author's collection*

Right The opposite end of the tool van, showing the handbrake wheel at the top of a column, behind which is a stove to keep the van sufficiently dry to prevent condensation on the metal tools. *BR, LMR, author's collection*

Below Although still more obviously a former passenger coach, reconstruction as riding vans was nonetheless often considerable. Ex-Midland Railway square-panelled No DM223418M at Kentish Town has a clerestory which has probably had a water tank fitted within. Other conversions had such tanks mounted on the roof. *Real Photographs, author's collection*

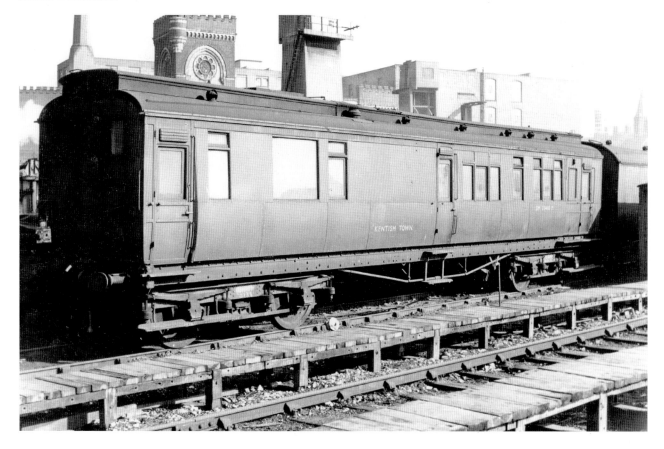

The breakdown riding and mess van for Inverness MPD was created out of an ex-WCJS low-arc-roof 50ft-bogie corridor third, which as No 245 to diagram D52 had entered service in 1902–3 and been withdrawn from revenue-earning service in November 1941. The short clerestory on the roof is not original, but due to the water tank added during conversion to a breakdown vehicle. Thanks to the efforts of the Depot Master, Duncan Burton, No (DM) 198614 was maintained in immaculate LMS livery as seen here in August 1965, and remained so until at least July 1971. By June 1973 it had been repainted in bright red, but the finish quickly deteriorated. It was taken into preservation in 1982, firstly on the Strathspey Railway, followed ten years later by the Scottish Museum Trust and moved to Bo'ness. *Neil Sinclair*

The Eastern Region made radical alterations to former Gresley coaches to provide for the MFD re-railing equipment they invested in. The ends have been cut back and an overhead gantry installed to enable heavier items to be offloaded on site. No DE320847 was photographed at Carlisle on 17 June 1969. *Author*

An example of an Eastern Region combined riding and tool van is No DE320604 of GER origin allocated to Leicester. The supervisor's compartment is at the left-hand end. *Unattributed*

underframe and an internal handbrake column. Two sliding doors were required at each side of the vehicle, with adjacent steps to gain access.

Riding vans

These were again usually converted from redundant coaching stock. They too had to be fully-fitted vehicles with a separate handbrake column inside. A compartment was provided at one end of the van for the officer in charge, and a separate access door was considered essential. Another separate access door was provided for the kitchen, often a separate compartment, which was equipped with a stove and full cooking facilities.

Combined tool/riding vans

To all intents and purposes, these were an amalgam on a smaller scale of the tool and riding vans.

All service vehicles

All service vehicles were to be fitted with screw couplings and, with the exception of officer's saloons, were all painted black according to the Railway Executive Committee's minute No 4619 of 14 August 1950. There were occasional exceptions to the types of vans employed, as depots serving areas with a large number colliery and dock railways, with tight-radius turn-outs, had to use four- or six-wheel box vans on account of movement restrictions.

The Committee appended the following diagrams to illustrate their recommendations:

Between 1983 and 1987, the fleet of breakdown vans was modernised by the introduction of vans based on BR Mark 1 coaching stock to convey specialist equipment for dealing with breakdowns and derailments of rail vehicles, three being provided to depots with cranes. These staff, dormitory, tool and generator vans were converted from

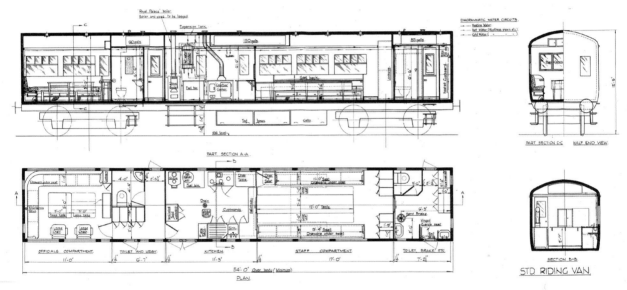

Figure 49 Drawings for standard riding van. *BR, author's collection*

Figure 50 Drawings for standard tool and packing van. *BR, author's collection*

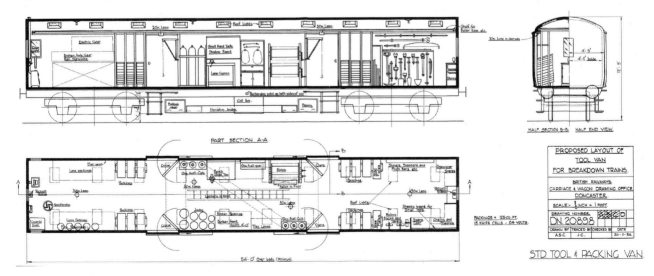

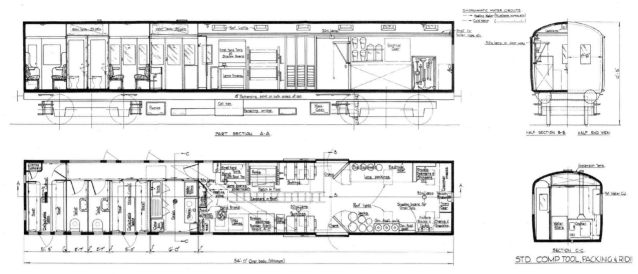

Figure 51 Drawings for standard combined tool, packing and riding van. *BR, author's collection*

Figure 52 Drawings for MFD equipment van. *BR, author's collection*

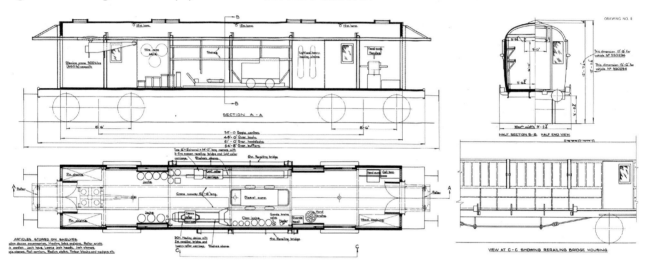

redundant coaching stock comprising former corridor third/second brake vehicles, originally built between 1951 and 1957, i.e:

Nos	Description	Code
ADB975453–975462	staff, tool & generator	QPX
ADB975463–975464	staff, tool & dormitory	QPX
ADB075465–975480	staff & tool	QPX
ADB975481–975499	tool & generator	QQX

These were extensively refurbished, fitted out for recovery and re-railing work and painted in yellow. They had dual-brakes and were permitted to run at a maximum speed of 75mph. Within the vans, provision was made for the stowage of re-railing equipment, including lightweight jacking equipment, and the accommodation of staff with mess and living facilities.

The tool vans had a maximum carrying capacity of 14 tons uniformly distributed. Each vehicle had four sliding doors, two each side, for loading and unloading of equipment. There were no windows, the interior walls being lined with timber. The floors were covered with light-alloy non-slip plate. Racking and bulkheads

were fitted internally for the stowage of lifting brackets and equipment, while tackle boxes were fitted externally on the vehicle underframe to give extra storage space. Fluorescent lighting was located inside the van, and outside on each side at solebar level to illuminate the trackside, the supply provided by 24-volt batteries fitted beneath the underframe.

Combined living and storage vans were provided to transport the breakdown team, consisting of a supervisor and team of up to ten, to locations without cranes. These vans were complete with mess facilities and stowage space for carrying lightweight jacking equipment. The riding half was equipped with seating and tables for ten people; a fully fitted kitchen with gas cooker, sink unit, water heater, gas refrigerator and storage cupboards; a separate supervisor's compartment with table, seating and cupboard space; and a drying room. Heating was by means of Calor gas convector heaters. The storage area was a scaled-down version of that in the tool van, with just one sliding door each side, but included two toilets at the remote end.

The quality of meals that could be prepared naturally depended on the expertise of the 'van man'. Nonetheless, most gangs looked after themselves remarkably well.

Newcastle's breakdown train behind No 37062 passes W.D. & H.O. Wills' factory. The train is made up of a 76-tonne diesel conversion of the Cowans Sheldon steam crane marshalled between a tool van and riding vans converted from BR Mark 1 coaching stock. *J.A.G.H. Coltas*

Figure 53 Plan of combined riding and tool van converted from BR Mark 1 coach. *Author*

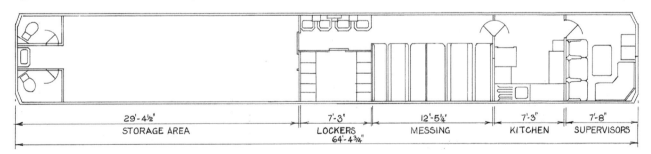

Margam's team had a first-class chef and he served up a full three-course meal during a break in operations, dressed for the occasion with traditional chef's hat!

For decades, heavy wrought-iron chains were the norm. These weighed almost as much as one or more men could lift. In more recent times these have been superseded by steel-alloy chains, which are only about half the weight of the old ones for the same capacity.

The Southern Region's version of a brake riding van for Nine Elms was ex-LSWR 'Ironclad' corridor brake third to diagram 135, built at Eastleigh in 1921 as No 3182, converted in 1959 and renumbered DS231. It was photographed at New Malden on 20 September 1959. *J.H. Aston*

A further generation of the Eastern Region's breakdown train vehicles is exemplified by those on show at Neville Hill, Leeds, on 28 April 1973, the oldest being a former Great Northern coach of Gresley design in use as a staff riding van No DE320807. *J. Bateman, courtesy HMRS*

Seen on the same occasion, ex-LNER Gresley passenger brake van No DE321106 has become a tool van with a pair of sliding doors. *J. Bateman, courtesy HMRS*

Thompson was represented by a former LNER passenger brake van as another tool van with folding doors and still fitted with the guard's lookout. All vans are in pristine condition, in red livery with wheel tyres and steam pipes picked out in white. *J. Bateman, courtesy HMRS*

Improvement in lighting levels during the hours of darkness is demonstrated by this view of a Cowans Sheldon, converted to diesel propulsion, recovering some de-railed hopper wagons at Constable Burton on 17 March 1989. As well as lanterns halfway up the jib and at the front of the superstructure, some lineside lighting seems to have been provided. *R. Watson*

A former BR Mark 1 coach converted into a staff riding and tools van for the Recovery Units, at Cheddleton on 12 April 1997, soon after being taken out of service and acquired by the Churnet Valley Railway. *Author*

Brighton breakdown gang's riding van. *M. House*

Clothing and Management Staff

The aforementioned Ad Hoc Committee of 1955 had given considerable thought to suitable clothing for the staff of breakdown gangs; however they overlooked the requirements of the supervisory and management staff that necessarily had to attend the scene of each incident.

Despite the best efforts of man, events can sometimes conspire to defeat him. For instance, as a consequence of the derailment of a tanker train at Ebbw Vale, fuel oil was spilt over the ground. This 'Bunker D' grade of oil had a thick, tarry consistency and the cold weather turned it into an even thicker mass. Following the initial derailment, it had snowed heavily and there was soon no indication to those newly arrived at the scene that the ground was covered by a layer of oil, hidden by the thick layer of snow, which at times led to the propping-girder jacks having to be used to force the thick oil out from under the packing.

It was only after some activity on site that the oil started surfacing and the mixture of oil and snow made underfoot conditions very slippery. One member of the management staff on site had the misfortune to fall over,

covering his suit with thick oil. He subsequently had it cleaned and submitted the cleaning bill on his expense return. Payment was rejected by the Staff Office as they said that such a claim was not detailed in the agreed scale of expenses! In addition, at the end of the operation the staff riding vehicle was so badly contaminated with oil that it was scrapped and a replacement vehicle provided.

In the 1960s, management staff were not paid overtime for the extended hours spent on recovery work and the annual 'on-call' allowance had yet to be introduced. No protective clothing was provided, so if called out during working hours they went as they were in their everyday suit and top coat, while outside office hours probably wearing more casual clothing. The only extra payment was standard expenses. If called out in the early hours, they could claim the breakfast allowance, or if out after 7.00pm could claim for dinner. On the other hand, if they were called out after 9.00pm and returned home before 7.00am they received no payment because the scale of expenses did not allow for this method of working! The 'on-call' duties were incidental to the post's main responsibilities, but at times such as example given, they could prove to be a major distraction.

12
Cranes at War

Just as the advent of railways revolutionised the logistics and movement of troops in warfare, so the acquisition of breakdown cranes by the military authorities soon followed. It was not long into the First World War before the War Department was seeking the assistance of our national railways by both requisitioning and purchasing steam breakdown cranes to assist the war effort on the Western Front and elsewhere. The individual cranes involved are noted in Volume 1, while a more general description of their work in Flanders will be found in *R.O.D. The Railway Operating Division on the Western Front, The Royal Engineers in France and Belgium 1915–1919*, by William T Aves.

As already explained, the implications of the aerial bombardment of Britain anticipated with the outbreak of the Second World War led to various preparations as part of the Air Raid Precaution programme, including the purchase of twelve 45-ton steam breakdown cranes. This was followed the military themselves acquiring two 36-ton cranes, and requisitioning two of the ARP cranes from the LNER, followed by the purchase of further 45-ton cranes later during the war.

As well as the additional cranage, in preparation for war it was considered advisable to institute a measure of general inter-company availability for the new and existing plant and equipment, particularly breakdown cranes. As the dozen new 45-tonners arrived on the LNER (6), GW (4) and SR (2), their existing cranes were reallocated so that eventually the locations of all the breakdown cranes throughout the country, including those of the LMS, had been reassessed. Each crane was located at an appropriate vital point and was available for use not only on the lines of the company owning the crane, but also over the lines of any other company's system adjacent to the individual stabling points. Inter-availability necessitated the assessment of important sections of lines over which the crane of another company might be required to work in the event of the line-owner company's own cranes being occupied elsewhere, or being prevented by blockages from reaching the scene of the damage.

For example, the LMS 50-ton crane at Motherwell was available, if requested, for incidents on the LNER line between Edinburgh Waverley and Glasgow Queen Street. In return, the LNER 36-ton crane at Edinburgh (St Margaret's) was sanctioned to attend incidents on the Edinburgh to Carstairs, Midcalder Jct to Glasgow Central, and Uddington to Carstairs lines if required. Likewise, route constraints on the GNS Section of the LNER led in November 1939 to the exchange of the LMS 15-ton cranes at Inverness and Hurlford, because the latter crane was passed to venture east of Keith or Elgin, while the former was still able to operate on ex-GSWR territory. The extent to which this procedure was implemented during the war is not known, but it stood BR in good stead during the clearing up operation after the disaster at Harrow and Wealdstone on 8 December 1952, when not only did the London Transport breakdown organisation offer assistance, but the Western Region's 45-ton crane stood in for one of the London Midland Region's 36-ton cranes which had to retire due to a defect.

During the war years, breakdown train and permanent way/bridging emergency repair trains became of 'frontline' importance and a high priority was given to both staffing and crew welfare. This was essential, as most of these emergency teams were sent out from their home depots in industrialised areas and stabled outside in the country, from where they would be ready to return to sort out any disruption caused by enemy bombing. The crews were relatively well looked after in their 'out of town' billets, and withdrawn mainline express sleeping cars or restaurant cars were used for this purpose at some locations. After the war it was another matter, and the crews who had provided the service felt downgraded. Their tool and riding vans were ancient, and as one crew member stated, 'prone to have leaking roofs, mildewed or mould-covered interiors and often infested with rats'. Progressively then, as other (less arduous) work became more plentiful, the numbers of men on the 'call-out list' rapidly declined.

Following the collapse of France in June 1940, urgent steps had to be taken to strengthen the defences along the south-east coast, in particular the installation of heavy naval guns in batteries overlooking the Channel in the Straits of

Three Ransomes & Rapier steam breakdown cranes in the process of installing a gun barrel on 30 April 1942 at the heavy batteries at Wanstone Farm, overlooking the Straits of Dover. The date suggests this is the second 15in gun 'Clem'. *Courtesy, After the Battle*

Dover. To meet the threat posed by the German heavy guns mounted at Cap de Gris-Nez, the War Office called for the assistance of three powerful breakdown cranes to provide lifting power for the installation of 14in calibre guns, nicknamed 'Winnie' and 'Pooh', at St Margaret's Bay. The cranes were also used in support of the 15in guns 'Jane' and 'Clem' located at the Wanstone Down anti-shipping batteries, along with the refurbished ex-First World War rail-mounted guns – the 18in 'Boche-Buster', and three 13.5in guns, 'Scene-Shifter', 'Piece Maker' and 'Gladiator' – in effect all the heavy coastal batteries, together with the hyper-velocity 8in gun 'Bruce'. To lift a gun barrel, either a lifting bracket was attached at the breach end and two cranes hoisted this end, while a third handled the muzzle end, or a chain was passed round the breech end and another about quarter of the length from the muzzle. The latter may have been for the barrels of smaller 9.2in guns.

As the SR's 45-ton cranes had barely arrived by July 1940, the 50-ton cranes located at Rugby and Willesden, together with the 45-ton crane from King's Cross, were sent south to the Martin Mill Military Railway, accompanied by the respective crane crews and supervisory officials. After a stay of nearly three weeks, during which time the

railway staff were housed and maintained in accommodation provided by the military, the cranes were returned to their bases. Winston Churchill, the Prime Minister took a personal interest in the task of installing the guns and afterwards forwarded letters of appreciation to the companies concerned, acknowledging the assistance provided.

In September 1940, the same LMS cranes were again requisitioned for a shorter period and similar arrangements were made. After meeting two further calls in the following October and November, the movements of LMS cranes to and from the Dover area at military behest finally ceased. Thereafter, three of the 45-ton ARP cranes, two Ransomes & Rapier from the SR and the Cowans Sheldon from King's Cross, were used at St Margaret's Bay, changing gun barrels at times in preference to the Craven crane, due to them now being available and supposedly having a more suitable jib-head detail. At some time, three Rapier cranes tackled the job, one of which may have been a 36-tonner.

During the Second World War, breakdown gangs were trained to carry out their work under conditions of gas attack. Undertaking heavy manual labour with a gas mask on and wearing waterproof gas caps, legging, wellington boots and hoods must have been highly uncomfortable.

In preparation for the invasion of Europe in 1944, sixteen complete breakdown trains were assembled, including building cranes, with breakdown teams gathered from both the Allied armies, trained and made ready for despatch across the Channel. Orders for 45-ton steam cranes were placed with both Cowans Sheldon (eight) and Ransomes & Rapier (six) in September and October 1942, to supplement a pair of 30-ton cranes ordered from Cowans in February that year. Sixteen breakdown trains, with twelve of the 45-ton cranes, are known to have been shipped to the North-Western European theatre, some via Harwich, by June 1945, together with fifteen Brownhoist cranes of 20 tons, seven generator vans, sixteen workshop vans and two special piling wagons plus, at sometime, one of the 30-ton breakdown crane.

From 1943, the LMSR responded to an order of the War Office to provide sixteen, fully equipped, four-wagon, breakdown trains. These utilised French and Italian continental ferry wagons which remained in Britain after Germany's conquest of mainland Europe. Upon arrival back in mainland Europe, they were put to work maintaining traffic on the railway lines operated by military authorities until such time as they were either returned to UK, or were handed over to the local railway networks.

The records of No 181 Railway Operating Company and No 3 Railway Operating Group both state that breakdown train No 7, with three covered wagons and an SNCF kitchen car, arrived at Lison, France on 7 August 1944. The means by which the kitchen car was acquired is not recorded! The Canadians are also believed to have operated two 45-ton cranes with their No 1 and No 2 Railway Operating Companies, Royal Canadian Engineers, while the US Army 724th Railway Operating Battalion is known to have had a British-built Cowans Sheldon breakdown crane, nicknamed 'Big Baby'.

An early exercise, probably in 1942, was performed by an LMS crew, in front of an audience of officers from other companies, on the section of the Strathaven to Darvel line in the Southern Uplands of Scotland, this having been closed to all traffic on 11 September 1939. The 50-ton Motherwell crane No RS1054/50 is seen lifting an ex-Caledonian Railway 4-4-0 Dunalastair II class, LMS No 14330, this having previously been withdrawn in February 1941. *S.C. Townroe*

Men dressed in mustard-gas-protective gear, consisting of oilskin hoods, jacket and trousers, rubber gloves and wellington boots, and wearing masks while handling sleepers as part of the exercise, while officials look on. *S.C. Townroe*

The crane driver of No 961601 wearing his gas mask. *Unattributed*

On the LNER, the 35-ton Ransomes & Rapier
No 961601 lifts one end of ex-GER 0-6-0 J15
Class No 7857 on 3 November 1943, while
undertaking training under simulated gas
attack at an undisclosed location.
Unattributed

13
Railway Crane Accidents

Breakdown cranes are of course intended to deal with the consequences of accidents of some sort to trains, be they locomotives, carriages or wagons, derailing or having suffered some other kind of unfortunate incident. However, due in part to the delicate balancing act that a crane performs, they are not past getting into a spot of difficulty themselves, although outside causes can also lead to their coming to grief.

One of the chief causes is instability of the ground under the crane, usually under the propping-girder support nearest the load to be lifted, especially if it is near, or beyond, its safe limit. Another unfortunate cause is the failure to employ the propping girders when the load is such that they are necessary, usually due to a failure to recognise the magnitude of the load to be lifted. Few accidents seem to have occurred as a result of mechanical or structural failure

An NER 25-ton Craven Bros crane from Darlington, at Lartington Quarry on the Darlington to Tebay line on 15 December 1911. It had been called out to deal with a derailed goods train and while swinging round with its own match wagon, presumably without its propping girders in use, overturned. It will not have been the first, nor the last time such an occurrence took place! *M.S. Welch collection*

A 15-ton Cowans Sheldon Mk 2 crane, thought to be ex-SER No DS202, came to grief at Ashford Sidings.
Unattributed

of the crane itself, although a couple of instances of buckling of the jib are recorded, one due to it having struck a lineside obstruction.

In the early days, the supervisor and the crane driver usually learnt by experience, supplemented perhaps by an initial briefing by a representative of the crane manufacturer at the time of delivery. As unfortunate events occurred, edicts would be issued from on high, instructing staff to do, or not do, this and that in an attempt to avoid re-occurrence. More recently, specific training has been instituted, training videos prepared and a breakdown training facility set up at Toton.

On the evening of 28 November 1948, some wagons derailed in the loop, and the goods brake van was thrown onto the down line, at Griseburn Ballast Sidings in the Upper Eden Valley, between Crosby Garrett and Ormside on the former Midland Settle to Carlisle line. The ex-LMS 50-ton Cowans Sheldon crane No RS1001/50 from Kingmoor, Carlisle, was summoned to clear the line, arriving at 00.35 hours. The line is on a 1-in-100 gradient at this point, so once it was separated from the rest of the breakdown train, arrangements were made to scotch the crane with a single wedged-shaped block of wood. On completion of the work, at about 02.30 hours, the crane and its equipment were being packed up and it was deemed time to bring the rest of the train closer prior to re-coupling. Despite the cautious efforts of the guard, Cook, when the front portion of the train met the match wagon, there was still sufficient force to push the crane over the scotch block, after which the crane and match wagon started to run away down the hill.

Whilst no efforts had been made to sprag the wheels, Cook had attempted to apply the handbrake wheel on the crane, but to no avail. Unable to read the labels in the dark,

he failed to realise that, because a single brake-lever shaft ran from one side to the other, its operation was handed, and in fact he had been releasing the brake rather than applying it! In any case, it required three complete turns to apply the brake fully. The foreman fitter George Campbell, applied the handbrake of the match wagon on the cess side as soon as the crane started to move off, ending up standing on the lever to gain extra purchase. Another fitter, named Charles Campbell, was endeavouring to make his way along the crane on the same side towards the driver's position in order to lower the jib, while crane driver TS Baty was trying to do the same from the 6ft side.

As if the runaway was not serious enough, 660 yards from the start of the crane's involuntary journey the crane struck an over-bridge. The jib was almost lowered back on to the match wagon and was being held 2ft above the jib rest, while the hook was stowed, as the crane approached the bridge. Unfortunately, instead of lowering the jib the rest of the way, on hearing the shout of warning, Baty's impulse was to jump clear. At this moment, the sheaves to the derricking tackle struck the soffit of the bridge. At least one sheave fractured, allowing the jib to fall violently fracturing the jib rest. As a consequence, George Campbell was struck and fatally injured by flying debris. Charles Campbell and Baty were thrown off the crane and found at the lineside, having respectively sustained a broken thigh and merely being dazed, while the crane continued on its way unhindered.

The line North from Ais Gill Summit generally falls all the way to Carlisle, 36 miles away from the scene of the accident. Fortunately, a mile or two of near-level track between Little Salkeld and Lazonby, followed by a short adverse incline beyond, was sufficient to bring the crane to a halt. Nonetheless, it had run for nearly 23 miles, after

Above Ex-LMS 30-ton Ransomes & Rapier crane No RS1069/30 in ungainly pose, having run forward and fallen into the gap over the highway during the renewal of the bridge on 23 October 1966 at Charnock Richard. Sadly, the crane did not survive its adventure. *P.G. Reed*

Right The end of ex-SR 36-ton Ransomes & Rapier crane, No DS1196 after tipping over at Lover's Walk, Brighton, on 25 October 1964 while lifting a motor bogie without the propping girders in use. *Evening Argus*

which it rolled gently back into the station where it was secured by the somewhat relieved signalman. Nonetheless, prior to this, Control had felt it necessary to make arrangements to clear the line through Carlisle station in case it continued that far. Intercepting the runaway crane by locomotive was even considered, but in the event such drastic action was fortunately not required.

Most modern cranes are capable of propelling themselves at slow speed at the scene of operations and therefore ordinarily do not need a locomotive constantly attached. Any damage to the track, or a deliberate gap, such as during planned bridge works, however, poses a greater threat. Once on site with its jib raised, the crane will move cautiously forward to the correct point of work. If the track has been broken, an upturned sleeper or wheel scotch should be placed across the rail ends. Particular care needs to be exercised when operating on steep gradients, however, because not only may a runaway occur, but also the crane may fall into the gap created by the bridge works.

On 23 October 1966, ex-LMS 30-ton Ransomes & Rapier crane No RS1069/30 was working near Charnock Richard on a gradient of 1 in 109, when it ran out of

control and fell, jib leading, into the roadway below, resulting in injuries to three men. Until shortly before, a locomotive had been attached to the crane, but this had gone to fetch water eight miles away when the moment arrived for the last girder to be removed. This required a reach with the jib of some 35ft and it was decided to bring the crane forward 3ft to within 3ft of the end of the rails. Having done so, the driver had been asked to move back some 6in, but as he disengaged the gears, the crane ran forward and although he attempted to control it, he was unsuccessful. Scotches had been applied, but these slipped off the rails when the crane started running away, with catastrophic results.

Despite a gradient post clearly marked 1 in 109, located about 10 yards from the northern end of the bridge, the shed-master in charge of the crane had not noticed the gradient; nonetheless, until shortly before the accident a locomotive had been attached to the crane. The accident occurred because the regulations had not been followed. The crane should not have been moved on a gradient of 1 in 109 without a locomotive attached, while a baulk timber also fastened to the rails might have prevented the accident. Following this disaster, instructions were issued

Cowans Sheldon 30-ton steam crane No 139 lying in an undignified pose, with the jib across the wagon it was trying to lift, in a field beside the line at Rhiwderin having fallen over on 7 February 1964. *E. Mountford*

Members of the breakdown gang gather round the bogie of No 139 during preparation for recovery. *E. Mountford*

Recovery in full swing with a pair of Cowans Sheldon 75-ton steam cranes, Nos 141 and 142 from Swindon and Canton, seen here individually lifting the jib and boiler on 26 February 1964. *E. Mountford*

As if bomb damage in Wimbledon Upside Yard in 1944 was not bad enough, the tipping over of Ransomes & Rapier 36-ton crane No 81S, without its counterweight in position, added to the confusion, leading to the need for 36-ton sister Rapier and 36-ton Cowans Sheldon cranes to come to its rescue. *S.C. Townroe*

Ex-LMS 30-ton Cowans Sheldon steam crane No RS1074/30 capsized on the Waterloo branch, Aberdeen, in May 1970. Sister crane No RS1073/30 did likewise at Belston Jct lifting a 20-ton brake van in February 1971 and was recovered by Cowans Sheldon 45-ton No RS1058/45 and taken into St Rollox on 8 February. *J. Templeton*

that on a gradient steeper than 1 in 260 it was required that timbers be placed across the track, while on anything steeper than 1 in 150, the crane must be coupled up to a locomotive throughout the duration of the work.

While a train of empty Portsmouth stock was waiting on the buffer stops of the exit road to the Lover's Walk depot, Brighton, prior to going into the station, it was run into by a twelve-car made up of a 6-PUL and 6-PAN set, creating quite a mess. The 36-ton Ransomes & Rapier crane No DS1196 of Brighton was duly summoned to clear the wreckage. While attempting to pick up a motor bogie from an EMU side on, without the benefit of having the propping girders extended and properly supported, the crane tipped over across all the lines from London into the station. In retrospect, to some, the organisation appeared far from what might have been expected, with too many bosses telling those that mattered how to do their jobs. The driver was seriously injured and the crane a total loss. The Stewart Lane's crane was called to Brighton to deal with the consequences and went on to deal with the original collision.

On the Western Region, Cowans Sheldon 30-ton crane No 139 overturned at Rhiwderin on the Newport to Caerphilly line on 7 February 1964, while slewing a 16-ton steel coal wagon through 90°. Unfortunately, the driver was killed in the incident. Two weeks later, the boiler was removed prior to re-railing the crane. Two Cowans Sheldon 75-ton cranes Nos 141 and 142 from Swindon and Canton recovered No 139 on 26 February 1964, the jib being loaded first, after which the frame and wheels were placed back on the track.

On 6 January 1968, a 120-ton electric transformer was being transported under police escort on a short road journey from English Electric's works at Stafford to a

disused airfield at Hixon, where the company's abnormal loads were held pending onward transfer. Having failed to heed the notices to phone the signalman before crossing with a long, low vehicle and exceptional load, while taking the loaded heavy-duty, thirty-two-wheel transporter and tractor over the automatic half-barrier level crossing in Station Road, difficulties were experienced. The problem was that the trailer needed raising to clear the ground, but contact with 25kV overhead lines had to be avoided. Whilst the transporter was stationary astride the line, the crossing's warning bells and lights were activated and the barrier came down onto the transformer. Barely 30 seconds later, the transporter was hit by the 11.30am twelve-coach Manchester to Euston express train travelling at speed, resulting in the deaths of eight passengers and three staff on the train.

During the clearing up operation, the transformer involved in the collision was being cut into manageable pieces when the insulation caught fire, to be doused by the fire brigade with liberal quantities of water. There followed a sharp drop in the ambient temperature, causing the water that had soaked into the ground to freeze. Temporary tracks were laid over this ground to give access for the breakdown cranes, however, a rapid rise in temperatures led to thawing of the ground. This then subsided under the weight of the 75-ton Cowans Sheldon crane No RS1092/75 from Derby, perhaps aided by an unknown land drain under one of the supporting propping girders, as it was making a tandem-lift of a coach with Crewe's 50-ton Cowans Sheldon crane No RS1005/50. The Derby crane fell over, causing an inspector on the footplate who jumped, to break a leg, while the driver was unhurt.

Unfortunately, cranes continue to fall over and 76-tonne crane No ADRC96705 did so at Ryhope Grange on 5 December 1992, where it is seen lying on its side with a severely buckled jib which proved fatal to the crane. *R. Watson*

14

Future Policy

In more recent years, the increasing use of alternative means of re-railing and recovery has led to a decline in the need to rely on rail cranes for such operations. Improvements in sophisticated lightweight portable power-driven jacking systems; the availability of inflatable air bags for lifting and righting vehicles; the introduction of road-mobile and road/rail recovery vehicles, suitable for small incidents; and the hiring of large road-mobile cranes, where appropriate, have all been the cause for a substantial reduction in the dependence on rail-mounted cranes for such operations.

In the civil engineering field, the increasing size and capacity of road-mobile cranes has led to their adoption for bridge works more often than in the past. Their use frequently permits the setting up of the crane adjacent to the line in advance of taking possession of the track, with a consequential saving in time over bringing a rail crane to site and setting up, together with subsequent packing up and clearing off the site all within the overall possession period. In addition, since the advent of the space programme and developments in the oil industry, there have been significant advances in equipment to lift and transport extremely heavy loads and these are now being used for bridge works, particularly when space allows the removal and installation of rail bridge decks over highways.

As a result, by 1988 only twenty breakdown cranes were left, consisting of six telescopic-jib 75-tonne, eleven 76-tonne and three 50-tonne strut-jib cranes, all diesel powered. For breakdown work, these were supplemented by 30 road/rail and 29 road recovery vehicles at 37 locations, together with four sites with rail vans only. The cranes were generally spread around England, with three in the London area, but only one in Wales, at Cardiff, and two in Scotland, at Haymarket and at Motherwell. The remainder of Wales, the north of Scotland and East Anglia became dependent on vans of one description or another, or for heavier work cranes brought in from some distance.

At long last, standardisation of lifting brackets has been adopted, with two capacities of 35- and 17½-tonnes. Costly and heavy wrought-iron chains, requiring regular annealing, or in some cases steel-wire ropes, have largely been replaced by synthetic-fibre slings of much lighter weight, or high-strength shock resistant alloy-steel chains. High-pressure sodium floodlighting was developed late in the conversion programme and first fitted to Doncaster's 76-tonne strut-jib crane and subsequently added to the telescopic-jib cranes. Staff training was undertaken on a dedicated site at Toton allied to the College of Railway Technology, Derby, in due course trading independently as Catils.

By early 1995, the number of cranes had been reduced to fifteen and the 50-tonne type made extinct, with Scotland having just one crane and the West Country joining the regions without any rail-mounted crane power for breakdown work. By 1998, most of the remaining strut-jib 76-tonne cranes had been withdrawn, leaving just two retained, while five of the telescopic-jib cranes were overhauled by Clarke Chapman of Gateshead. Telescopic-jib crane No ADRC96711, on the other hand, was withdrawn and cannibalised to provide spares for the remainder.

With the break up and privatisation of British Rail, ownership of breakdown facilities, including cranes, fell to Railtrack and later Network Rail. They made arrangements with English, Welsh and Scottish Railway (EWS) to base the cranes at sites owned or leased by EWS and for the latter to man, maintain and operate the cranes when required. In the event of an incident, following the release of any passengers, greater priority is now given to the investigation and recording of any evidence relating to the incident as a potential 'scene of crime', rather than clearing the line and restoring traffic, which would minimise delay and inconvenience to rail customers at large. It is usual for the EWS crane supervisor to travel to the site, assess the situation with respect to recovery and then liaise with Network Rail's Incident Officer with regard to the programming of his operations. In such circumstances, it may be some time before any cranes, either rail- or road-mounted are able to move onto site and set to work. During this period, risk assessments will have been undertaken, careful plans will have been fully developed and method statements prepared.

The increase in freight traffic on the rail network following privatisation, however, means that, instead of

Bridge sites inaccessible by road, such as rail over rail intersection bridges, may continue to challenge the ingenuity of engineers charged with say renewing a bridge deck without employing rail-mounted cranes. In this example from the past, shows a relatively new BR 75-ton Cowans Sheldon crane No. RS1092/75 from Willesden and the Chief Civil Engineer's ex-WD Cowans Sheldon 45-ton breakdown crane No. RS1085/45 undertaking a two-crane lift during the reconstruction of Bridge No. 13 just north of Primrose Tunnel outside Euston station. This was on the Marylebone to Neasden line (ex-GC) over the West Coast main line (ex-LNWR) at South Hampstead on 15 November 1964. *MS Welch*

there being a steady fall-off in derailments, and despite other methods of coping with them, when they occur, the need for a few high-capacity rail-mounted cranes strategically located around the country remains a requirement. At the beginning of September 1998, when two of the telescopic-jib cranes were out of service for overhaul, the Thornaby 76-tonne strut-jib crane overturned at Denthead while clearing up after the derailment of a coal train. Cranes from Crewe and Toton were then sent to deal with the toppled crane, leaving only two cranes, located at Old Oak Common and Cardiff, available for duty elsewhere.

Whilst since 2001, two 100-tonne and three 125-tonne telescopic-jib cranes, of similar or greater capacity than breakdown cranes, have been acquired by track-maintenance companies from Kirow of Leipzig in Germany, at a cost of approximately £1.4 million each, during the ensuing decade little attempt to employ them in accident or derailment recovery work appears to have been made.

At the time of concluding this text, it is understood that four 75-tonne telescopic-jib cranes remain in the ownership of Network Rail, three allocated to Bescot, Knottingly and Wigan, with one spare and available to stand in as necessary.

Conclusions

To design a rail-mounted crane for breakdown work that is capable of lifting any substantial load and yet remains stable while standing free on rail and within a limited maximum axle load invariably leads to some compromises. The narrowness of the distance between the rail heads limits the stability when free on rail. For a given load and radius this can be counteracted by increasing the counterbalance at the tail end of the crane superstructure, but this is in turn restricted by the risk of overturning backwards with no load. This can be offset by increasing the total dead load acting about the centre of gravity of the crane, and usually this is put in the carriage. For a given number of axles, however, the maximum permissible axle load will constrain the extent to which the overall weight can be raised. This might be overcome by adding to the number of axles, but minimum permissible axle spacing means that the length of the carriage has to be increased, which has an adverse effect on the outreach to the point of lift for maximum load in front of the crane.

From the 1930s, the usual solution for all larger cranes in the United Kingdom has been to adopt a four-axle carriage with relieving bogies at each end. Even then, to make the most of the permitted axle loads, it is desirable to utilise the maximum load on each axle. In train formation, however, with the weight of the jib

Ex-LNER 4-6-0 B17 Class No 61643 *Champion Lodge* passes Hatfield on 11 November 1951 with a breakdown train including a 45-ton Cowans Sheldon steam crane, thought to be from Cambridge. *Unattributed*

On 5 August 1966, Cowans Sheldon 75-ton diesel No DB965186 from Nine Elms, and Ransomes & Rapier 36-ton steam crane No DS80 from Guildford, work on in the evening light to restore a Sulzer Type 3 diesel locomotive which had run through the trap points at Cox's Mill, Addlestone. *Author*

The sad end to Cowans Sheldon 50-tonne crane No ADRC96716 as its dismantled component parts stand on the ground outside the works at Ashford (Kent) in July 1973, awaiting final disposal in 1993. *M. House*

largely resting on the match wagon, the counterweight in the tail of the crane would place the longitudinal centre of gravity to the rear of the middle of the carriage and hence give an unequal distribution of axle loads. This has often led to the placing of the king pin just forward of the second axle to optimise the axle loads.

In conclusion, it can be seen that from 1930 onwards, the general trend was towards high-capacity cranes with relieving bogies capable of lifting 36 tons at 24ft radius. The possibility that greater loads at reduced radii would be lifted under emergency conditions was acknowledged by the LMS in their strengthening of this type to 50 tons and subsequently in 1940 by the introduction of 45-ton cranes by the other three mainline railway companies.

At the same time, the LMS also recognised the need for a modern intermediate-capacity handy crane with a long jib, whereas the other companies merely cascaded their older, lower-capacity cranes to less-important districts. Older cranes were usually limited to a speed of 25mph in train formation, which clearly restricted their ability to reach the site of any derailment or accident promptly, but perhaps this did not matter when there was always a crane based not too far

away. More-modern cranes of the grouping era were usually allowed to run at up to 40 or 45mph, while BR's cranes of the 1960s could run at 60mph.

Finally, railway cranes followed the practice developed for road-mobile cranes of adopting telescopic jibs when 75-tonne cranes were introduced in 1977. Equipped with a moveable counterweight and relieving bogies, but without the need for a match wagon, these cranes achieved an equal distribution of axle loads and were capable of running at 75mph.

Readers will recall that my initial enquiries into the subject of breakdown cranes were brought about by Hornby-Dublo launching a model steam breakdown crane in 1960. It was stated at the time that this was based on a Cowans Sheldon 45-ton crane from the Eastern Region of British Railways, but that was all. Faced with this challenge, my keeping an eye out for any information, drawings, diagrams and photographs gradually grew into dedicated research, on and off, over several decades and resulted in this work. It has been absorbingly interesting and has brought me into contact with many people, both professional and amateur, who have shared my interest, be it through their business or through an enthusiasm for the subject.

Appendices

Appendix 1: British Railways Statistics

Year ending 31 Dec	1923	1938	1948	1955	1966	1970	1980	1987	1995
Route miles	20,314	19,881	19,598	19,061	13,721	12,000	10,964	10,358	10,339
Passenger journeys	1,772M	1,205.6M	996.0M	966.9M	975M	805M	760M	727.2M	718.7M
Passenger miles	-	19,702M	21,259M	20,309M	18,453M	18,400M	19,700	19,150M	18,256M
Freight traffic (t)	343M	267.9M	277.6M	278.6M	214M	201M	144M	138M	97.3M
Passenger carriages (including DMU/EMU)	51,015	43,197	40,351	41,715	22,492	18,869	17,012	12,685	10,637
Steam locos	24,184	19,587	20,211	17,955	1,686	0	0	0	0
Diesel locos	6	37	69	456	4,062	4,183	3,078	2,398	1,619
Electric locos	41	13	17	71	340	328	301	240	258
Freight vehicles	714,246#	1,243,944	1,179,404	1,124,812	551,422	415,832	119,507	74,247	13,397*
Number of derailments	-	-	-	-	-	10,182	4,843	3,171	159
Breakdown cranes	74	86	107	101	83	64	45	25	6

Excluding private owner wagons.
* For 1994.

Appendix 2: Mechanical Details

			Works/ Order Nos (No if not clear from works Nos)	Max load @ radius (Tons/ ft-in)	Wheel arrangement	Cylinders dia. x stroke (inch)	Boiler		Jib length (ft-in)/ source	Tare Wt (T-c)
RAILWAY BREAKDOWN CRANES – MECHANICAL DETAILS										
Maker	Year	Purchased by					Pressure (psi)	Dia. x ht (ft-in)		
R&R	1915	MR	7608	36/20 40/18	4-8-4RB	8 x 14	120	4-6 x 7-8	41-5	82-10/ 96-15
CS	1930	LMS	5111-3	36/25-0 50/18-0	4-8-4RB	8 x 12	120	4-6 x 6-8	40-7½	95-0
Craven	1931	LMS	12683(2)	36/24-0 50/18-0	4-8-4RB	8 x 14	120	4-6 x 6-6	41-9	
R&R	1931	LMS	2958(1)	36/20 40/18	4-8-4RB	9 x 14	120	4-6 x 6-8	41-10	92-2
R&R	1932	LNER	D4648(1)	35/25-0	4-8-4RB	9½ x 14	120	4-6¾ 6-8		92-8#
CS	1936	LNER	5755	36/25-0	4-8-4RB	8 x 14	120	4-6 x 6-8	41-0	95-17
CS	1937	LNER	6080	35/25-0	4-8-4RB	8 x 14	120	4-6 x 6-8	42-0	95-17
R&R	1937	SR	E4334(2)	36/20-0	4-8-4RB	9½ x 14	100	4-6 x 6-5	41-10	99-18#
R&R	1940	WD	E9085(2)	36/20-0	4-8-4RB	9½ x 14	100	4-6 x 6-5	41-10	
CS	1940	LNER	6870-5	45/20-0 50t/	4-8-4RB	8 x 14 diesel	120 -	4-6 x 6-8 -	42-0	95-17 102-9
R&R	1940	SR	E8137(4)	45/20-0	4-8-4RB	9½ x 14	120	4-6x6-11	41-10	112-7
R&R	1940	GW	E8136(2)	45/20-0	4-8-4RB	9½ x 14	120	4-6x6-11	41-10	111-19
CS	1941	LMS	7117	30/16-0	0-6-4	8 x 12	120	4-6 x 6-8	40-6	
R&R	1942–3	LMS	GF3878(5)	30/16-0	0-6-4	8½ x 12	120	4-6 x 6-8	41-0	58-10
CS	1942	MoS	7871-2	45/20-0	4-8-4RB	8 x 14	120	4-6 x 6-8	41-10	
CS	1943	MoS	8052-9	45/20-0	4-8-4RB	8 x 14	120	4-6 x 6-8		
R&R	1943	LNER	F4991(2)	45/20-0	4-8-4RB	9½ x 14	120	4-6x6-11	41-10	112-2
R&R	1943	MoS	F5937(6)	45/20-0	4-8-4RB	9½ x 14	120	4-6x6-11	41-10	
CS	1943–4	LMS	F7519-23	30/16-0	0-6-4	8 x 12	120	4-6 x 6-8	40-6	60-8
CS	194?	MoS	7869-70	30/16-0	0-6-4	8 x 12	120	4-6 x 6-8	40-6	
R&R	1945	SR	GF9162(1)	45/20-0	4-8-4RB	9½ x 14	120	4-6x6-11	41-10	111-17
R&R	1946	WO	GG2144(1)	45/20-0	4-8-4RB	9½ x 14	120	4-6x6-11	41-10	110-19
CS	1948	LNER	9017	36/25-0	4-8-4RB	8 x 14	120	4-6 x 6-8	41-10	99.25
CS	1961	BR	C58-65	30/16-0	0-6-4	8 x 14	150	4-6 x 6-6	45-0	67-16
CS	1962	BR(S)	C66-7	30/16-0	0-6-4	diesel	-	-	45-0	63-8½#
CS	1961	BR	C78-87	75/18-0 76t/5.5m	4-8-4RB	8 x 14 diesel	150 -	6-6 x 6-9 -	49-0	131-4 140.8t
CS	1964	BR(S)	C88-89	75/18-0	4-8-4RB	diesel	-	-	49-0	117-0#
CS	1977	BR	31145-31150	75t/7.5m	4-8-4RB	diesel	-	-	10,897-15,926	153t
Note: # Jib resting on match wagon.										

Left Holbeck's ex-LMS 40-ton Ransomes & Rapier crane No. DE 331159, together with replacement match wagon No. DE 961652 on 10 June 1972, both in bright red livery. *Author*

Appendix 3: Speed of Motions

RAILWAY BREAKDOWN CRANES – SPEED OF MOTIONS								
Maker	Year built	Purchased by	Works/ Order Nos	Max speed Lifting (ft/min)		Max speed travelling (ft/min)	Slewing 1 revolution (min)	Raise Jib (min)	Remarks
				Max load	Reduced load				
R&R	1915	MR	7608						
CS	1930	LMS	5111-3	13	35	150	2	3	
Craven	1931	LMS	12683	15	30	260	1½		
R&R	1931	LMS	2958	10	40	85	1	6ft/min	
R&R	1932	LNER	D4648	10	40	85	1½		
CS	1936	LNER	5755	20	52	100	1½	3	(1)
CS	1937	LNER	6080						
R&R	1937/40	SR & WD	E4334/9085	10	30	80	1		
CS	1940/43	LNER & MoS	6870-5/8052-9	15	45	180/270	1		
R&R	1940	SR & GW	E8136/7	10	30	180/270	1		
CS	1941/43–4	LMS & MoS	7117/7519-23/ 7869-70	15	40	300	1	2½	
R&R	1942–3	LMS	GF3878	15	45	300	1	8ft/min	
CS	1942	MoS	7871-2						
R&R	1943/5-6	LNER, MoS, SR & WO	F4991, F5937, GF9162, GG2144	10	30	180/270			
CS	1948	LNER	9017						
CS	1961/2	BR	C58-65	25	75	150/300	1	15 ft/min	(2)
CS	1962	BR(S)	C66-7	25	50	150/30	1	15 ft/min	(2)
CS	1961	BR	C78-89	10	20	300	2	2½	(3)
CS	1977	BR	31145-31150	10	42	432	2	1.9	(4)

Note:
(1) 6 tons @ 120 ft/min on auxiliary hoist
(2) Haul 6 tons @ 125 ft/min
(3) 12 tons @ 45 ft/min or 6 tons at 90 ft/min on auxiliary hoist
(4) 6 tonnes @ 10 ft/min

Six 45-ton cranes were built by Cowans Sheldon in 1939/40 as part of the ARP arrangements and supplied to the LNER. As Scottish Region No. RS1058/45, it stands outside Eastfield motive power depot in red livery on 11 June 1978. Eight years later it was converted to diesel power. *Colour Rail*

Appendix 4: Breakdown Cranes out with the National Network

RAILWAY BREAKDOWN CRANES OUT WITH THE NATIONAL NETWORK

Company	Group/BR Nos			Maker	Year built	Makers Works No	Max Cap	Match wagon No	Locations & Remarks	Date of Withdrawal from BR
	1st	2nd	3rd							
LMS	MP 2	RS1001/50	ADRC95202	CS	1931	5112	50T	299854	Midland Rly Centre ex Spring's Branch 25/5/80, sold to MR Trust, Butterley	c8/80
LMS	MP 3	RS1004/40	DE331159 ADRR95207	R&R	1931	D2958	40T	299850	Sold Wath Skip Hire, resold to Nene Valley Rly ex Doncaster 12/82, Wansford 1/83	12/82
LMS	MP 4	RS1005/50	ADRC95203	CS	1931	5111	50T	299851	Sold to K&WVR ex Spring's Branch 5/82, K&WVR 20/5/11	5/82
LMS	MP 8	RS1013/50	ADRV95205	Craven	1931	12683/6	50T	299852	Sold to E Lancs R ex Carlisle 26/8/82, Bury 11/82	4/82
LMS	MP 9	RS1015/50	ADRV95206	Craven	1931	12683/6	50T	299853	Dinting ex Allerton 2/82, KWVR, 30/9/90	2/82
LNW	MP 20	RS1020/30	-	CS	1908	2987	30T	284???	Preston Park, NRM York 1977 Carnforth 1978, Oakmoor, Churnet Valley Rly 1998, Crewe Heritage Centre 10/11	6/64
LMS	1250	RS1054/50	ADRC95204	CS	1931	5113	50T	299855	Sold to GWS ex Haymarket 9/87, GWS Didcot 9/87	9/87
NER	CME ?	-	-	Craven	1912	9372	35		Gateshead 1912, To WD 1914, to SNCB, Leuven 1996.	
NER	CME 13	901638	(DE331)153	Craven	1907	8153	25T	320952	NRM York ex Shirebrook & Doncaster 1975, NYMR 2/78 to 7/85, NRM York 7/85, Cheddleton, Churnet Val Rly early 1998, NRM 05/04	3/71
LNER	SB 1 39A	941590	(DE330)107 ADRC95224	CS	1926	4524	45T	39AA, 941751	Sold to NYMR ex Healey Mills 4/81, Grosmont MPD 4/81	3/81
LNER	941591	124	RS 1106/36 ADRC 95223	CS	1936	5755	36T	941753	Sold to Peak Rail ex Toton 12/87, Matlock 12/89	6/87
LNER	941599	ADE330110	ADRC95218 ADRC96719	CS	1940	6871	50t	DE 941776	Replacement all welded articulated jib following accident c1968, Crewe Heritage Centre 11/01-6/06	c1996/7.
LNER	941600 &/or 951515	WD u/k &/ or 210	-	CS	1940	6875 &/or 6874	45T	u/k &/ or 951675	King's Cross &/or Gorton, to Persia (Iran), Tehran 10/05 & other?	c1941
LNER	941601	(DE330)102	ADRR95214	R&R	1943	F4991/3	45T	941767	Sold to NYMR ex Tinsley 7/86, Pickering CE Dept 26/3/02	27/11/85
LNER	951516	(De330)122	RS1083/45 ADRR95215	R&R	1943	F4991/3	45T	951676	Sold to Bluebell Rly ex Newton Heath 11/81, Sheffield Park 11/81, OOU Horsted Keynes 21/2/12.	c1981
NB	770517	971567	RS1062/36 ADRC95200	CS	1914	3310	36T	770518 971568	Sold to SRPS 6/79 Falkirk to 23/8/85, Bo'ness 22/7/90-5/5/02	17/11/78
LNER	-	966103	ADRC95222	CS	1948	9017	45T	DB 998500	Dean Forest Rly, Norchard ex BREL Derby 4/4/86– 11/8/95, GCR, Ruddington 4/96.	c1985
GW	2			R&R	1908	B4411	36T		Dart Valley, Buckfastleigh ex BREL Swindon 25/11/75, Torbay Rly, Swindon Wks 24/5/90?, E Somerset R, Cranmore 1995.	1975
GW	17	RS1097/45	ADRR95208	R&R	1940	E8137	45T		Sold to GCR ex Crewe 2/82, Loughborough 2/82	c1981
GW	18		ADRR95212	R&R	1940	E8137	45T		Sold to Flying Scotsman Enterprises ex Old Oak Common 2/84, Carnforth 2/84-3/10.	c1983
GW	19		ADRR95213	R&R	1940	E8137	45T		Swindon Works Ltd ex Stewart's Lane 12/87, Swindon & Cricklade Rly, Blunsdon Rd 26/4/94-5/10/96. Flour Mill, Bream 2006.	c1987

RAILWAY BREAKDOWN CRANES OUT WITH THE NATIONAL NETWORK

Company	Group/BR Nos			Maker	Year built	Makers Works No	Max Cap	Match wagon No	Locations & Remarks	Date of Withdrawal from BR
	1st	2nd	3rd							
SR	1561S	DS1561	ADRR95210	R&R	1939	E8136	45T	DS3095	Sold to Swindon Rly Engrg 6/89, Swindon 12/90–27/8/00, Southall 2/06–29/11/11, Swanage 4/12	c1989
SR	1580S	DS1580 ADW 151	ADRR95216	R&R	1945	GF9162	45T	DS3096	Gloucester Warwickshire Rly, Toddington ex Old Oak Common 11/83, Llangollen Rly c1989, Mid-Hants Rly, Alton 7/92	1982
WD	Army 62006		WD214	R&R	1943	5937/49	45T		Gloucester & Warwickshire Rly ex WD 1992–3/10	
Ex-WD	RS 1085/45	ADRC 95221	ADRC96718	CS	1943	8053	50t	DB 998523	Llangollen Rly ex Laira 30/3/97	c1996
Ex-WD			XL1	CS	1943	8056/4-9	45T		Ex Gözdaru, Hungary	-
MoS			966 300		1944	7869/70?	.		OBB, Austria No. 966 300' Preserved at Strass Hof, 1998	
BR		139		CS	1960	C58	30T	DB 998526	Birmingham Rly Museum, Tyseley ex Worcester c1976	c1976
BR	-	RS1087/30	-	CS	1961	C60	30T	DB 998520	KWVR c7/76, SVR Bridgnorth 26/7/82	12/76
BR		RS1091/30	-	CS	1961	C65	30T	DB 998524	To SVR, Bridgnorth ex Chester 24/6/77, scrapped 2010/11	11/77
BR	DB 965183	ADB965183	ADRC96100	CS	1962	C66	30T	DB 998531	Horsham 9/80–3/05, Doncaster Electrification Construction Depot 4/03–07/05, Carnforth 4/12	c1996
BR	DB 965184	ADB965184	ADRC96101	CS	1962	C67	30T	DB 998531	Horsham 9/80–3/05, Doncaster Electrification Construction Depot 4/03–07/05, Dean Forest 3/05–2/08, Scrap Booth Rotherham 3/08.	
BR	DB966111	ADB966111	ADRC96701	CS	1961	C78	75T	DB 998517	Selhurst OOU 3/97 to 9/98. Sold to Phillips & bought by Needle, MOD Knighton 10/6/00–9/06, for scrap 5/08	3/97
BR	RS 1092/75	-	ADRC96706	CS	1962	C80	75T	DB 998534	Toton 9/94– 4/98. To Oakmoor, Churnet Valley Rly 1998–9/01, scrapped	by 7/95
BR	RS 1094/75	ADB365	ADRC96704	CS	1962	C82	75T	DB 998536	Toton 3/95. sold to Midland Rly Trust 22/10/97	10/96
BR	142	RS1095/75	ADRC96708	CS	1962	C84	75T	DB 998539	Tyseley 4/88–2/06. To Fragonset Rlys early 1998–10/06, Battlefield 12/09.	10/96
BR	141	ADB141	ADRC96707	CS	1962	C85	75T	DB 998538	To East Lancs Rly 3/97, ex Eastleigh, Riley Engrg at Bury 2003, ELR 5/12.	c1996
BR		ADB967159	ADRC96709	CS		C86	76t	DB 998540	Tees Shops (C&W), 02/04–5/08, to GCR Loughborough 2/09.	

Notes:

CS = Cowans Sheldon of Carlisle

R&R = Ransomes & Rapier of Ipswich

Craven = Craven Bros of Manchester and later Loughborough

OOU = Out of use

Wthl/Wthn = Withdrawal/Withdrawn

T = Ton

t = metric tonne

N/A = not applicable

Dates shown in *italics* are spot dates upon which the crane is known to have been at the depot concerned.

Appendix 5: Recovery Following a Derailment at Tremains East

Report on the Re-railing Operation carried out at Tremains East – 12 January 1964
The 6.20pm. Margam to Hafodyrnys, comprising thirty-five empty steel coal wagons with brakevan, and hauled by two English Electric Type 3 Diesel Electric Locomotives Nos D6843 and D6878 working in multiple, was derailed at Tremains Up Loop at 6.32pm on Friday, 10 January 1964. In the derailment, the train went through the stop block situated at the end of the trap point spur at the Up End of the Loop and came to rest with the rear end of the trailing locomotive D6843 approximately 12ft off the remaining end of the trap point spur and the front end of the leading locomotive fouling the Up Main Line. The leading wagon in the train had been forced up through the rear nose and cab of D6843, losing its front wheels and axle-box guides in the process. No other vehicles were derailed, but the front buffers of the second wagon in the train had been forced through the back of the leading wagon. A section of the Up Main Line adjacent to the stop block was also slewed and damaged by the derailment.

Description of site
The point of the derailment was at Tremains East, which is approximately one mile on the Up Side of Bridgend Station. At this point the Up Loop Line rejoins the Up Main Line, there being also a Down Loop Line which leaves the Down Main Line near Tremains East Box, approximately 200 yards on the Up Side of the derailment point. A crossover exists opposite Tremains East Box. At the point of derailment, the Main Line is level and there is a very little super elevation. A public road runs adjacent to the railway line at this point and there is an embankment running up from the line to the road, this embankment coming within 12ft of the Main Line where the leading derailed locomotive came to rest.

Description of locomotives
The two locomotives involved in the derailment were both of the Type 3 English Electric 1,750hp. The weight in working order of this class of locomotive is 102 tons 12cwt. The body is carried on two six-wheeled bogies, each bogie weighing 20 tons, and being connected to the main body by four safety links to either side of the locomotive. Four lifting points are provided at each end of the locomotive, the centre of each group of lifting points being 12ft 2in from the heads of the buffers.

Action taken on the evening of the derailment
Single Line working was introduced over the Down Main Line between Tremains West and Tremains East and the Tondu Breakdown Vans and Canton 75-ton Crane were ordered to the site.

Movements and Maintenance representatives were called to the site and after viewing the situation and discussing same it was eventually decided to postpone re-railing operations until the following Sunday, 12 January. This decision was prompted by the following factors:

1 The extent of the derailment of the two locomotives ruled out the possibility of re-railing by jacks or by towing back on over the trap point spur.
2 To carry out the operation as expediently as possible, two 75-ton Cranes would be necessary. Only two of these units are allocated to the Region and it would be necessary to bring one of these from Swindon.
3 Re-railing these locomotives can only be carried out by crane by utilising special lifting equipment. Except for eight combined lifting and jacking brackets, all at Canton, none of this equipment is in existence on this Region. There are in fact only two sets on British Railways, both allocated to the Eastern Region.
4 The damage to the permanent way would prevent the cranes being positioned close to the derailed locomotives. Due to the weight of the locomotives and the lifting characteristics of the 75-ton cranes, lifting could not be carried out from any other adjacent line.

Following this decision, arrangements were made with Paddington HQ for the Eastern Region equipment to be forwarded from Stratford to Cardiff during the following day and for the Swindon 75-ton crane to be sent down early on Sunday morning. The District Engineer's representative undertook to carry out temporary repair of the Up Main Line before Sunday and to remove any super elevation that did exist to enable the cranes to be positioned close to the derailment and the Movements representative undertook to arrange occupation for the duration of the operation.

Further operations on the Friday night were limited to withdrawing the remainder of the train from the Up Loop and extracting and removing the second wagon from the derailed wagon.

Arrangements made on Saturday 11 January
On the following day, the arrangements made with Paddington HQ the previous night were confirmed. The special lifting equipment had already been despatched from Stratford in a GUV and had left London on the 4.20am ex-Acton, eventually arriving at Canton at 7.00pm Saturday evening. A Lowmac vehicle was directed from Radyr to Canton to go with the Breakdown Special and to be used to load up the damaged wagon.

It was arranged for the Swindon Crane Special to form up with the Canton Crane at the latter depot and proceed to the site, together with the above vehicles, to arrive at 7.00am on Sunday morning. The Tondu Breakdown Vans were also ordered out to be on site at the same time.

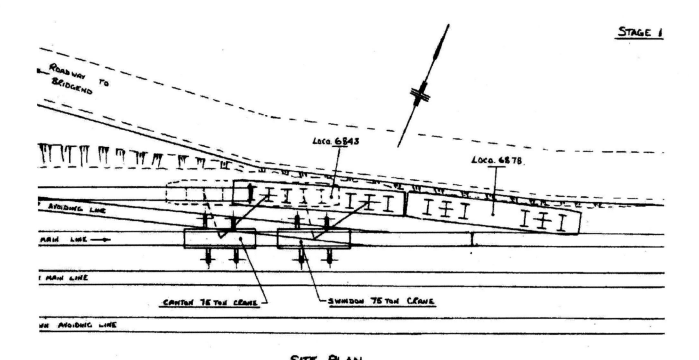

Figure 54 Site plan for first stage of the recovery of two English Electric Type 3 diesel locomotives derailed at Tremains East in January 1964. *BR, courtesy B. Penney*

On Saturday afternoon, the lifting brackets held at Canton were loaded on to a light Diesel Locomotive and conveyed to the site. Staff from Tondu Depot were on hand to fit these brackets to the trailing Locomotive D6483.

Operations carried out Sunday 12 January

The Special train left Canton at 6.00am on Sunday 12 January, but due to a late start and delays en route, the Swindon Crane Special was running 2 hours late and it was found necessary to form the train at Cardiff General Station.

The train left Cardiff General at 5.55am with the following formation: Diesel-hydraulic Locomotive D1045, Lowmac; GUV, Canton Riding Van; 75-ton Crane; two Brakevans; Swindon 75-ton Crane; Riding Van; arriving at Tremains East at 7.20am. Complete occupation of the Up and Down Main Lines and Up Loop had been given, single-line working being in operation over the Down Loop. The Crane Special was brought to a stand in the Down Main; opposite the site and the task of preparing the cranes was commenced.

The Up Main had now been temporarily repaired and re-aligned and the Up Loop connection taken out and it was now possible to plan the operation in the following sequence.

1 Bed down Swindon Crane on Up Main adjacent to back end of D6843
2 Position Lowmac on Up Loop near site
3 Lift damaged wagon off D6834, load on to Lowmac
4 Bed down Swindon Crane on Up Main adjacent to front end of D6843
5 Bed down Cardiff Crane on Up Main adjacent to rear end of D6843
6 Lift D6843 bodily with the two cranes and:
   a) If clearance between loco and the embankment was insufficient to permit slewing, build temporary track under loco leading up to trap point spur
   b) If clearance between loco and embankment was sufficient to permit slewing, slew round loco and put it down as near as possible to the trap point spur
7 If (a) above, position D1045 on Up Loop and endeavour to drag D6843 on to the trap point spur, utilising a chain from the Breakdown Van
   If (b) above; reposition cranes and lift D6843 on to the trap point spur
8 Reposition and bed down Swindon Crane adjacent to rear end of D6878
9 Run-round Cardiff Crane via Down Loop and reposition and bed down on Up Main adjacent to front end of D6878
10 Lift D6878 bodily with both cranes, slew round and lower D6878 on Up Main between the two cranes

In practice the above plan worked out quite well, but a certain number of operational and technical difficulties arose. These are given below where the re-railing operations are described in chronological order:

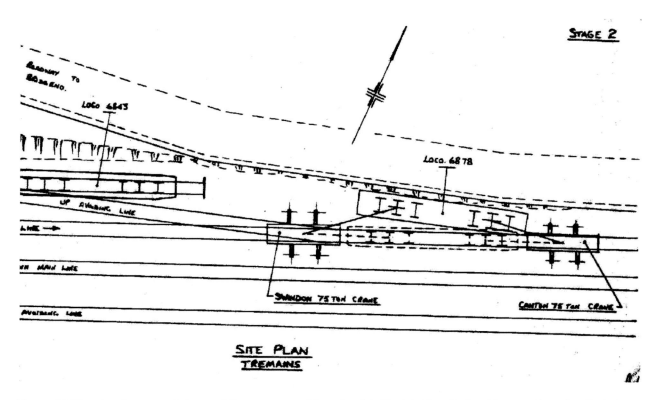

Figure 55 Site plan for second stage of the recovery of two English Electric Type 3 diesel locomotives derailed at Tremains East in January 1964. *BR, courtesy B. Penney*

7.20am   Crane Special arrived on site; stopped on Down Main opposite derailment. Tondu Breakdown Vans already at site standing on Up Loop.
Swindon Crane jib raised, train parted between Swindon Crane and its match truck.

8.00am   Front portion of train moved off along Down Main to crossover point at Tremains West, approx 1 mile from site. Necessary to lower jib of Swindon Crane to clear footbridge to Tremains Station.
In conjunction with this movement Tondu Loc and Vans taken to cross-over point and stood clear on Up Main. D1045 off, Tondu Vans pick up Lowmac and propel back along Up loop to site.
D1045 on train, picks up GUV and Canton Crane; stands clear.
Swindon Crane works over crossover road and proceeds along Up Main to site.
Canton Crane jib raised and follows Swindon Crane along Up Main to site.
D1045 propels GUV and Canton Match Wagon on to remainder of train and then propels back Down Main to site.

9.30am   Cranes arrive at site. Difficulty experienced en route due to cranes having to lower jibs to clear footbridge. (Note: It was decided to shunt the match wagons rather than lift them, due to the necessity of bedding down the cranes to carry out this operation.)

10.20am   Swindon Crane bedded down adjacent to back end of D6843. Both Stokes Bogies had to be lifted clear before this could be done and as there was insufficient clearance between the Up Main and Up Loop Lines to place them down in front of the Tondu Loco on the Up Loop. Due to their design with draw gear at one end only, each bogie had to be conveyed separately by Tondu loco and stood clear at Tremains West.

11.00am   Wagon loaded on to Lowmac. Due to the front buffers of the wagon being entangled in the cab superstructure of D6843 it was not possible to lift the wagon clear of the loco. and it was necessary to drop off the lifting chains and drag the wagon clear, using the Tondu train and chain from the vans. The wagon was then re-slung and lifted on to the Lowmac; following which the light hoist on the crane was used to lift the one pair of wagon wheels remaining on the ground into the loaded-up wagons. Meanwhile, the Canton crane had lifted its front Stokes Bogie and placed it to the rear on the Up Main. The special lifting equipment had been offloaded from the GUV on to the ballast and was coupled up to the 73½-ton lifting beam; which by now had been attached to the crane from the match truck. Following the loading up of the wagon, some considerable time was taken in improvising lifting equipment for the Swindon crane. Only two equalising beams were available from Stratford and the problem was eventually overcome by using two 25-ton shackles in conjunction with the main shackle and the four 21-ton large eyed ropes sent from Stratford.

During the above operation, opportunity was taken to remove three bogie safety slings from D6878 and replace three slings on D6843 which had been broken during derailment.

1.30pm   Both cranes moved up and bedded down in the pre-determined positions with the jibs at 22ft radius above the centre of the lifting points.

Some difficulty was experienced in securing the spreader beam to the lifting brackets due to the close fit of the pins in the brackets.

The weight of the loco was taken by both cranes and although there was no tendency for either crane to lift off the rails, the load was eased off and the extension-girder jacks tightened as a precautionary measure.

The weight was again taken and by jibbing in 2ft it was possible to part the two locos sufficiently to allow the couplings to be burnt apart.

By jibbing in and slewing it was then found possible to carry D6843 back sufficiently to drop the trailing bogie on to the end of the trap-point spur. This operation had to be carried out in a series of movements owing to the close proximity of the road embankment.

2.30pm   Back bogie of D6843 dropped on trap-point spur, front end dropped on the ground. Spreader beams released from lifting brackets, Canton crane packed up and moved back to pick up its leading Stokes Bogie.

Swindon Crane rebedded down adjacent to rear end of D6843. Coupled up to lifting brackets, procedure above repeated to lift front end of loco and move slowly back until front bogie over trap-point spur.

3.30pm   D6843 re-railed.

The ground around the rear of D6878 had a tendency to be soft and PW Staff were employed in making a firm foundation for the crane with ballast and old sleepers.

The lifting brackets were removed from D6843 by the Tondu gang and a start made on fitting these to D6878. The left rear end of this loco was hard up against the embankment and it was necessary to dig away the earth to allow the fitting of the bracket at this point.

The Swindon crane was bedded down adjacent to rear end of D6878 with jib set at 27ft radius over centre of lifting point. At this radius the crane would be overloaded, but this was the minimum radius at which the loco could be dropped between the two cranes.

The Canton crane was taken round to the up side of the derailed loco via the Down Loop and after depositing the rear Stokes Bogie on the Down Main was propelled along the Up Main and bedded down adjacent to the front end of D6878 with jib radius set at 26ft above the centre of the lifting points.

Spreader Beams attached to lifting brackets. Again difficulty experienced in entering pins.

5.15pm   Strain taken by both cranes. Canton crane holds firm, but rear wheels of Swindon crane start to lift off rails. Weight released and extension-girder jacks tightened. Process repeated four times before Swindon crane stable enough to take weight of loco.

Loco lifted off ground and Swindon crane jibs in to 26ft radius. Both cranes then slew in toward Up Main, bringing D6878 between them over latter line. Before lowering it was necessary to burn off a section of AWS casting hanging from underside of loco.

6.30pm.   D6878 re-railed.

Following the completion of the re-railing operation the cranes were utilised to assist the PW staff in replacing the connection from the Up Loop to the Up Main, which had been removed during the temporary repair of the track.

The disposal of the lifting equipment and the reforming of the cranes followed. This took a considerable time owing to the necessity of having to shunt each Stokes Bogie separately for the Swindon crane and of having to take both cranes with jibs raised back down the Up Main to connect up with their match trucks. This work was eventually finished at 10.00pm.

The Crane Special eventually left the site at 2.30am and arrived at Canton Depot 4.45am.

Summary of technical difficulties encountered during re-railing operations

1. The lifting equipment supplied by Stratford proved to be satisfactory. No difficulty was encountered in connecting the special equipment to the standard 73½-ton spreader beam supplied with the crane when two equalising beams were used. Some time was taken in selecting suitable shackles for adapting the equipment for use with Swindon crane's standard beam, but now that it is known what shackles can be used, this problem should not arise for future operations. Without this special equipment the operation could not have been accomplished and the question of supplying

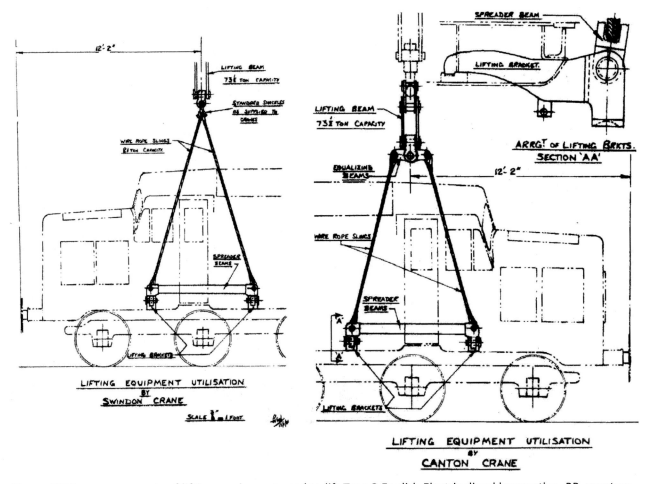

Figure 56 The arrangements of lifting equipment used to lift Type 3 English Electric diesel locomotive. *BR, courtesy B. Penney*

a set of this equipment for the Division should be followed up as a matter of urgency. Swindon DO representatives state that the necessary drawings were supplied to the Works last March.

2. The combined jacking and lifting brackets were fitted to the locomotives without difficulty, apart from the physical effort required to lift them into position (each weighs 220lbs, there being eight per locomotive). The brackets had been used on two previous re-railing operations.

3. Some difficulty was experienced in connecting the spreader beam to the lifting brackets due to the pins being a close fit through the two components. This can be overcome by grinding a lead on each pin. This can be arranged locally.

4. Three bogie safety links were broken during the derailment and it was necessary to transfer three from the second locomotive to aid the first re-railing operation, and then transfer them back again for the second operation.
    As this trouble might be experienced in other derailments it would no doubt be beneficial to retain a number of spare safety links in Breakdown Vans. This will be followed up.

5. One of the major difficulties encountered, which is due in the main to the design characteristics of the cranes, was the excessive overloading necessary to re-rail D6878. As stated previously, it was necessary to jib out to 27ft with the Swindon crane to carry out this operation, which resulted in a 46% overload being imposed on this crane and it will also be noted that before repeating tightening down of the extension-girder jacks, this crane was unstable with this overload.
    To bring the derailed locomotive down between the two cranes, which would be equivalent to an end-on lift, it was necessary to jib out the Canton crane 26ft which imposed an overload of 41% on this crane. Clearly to impose such an overload is most undesirable and it must be mentioned that similar overloads occur when corresponding lifts are taken with the majority of Diesel Main Line Locomotives supplied to this Region. This is however, due entirely to the limited lifting characteristics of this type of crane and this problem should be investigated as a matter of urgency by the British Railways Board.

On 30 August 1969, No. RS1075/30 from Shirebrook having recently arrived at Ripple Lane to relieve ex-LMS Rapier 30-ton, which was about to be sent to Doncaster for overhaul. *Author*

Notes:

1. The lifting characteristics of the 75-ton Crane are as follows:

MAIN HOIST		
Radius	**Level track**	**2in superelevation**
18ft-0in	75 tons	Not to be used
20ft-0in	65 tons	64.25 tons
25ft-0in	40 tons	39.75 tons
30ft-0in	30 tons	29.50 tons
35ft-0in	20 tons	19.75 tons
40ft-0in	15 tons	14.75 tons

2. When standing on a superelevated track, the crane must not work laden or unladen at less than the following radii:

2in superelevation	Main Hoist	Not less than 20ft-0in radius
2in superelevation	Aux Hoist	Not less than 22ft-9in radius

The radius for all superelevation duties is measured with the jib at right-angles to the carriage and pointing towards the low side of the track.

B.J. Penny Assistant Locomotive Engineer

Appendix 6: The Breakdown Crane Association (BDCA)

Studying the past and protecting the future of the railway breakdown crane

The Breakdown Crane Association exists to encourage and promote the preservation and operation of historic railway breakdown cranes. To this end it is working to create a core of expertise in the operation, maintenance, preservation and restoration of the cranes that exist, to promote common standards and procedures for trainee induction into a crane team, crane team training and safety in operation, and to develop the engineering processes and standards and to locate the specialist suppliers and services needed to keep historic breakdown cranes operating.

The BDCA aims further to present a single unified interface between regulators and historic breakdown crane owners and operators, to research, record, share and make public the history of railway breakdown cranes, and to raise awareness of the historical contribution of breakdown cranes to British railway development.

It is hoped that meeting the Association's aims will be encouraged by its forum for the interchange of information between breakdown crane owners and operators, the forum having a restricted Members' Section for discussions on Safety and Training, Operation, Maintenance and Servicing, and Processes and Suppliers, but also an area for public discussion on general breakdown crane matters.

Membership is open to all breakdown crane owners and operators, and to any other person with hands-on involvement or relevant technical/historical expertise. Communications are normally conducted by electronic means and there is no membership fee (this may need to be reviewed from time to time).

If you would like to become a member, please go to: www.bdca.org.uk and follow the menu through 'The Association' – 'About the Association' – 'Membership'.

Received too late to include in Volume 1 is this splendid view of the interior of the Rugby breakdown train in 1920, with the shed foreman J.C. Beck and the leading fitter sitting in the riding van. Note the photographs and route map on the walls. *J.P. Richards, courtesy LNWR Society*

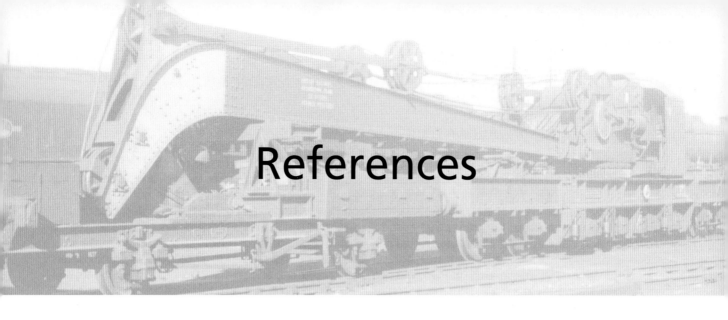

References

Alves, A.T. *The Railway Operating Division on the Western Front* (Shaun Tyas, 2009, pp192–195)

Appleby C.J. *Appleby's handbook of machinery* (E&FN Spon, 1869)

Ashcroft W. *Derailed at Hest Bank* (*Steam World*, August 1998, pp58–61)

Atherton W.H. *Hoisting machinery* (The Technical Press, 1940)

Atkins A.G., Beard W., Hyde D.J. & Tourret *A history of GWR goods wagons* (David & Charles, 1975 & 1986)

Bishop W. *Off the rails* (Kingfisher Railway Publications, 1984)

Breakdown cranes for British Railways (*Railway Gazette*, 27 May 1960)

The breakdown squad (*Locomotive Magazine*, p 171, Vol 5, Nov 1900)

Bridge E.K. *Practical aspects of bridge reconstruction in the Southern Region of British Railways* (*Railway Gazette*, 13 July & 10 August 1956)

Brownlie J.S. *Railway steam cranes*, (Author, Glasgow, 1973)

Cameron K.R.M. *Railway breakdown services* (*Railway Division Journal*, Institution of Mechanical Engineers, pp 213–285, Vol 2, Part 3, 1971)

Cooper A., Leggott & Sprenger C. *The Melbourne Military Railway* (The Oakwood Press, 1990, pp51–58)

Crafter R. *Rapier petrol-electrical mobile cranes & steam breakdown cranes* (Locomotive & carriage Institution of Great Britain, 1937)

Designing for mobility – cranes on rails (*Engineering*, Nov 1977, pp 962–3)

Dunn J.M. *Reflections on a railway career* (pp 22–23)

Early steam cranes and hoists (*The Engineer*, 28 May 1909, pp 551–554 & 11 June 1909, p614)

Earnshaw A. *Trains in trouble Nos 5–8* (Atlantic Transport Publishers, 1989, 1990, 1991, 1993)

Earnshaw A. *An illustrated history of trains in trouble* (Atlantic Transport Publishers, 1996)

Essery R.J. *An illustrated history of LMS wagons, Vol 1* (Oxford Publishing Co, 1981, p152)

General Instructions 10 – Covering the repainting and treatment of …. breakdown cranes and other service stock (British Transport Commission, No BR 9210, July 1959)

Highland Railway Journal (No 49, Spring 1999, p18)

Hoole K *Trains in trouble, Vol 3 & 4* (Atlantic Transport & Historical Publishers, 1892 & 1983)

Industrial rail cranes of the British Isles (Industrial Railway Society, January 1997; Amendment List Nos 1 and 2, July 1997 and May 1998)

Ivatt H.A. *Breakdown tackle for railway work* (Transactions of the Institution of Civil Engineers of Ireland, Vol XVI, June 1886, pp89–106 and figs 1–10)

Kidner R.W. *Service stock of the Southern Railway* (The Oakwood Press, 1993)

Locomotive breakdown steam crane – Taff Vale Railway (*The Engineer* 1885, p 48)

Locomotive Magazine (15 February 1943, p23)

Lund G.H.K. *Railway breakdown and re-railing equipment* (*Journal of the Institution of Locomotive Engineers*, May/June 1950, pp 226–303)

Nichols M. *Mishaps and recovery facilities on British Rail* (Conference on vehicle recovery road and rail, Institution of Mechanical Engineers, 1983, pp 37–43)

The Operating Department of the LMS during the Second World War 1939-1945 (TNA, RAIL418/197, pp 195–196 and RAIL418/201, pp 22–23)

Payne J. *Stothert & Pitt, the rise & fall of a Bath company* (Millstream Books, 2007) Patent Specifications:
a) No GB 12,927, 1904, FW Scott Stokes, *Improvements relating to the distribution of travelling cranes and other heavy bodies upon a temporary extended wheel base*
b) No GB 323,723, 1929, Ransomes & Rapier and A Scott Stokes, *Improvements in or relating to travelling cranes*
c) No GB 346,348, 1930, Craven Bros and AE Horrocks, *Improvements relating to breakdown cranes*
d) No GB 1,498,859, 1975, Clarke Chapman and M Buttkereit, *Relieving bogie*

Permanent way locomotive crane, constructed by Messrs Appleby, Brothers, Engineers, Southwark (*Engineering*, 10 Sept 1875, pp205–206)

Reed J. *The cross-Channel guns* (After the Battle, 1980, No. 29 pp1–19)

Reid G.J.C. *Recovery techniques training in Scottish Region of British Rail* (Conference on vehicle recovery road and rail, Institution of Mechanical Engineers, 1983, pp 113–120)

Report of ad hoc committee on breakdown trains and cranes (British Transport Commission, 1955)

Robinson P.J., Baker S.M. and Hind J. *Design and development of the new 75-tonne high capacity rail cranes* (Railway Division, Proc Institution of Mechanical Engineers, Vol 193, 1979, pp425–438)

Robinson P.J. *Breakdown and recovery equipment modernization and improved techniques from new technology* (*Journal of Rail and Rapid Transit*, Proc Institution of Mechanical Engineers, Vol 203, 1989, pp14-24)

Robinson W.P. *From Steam to Stratford* (Author, 2005)

Sparks A.C. *Ex-CR 15-ton breakdown crane* (*Model Railway Constructor*, Vol 39, August 1972, p 309)

Sparks A.C. *Ex-HR 15-ton steam breakdown crane* (Model Railway Constructor, Vol 37, July 1970, p221)

Talbot E. *LNWR Recalled* (Oxford Publishing Co, 1987)

Travena A. *Trains in trouble, Vol 1 & 2* (Atlantic Books, 1981 & 1982)

Trotter E.B. *The breakdown crane* (*The Observer*, RCTS, July 1958 pp193–198)

Wainwright D. *Cranes and Craftsmen, The story of Herbert Morris Ltd* (Herbert Morris, 1974)

Webster H.C. *Locomotive running shed practice* (Oxford University Press, 1947, pp14–27)

Addendum and Corrigenda

Acknowledgements

As remarked in Volume 1, a work of this nature and length is not accomplished without the willing assistance and support of a large number of people and organisations. A wide range of source material on cranes, although often very focused on a specific niche area, nonetheless collectively assist building up of the overall picture. The National Archives, Kew, West Register House of the Scottish Record Office (now renamed and relocated the Scottish National Archives at General Register House) and the Library of the National Railway Museum at York, together with various county records offices, particularly Cumbria and Suffolk, were consulted and assistance kindly provided by their members of staff.

British Railway officials at all levels and of all regions have kindly assisted wherever they could, showing great friendliness and intense pride that one should be taking an interest in their work. Initial help came from the Public Relations & Publicity Officer of the London Midland Region at Euston. Access was granted to the archives by the CMEEs of the London Midland, Eastern, Western and Scottish regions at Derby, York, Swindon and Glasgow respectively. Permits to visit motive-power depots were issued to me and others, thereby enabling photographs to be taken of cranes. Similar facilities have been afforded on heritage railways, including the Bo'ness & Kinneil, Mid-Hants, North Yorkshire Moors and Swanage railways.

All the crane manufacturers still in business when this project started were kind enough to take time from their duties to answer my requests for information. Without exception this was graciously provided, but the records of some companies have survived to a greater extent than others. Facilities were afforded by Cowans Sheldon, Morris Cranes (Craven Bros), Ransomes & Rapier and Stothert & Pitt. Reference has been made to books and periodicals in many public collections, such as the Science Museum Library, Kensington and the Business and Patent Information Services, Leeds, and a few private libraries, together with papers read from some professional institutions, particularly the Locomotive Engineers Institution, now incorporated as the Railway Division of the Institution of Mechanical Engineers.

Whether a member or not, many railway societies have been of great assistance in responding to my enquiries over the years. Among these are: the Cumbria Railway Association, Great Eastern Railway Society, GNSR Association, Historical Model Railway Society, Industrial Railway Society, LMS Society, LNER Society/Study Group, LNWR Society, NER Railway Association, and Stephenson Locomotive Society. Correspondence has been entered into and meetings arranged with various fellow enthusiasts and railwaymen of which perhaps P.C. Appleyard, W.J. Barker, Bill Bishop, C.H. Burns, Duncan Burton, Manfred Buttkereit, Dave Carter, F.D. Carter, Francis Cooper, W. Dalkers, John Dawson, J.M. Dunn, Alan Earnshaw, Ron and Allan Garraway, Jack Hollick, Ken Hoole, Barry Lane, Walter Moffat, Eric Mountford, A.G. Newman, K. Noble, Jim MacIntosh, W.M. Roscoe Taylor, Ron Shepperd, John Steeds, Richard Taylor, Jack Templeton, Stephen Townroe, Harold Tumilty, Chris Verrinder, Mike Walshaw and Les and Peter Woad, deserve special mention. More recently, with the creation of the Breakdown Crane Association, great assistance and support has come from David Withers, Roger Cooke, Chris Capewell, Bill Lee and Mick House. My thanks to them all, for enabling me to offer this work and the accompanying drawings.

Picture Gallery

The Western Region's 75-ton crane No. 141, following an overhaul at Swindon Works, in the process of receiving the final touches of a repaint in plain red on 23 August 1971. *Author*

Thornaby TMD's 45-ton Cowans Sheldon No. ADRC95222 during the renewal of a bridge deck at East Cowton on 12 May 1984. *R Watson*

Cowans Sheldon 76-tonne crane No. ADRC96708, following its conversion to diesel propulsion and in yellow livery, stands adjacent to the M6 Motorway viaduct at Washwood Heath on 19 February 1990. *P Bartlett*

Cowans Sheldon 30-ton crane No. RS 1091/30 stands at Saltley MPD on 24 May 64, looking rather dirty in keeping with its Black Country location. It was later preserved on the Severn Valley Railway, but has recently been scrapped. The SVR does, however, still have sister crane, RS 1087/30, which was purchased from the Worth Valley Railway. *MS Welch*

One of the six Ransomes & Rapier 45-ton cranes were supplied to Ministry of Supply for War Department in anticipation of the invasion of Europe. This one found further employment on the Longmoor Military Railway in training railway troops for breakdown work. It was photographed on the last open day at Longmoor on 5 July 1969. *Author*

Above and below Ex-Midland Railway 40-ton Ransomes & Rapier crane No. RS1038/40 from Derby and recently repainted ex-LMS 50-ton Cowans Sheldon No. RS1005/50 steam crane from Crewe on 14 May 1961 are in the process of undertaking the renewal of the deck of under-bridge No. 9 close by Sedgeley Jct signal box at Dudley Port. *MS Welch*

Rugby's 50-ton Craven crane No. RS1013/50 on the left and Wellingborough's 30-ton Rapier crane No. RS1067/30 on the right lift out the old centre girder of Bridge No. 81 in October 1961, as part of the renewal of the deck. This bridge was at Hillmorton south of Rugby on the New Line from Roade via Northampton. *MS Welch*

Ex-GWR Ransomes & Rapier 45-ton crane No. RS 1097/45, formerly GW No. 17, on the Great Central Railway at Loughborough Central, circa 1999. Originally based at Wolverhampton Oxley MPD, in the early 1960s all Western Region territory North of Banbury inclusive was transferred to LMR control and thereby gaining its new number. The crane was then used on much of the West Coast Main Line electrification bridge renewal work. The original black livery has been re-applied to this crane since this photograph was taken.

A pair of Ransomes & Rapier 45-ton cranes from Nine Elms and Guildford (with the grey jib) during the early sixties engaged on the replacement of the bridge deck to Bridge No. 1 at Plough Lane between Clapham Jct and Wandsworth Town on the Windsor Line. *A Chiles*

Later in the operation at Windsor Street, Salford on the Liverpool to Manchester line illustrated on page 83, on 12 January 1969 the CCE's 45-ton crane, by now in yellow livery, lifts, with the aid of a lifting beam, a pre-tensioned precast concrete bridge beam from a wagon to within reach of a pair of 25-ton Coles road mobile cranes positioned one on each abutment. *MS Welch*

Ripple Lane's regular crane No. DE330136 on 19 July 1969, in faded red prior to its overhaul at Doncaster. *Author*

The construction of a new 2-span bridge to allow the dual-carriage M1 Motorway to pass beneath the GC main line south of Whetstone, a few miles South of Leicester. In wintery conditions of February 1963 ex-LNER 36-ton No. 124 and ex-WD 45-ton No. RS1085/45 Cowans Sheldon cranes unload from a bogie wagon a welded steel main girder and are about to place it onto a rolling path on military trestling beside and under the line. Once the rest of the steelwork has been erected on the roll-in path, the in-situ reinforced concrete deck cast and waterproofed: the whole assembly will be winched into a shallow excavation made in the line between newly constructed abutments and the track reinstated across the new bridge deck. *MS Welch*

At Oxford Road, Manchester, ex-LNER Ransomes & Rapier 45-ton crane No. RS1083/45 from Newton Heath gingerly lifts out a pre-cast concrete beam of a footbridge to be replaced by a wider one on 3 September 1968. Note the chimney raising tackle still in place. *MS Welch*

Freshly painted and so possibly overhaul, a Ransomes & Rapier 45-ton at Eastleigh being load-tested.

Cowans Sheldon 76-tonne crane No. ADRC967601 in May 1994 at Hove, soon after its transfer to Brighton, being tried out by the breakdown gang. In fact, it is understood that, it was never used in anger before being transferred away to Selhurst out of use and eventually scrapped. *M House*

Right Night draws on as two ex-SR Ransomes & Rapier cranes continue with the installation of a new deck to the bridge over Market Place within Haywards Heath station in October 1985. Nearer the camera is 45-ton crane No. ADRR95210, while 36-ton No. ADRR95201 is the other side of the gap, into which they are gently lowering a pre-cast pre-tensioned concrete beam. *John Goss Photographs*

Below A view looking down on No. ADRC95222 from a bridge abutment, while undertaking some work to a bridge at Bridlington on 9 April 1983. *R Watson*

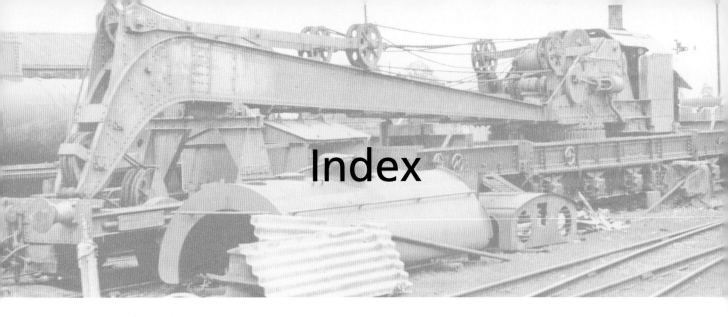

Index

Railways

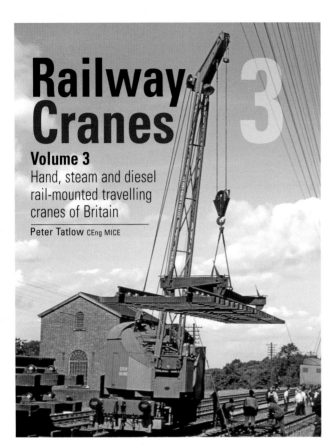

Railway Cranes Volume 3
Hand, steam and diesel rail-mounted travelling cranes of Britain

Peter Tatlow

Peter Tatlow's background as a professional engineer leant considerable weight to his two previously published volumes on *Railway Cranes* both of which have received unqualified praise from reviewers.

This new book looks at the smaller cranes used by the engineers and other departments mostly on track work though sometimes they operated at stations on other duties. These smaller cranes, which were mostly self-propelled, were powered either by steam or diesel though in order to present a complete picture of this range of specialist vehicles, some hand cranes are included.

In series with the two earlier volumes, the book's detailed text is accompanied by numerous colour and monochrome illustrations and the author's meticulous drawings are mostly reproduced to 4mm scale making them ideal for the modeller. The narrative transcends BR regional and railway company boundaries and records the history of these smaller cranes from the earliest days up to the present. Like the two previous *Railway Cranes* volumes, this new book covers a subject never before tackled and will be welcomed by railway enthusiasts, historians and modellers across the board.

ISBN: 9780860936848
Price: £35.00
224 pages